Revolution in Poetic Language

Revolution in Poetic Language

Julia Kristeva

Translated by Margaret Waller
with an Introduction by Leon S. Roudiez

Columbia University Press   New York

Library of Congress Cataloging in Publication Data

Kristeva, Julia, 1941–
    Revolution in poetic language.

    Translation and abridgment of: La révolution du
language poétique.
    Bibliography: p.
    1. Semiotics and literature.   2. Poetics.
I. Title.
PN54.K75   1984   808′.00141   84-12181
ISBN 0-231-05642-7 (cloth)
ISBN 0-231-05643-5 (paper)

Columbia University Press
New York   Guildford, Surrey
Copyright © 1984 Columbia University Press
La révolution du langage poétique © 1974 Éditions du Seuil
All rights reserved
Printed in the United States of America

p 10 9 8 7 6 5 4 3 2

Contents

Translator's Preface

THE TRANSLATOR's preface usually begins by assessing what is "lost" in the translation and this preface will be no exception. But prefatory references to metaphorical debits presuppose the "original" text as plenitude and presence as if to deny that it does not always already constitute a loss. Moreover, such an ostensibly self-effacing gesture glosses over the deferential submission and violent struggle by which the end result is achieved: the translation becomes a slave to the original in an attempt to master it. In representing what is textually "other," the translation inevitably appropriates the "alien" through the familiar. Indeed, inasmuch as it replaces the previous work, a translation is not only a transformation of that text but also its elimination: the homage paid is a covert form of parricide.[1] Although the traces of this conflict surface in the preface's allusions to a figurative balance sheet of gains and losses, they remain, of course, camouflaged within the translation itself.

A translation, its etymology suggests, is a carrying across, one that more or less conceals what is lost in transit. Following that idealized image, this text aims to carry *La Révolution du langage poétique* (1974) across a linguistic and sociocultural interstice so that it may be read in 1984 by an Anglo-American audience. Whether or not the name Julia Kristeva already speaks volumes to this audience, negotiating any such critical divide is always a hazardous enterprise. In presenting texts from that particular decade, the translator may succumb to two equally unproductive temptations: to look back nostalgically on 1974 as an apical moment of contemporary theory,[2] and/or to deprecate writings of that era in the light of subsequent critical preoccupations. To ensure any significant gain from this "carrying across," however, one must neither ignore the shortcomings of these time-bound works nor set them up as straw dogs for later arguments.

Revolution in Poetic Language counts among the emblematic works of the 1970s that extended the parameters of what could be said about texts and questioned the epistemological premises of critical theory. But Kristeva's text, her thesis for the *doctorat d'état*, makes this critique within the forms of scholarly convention with few signs of self-reflexive literariness. Despite the later evolution of her style from the starkly formalistic to a more personal mode, Kristeva describes her writing as a conscious resistance to the "strong post-Heideggerian temptation" of equating theoretical and literary discourse.[3] She argues that although epistemological honesty requires a recognition of the limits of scientificity, the assertion that theory and fiction are the same constitutes an abuse of power.[4] Although Kristeva's attitude may explain why her text refrains from actively engaging in the play of signifiers, this does not mean, of course, that *Revolution* may not be subjected to a symptomatic reading and translation.

Despite its academic format and its refusal of playful polysemia, *La Révolution du langage poétique* resists easy readability—and smooth translation. The text's density and difficulty force the translator to determine at every turn whether to separate the signifier from the signified and when to privilege, in the name of clarity, the latter over the former. These decisions, which are never innocent, were often reached in consultation (and complicity) with the author, but they inevitably entailed "saving" one aspect of the text only to deform another. In some instances, such alterations had stylistic, particularly syntactic, consequences: specifying antecedents, changing nouns to verbs, making passive verb forms active, breaking up and sometimes rearranging sentences, as well as inserting paragraph breaks.

These gains in clarity meant nuances lost. I have tried, of course, to minimize the losses by retaining—even when it meant occasional gallicisms—the meaning effects of the text's most important terminological distinctions and its most telling tropes. Such figures of speech, symptoms of the "blindness and insight" in modern theoretical discourse, permeate Kristeva's work: "the true," "the real," "the murder of the thetic," "the shattering of the subject," "the three points of the family triangle," and so forth. This rhetorical strategy is perhaps endemic to what Philip Lewis has called *Revolution*'s super-disciplinary approach to an inter-disciplinary subject[5]: such a strategy elucidates the meta-significance of concrete phenomena even as it seems to distance the object of analysis through ambiguity and abstraction. Similarly, the personal dissolves into the impersonal through the exclusive use of a democratic yet royal "we" (more common in French than in English) that paradoxically calls attention to its own self-effacement. Indeed, in one of the rare self-referential moments in the text, Kristeva calls attention to this pronoun and makes its use emblematic of metalanguage in general.[6]

 Revolution is the most wide-ranging metalinguistic elaboration of Kristeva's theories. As a result, although the translations of some of her later essays in *Desire in Language* have provided the basis for my own practice,[7] the vast scope of the earlier work presents its own terminological minefields. Most of these center around the critical Kristevan preoccupation with the "subject." "*Le sujet*" (the speaking/thinking agent) is of "masculine" gender but is usually rendered in English as "it." Unfortunately, using the impersonal pronoun in this instance would merely compound the already considerable difficulties of ambiguous antecedents. On the other hand, "s/he" and "his/her" would overly concretize what remains for Kristeva a highly abstract concept. I have therefore chosen to use the masculine "he" and "his" with their standard connotations of universality.[8] The individual subjects cited in *Revolution* are, in point of fact, exclusively male, and the psychoanalytic account offered for the emergence of the subject is rooted in a fundamentally masculine (Oedipal) model. Although the abstract "*il*" may point to a gender-specific foundation, the Kristevan subject is nonetheless always implicated in a heterogeneous signifying process: his identity, never become, ever becoming, questioned and questionable, is always on trial (*en procès*). Over and beyond this "subject in process/on trial," numerous other terms for the subject appear in Kristeva's text: *ego*, ego, Moi, moi, and "moi."

Since no systematic distinction is made among these variants, I have followed "standard practice" and specific English translations, using "ego" when the term denotes a psychoanalytic concept, but "self" in explicitly nonanalytic passages; "I" for its appearance in Frege, and "Ego" (capitalized) for this same notion in Hegel and Husserl.

For psychoanalytic terminology, I have generally followed Laplanche and Pontalis's *Vocabulaire de la psychanalyse* and its English translation.[9] Two important exceptions should be noted, however. "Drive" was preferred over "instinct" because it conveys more precisely the French "*pulsion*" and Freud's "*Trieb*." "Instinctual" always refers to the drives rather than to instincts and, whenever possible, I have used "drive" as an adjective ("drive bases," "drive movement," and so forth). Secondly, "investment" was chosen over "cathexis" for its similarity to the French ("*investissement*") and for its versatile verb form: invests, invested, investing, etc.

I have relied on published translations of texts cited in *Revolution* as much as possible, and have modified them only when inconsistencies between French and English terms would have obscured the argument. (Such changes are indicated in the notes.) All translations not otherwise attributed, however, are my own. The quotations from Mallarmé required particular attention because of their infamous "untranslatability." From the many translations of "Un coup de dés," I have chosen the attempt that coheres best with Kristeva's own emphasis on the interdependence of the "semiotic" and "signifying" modalities. For Mallarmé's prose essays and his *Igitur*, I have ventured my own English versions, with occasional borrowings from previous translations, in an attempt to ensure the intelligibility of Kristeva's analyses without incurring the net loss of Mallarmé.[10]

Although the balance sheet of any text remains indeterminable, credit for this trans-lation is largely due to Julia Kristeva herself. Her gracious and patient attention through numerous translating sessions and written queries helped me avoid a large number of misinterpretations. Many of the modifications for clarity and concision could not and would not have been made without her generous assistance and "authorization." I owe a similar debt of gratitude to Leon S. Roudiez for his invaluable readings of this work. His meticulous clarification of countless ambiguities were essential to my understanding of the text.

Given its scope and difficulty, this translation has been, perhaps more than some, a collaborative process of vision and revision. Specific chapters in early drafts of the manuscript benefited enormously from the informed and attentive scrutiny of various friends and colleagues: Alice Jardine on avant-garde practice, Mary Shaw on Mallarmé, and Rick Livingston on historical materialism. Avital Ronell helped resolve difficulties with passages on Hegel and Derrida, Ephrain Kristal with the Hegelian dialectic, and Dr. John Kafka with psychoanalytic concepts and terminology. For their excellent and timely suggestions on penultimate revisions, I thank Nancy K. Miller, Terese Lyons, and Kathryn Gravdal. Domna C. Stanton painstakingly edited some of the most difficult pages wisely and well. As always, Kate Jensen gave not only a reading of the manuscript but her unfailing friendship. And, finally, thanks in particular to Ken Bowman, the invaluable in-house editor who sustained me.

Had I taken full advantage of so much help from so many, what is inevitably lost in translation might represent a more substantial gain. For all errors and inadequacies, however, the liability is mine alone.

Introduction

JULIA KRISTEVA is a compelling presence that critics and scholars can ignore only at the risk of intellectual sclerosis. She is also, among the major theoreticians writing in France, the only woman—and that makes her contribution even more noteworthy as she challenges a long Western tradition of male-dominated thought. Perhaps we have, in the United States, been slow in recognizing the importance of her work, for it has not been translated as promptly as it has been elsewhere.[1] We are nevertheless closing the gap, and with *Revolution in Poetic Language* a large portion of her basic, theoretical work has now become available in English.

Her aim here is to investigate the workings of "poetic language" (a notion to which I shall presently return) as a *signifying practice*, that is, as a semiotic system generated by a speaking subject within a social, historical field. The "revolution" in her title refers to the profound change that began to take place in the nineteenth century, the consequences of which are still being sustained and evaluated in our own time. The change has affected what we commonly call "literature"; it also concerns other domains—in different but related ways. Indeed, philosophy and history have been transformed, linguistics and psychoanalysis have come into being, and without a knowledge of what is at hand in those disciplines it would be difficult to account for the revolution in "poetic language." What Kristeva actually does in the following pages is to impress large bodies of philosophical, linguistic, and psychoanalytic texts (concurrently submitting them to critical analysis) in the service of her main argument, namely that the nineteenth-century post-Symbolist avant-garde effected a real mutation in literary "representation"; and once the process of this alteration has been identified, one is able to detect a similar ferment in the essential writings of other historical periods.

A few definitions or clarifications are in order. That there has been a conceptual "revolution" is, I believe, a generally accepted fact. Louis Althusser, in 1970, expressed this in terms that are both challenging and, to my mind, quite accurate: ". . . there is a chance that our times will some day be seen as branded by the most dramatic, laborious ordeal one can imagine—the discovery of and proficiency in what are the 'simplest' acts of our existence: seeing, listening, speaking, reading."[2] He added that we owe this "bewildering knowledge" to a mere handful of men: Marx, Nietzsche, and Freud. But what about "poetic language"? In the context of this work it does involve notions of "literature" and "poetry" but without the preconceptions these usually carry; it does not connote "belles lettres" or verse, for instance. The phrase was coined by the Russian Formalists, specifically Ossip Brik, who founded the Society for the Study of Poetic Language in Moscow in 1917, whose members worked in conjunction with the Moscow Linguistic Circle. For Brik "poetic language" stands in opposition to spoken language, a language whose basic purpose is communication, and it includes what he and others called transrational language. As Roman Jakobson also emphasized, in a different context, "Any attempt to limit the domain of the poetic function to poetry, or to restrict poetry to the poetic function would only amount to an excessive and misleading simplification."[3] Neither Brik nor Jakobson's definitions, however, suffice to account for Kristeva's concept of "poetic language." While agreeing with Jakobson that "poetic language" cannot be viewed as a "deviation from the norm" of language, she does not see it as a sub-code of the linguistic code. Rather, it stands for the infinite possibilities of language, and all other language acts are merely partial realizations of the possibilities inherent in "poetic language." From such a point of view, "literary practice is seen as exploration and discovery of the possibilities of language; as an activity that liberates the subject from a number of linguistic, psychic, and social networks; as a dynamism that breaks up the inertia of language habits and grants linguists the unique possibility of studying the *becoming* of the significations of signs."[4]

It should be clear, incidentally, that Kristeva can be termed neither a formalist nor a structuralist; the Russian Formalists themselves, as a matter of fact, after an early, seemingly absolute formalism ("formalism" was first a pejorative term applied to them by their adversaries), evolved in the direction of a more sociological approach. Most French literary structuralists, with the signal exception of Lucien Goldmann, tended to leave aside history as well as what Jean Piaget has called the epistemic subject. As can be seen here as well as in previously translated works, Kristeva takes into account the historical dimensions of literary and artistic works and also analyzes the role of the subject, albeit a heterogeneous one, in their production.

Now the link between poetic language and revolution is neither causal nor immediate; what it entails is very different from what Sartre, for instance, had in mind when he elaborated the notion of *engagement*. Sartre saw Mallarmé as a consciously committed writer whose commitment, however, consisted in large part in a refusal of the "bourgeois stupidity" of his time; when he examines his poetic practice, he dismisses all references to "brutish instincts or the dark history of his sexuality."[5] Kristeva, on the other hand, emphasizes the signifying process in Mallarmé's texts, which, along with those of Lautréamont, are seen as the prototypes of modern avant-garde practice. Pointing to manifestations of the semiotic disposition she shows how closely their writing practice parallels the logic of the unconscious, drive-ridden and dark as it might be; such a practice thus assumes the privilege of communicating regression and jouissance. In the final analysis, it may be interpreted as an affirmation of freedom, as an anarchic revolt (even though it openly advocates neither freedom nor revolution) against a society that extols material goods and profit.

The idea that poetic language constitutes a "semiotic system" needs to be tempered with the reminder that the word "semiotic" has a very specific meaning when used by Kristeva. It cannot be understood properly unless it is considered within the polarity that characterizes what she has termed *the* symbolic and semiotic dispositions. The first chapter of the present volume deals with this in some detail, and there would be no point in summarizing a presentation that needs to be followed step by step. It is essential, just the same, to begin with as few misconceptions as possible. Her concern does lie within the field of *la sémiotique* (i.e., "semiotics" as a general science of signs) but it involves a more specific domain that she calls *le sémiotique* ("the semiotic") seen as one of the two components of the signifying process— the other being "the symbolic." While this divison is not identical with that of unconscious/conscious, id/superego, or nature/ culture, there are analogies here that could be usefully kept in mind. In all four instances there is a constant dialectical process at work, one that has its source in infancy, and is implicated in sexual differentiation. Such a dialectic comprises drives and impulses on the one hand, the family and society structures on the other. One difference, however, is that the semiotic/symbolic opposition as envisaged here operates within, by means of, and through language.

Hence the weight Kristeva assigns, in the elaboration of her concept of poetic language, to the ideas of Lacan and to contemporary linguistic theory. Lacan is sought after because he gave further emphasis to the role Freud had already assigned to language. In a noteworthy paper read in Rome in 1953 he said, "The resources [of psychoanalysis] are those of speech to the extent that it endows a person's activity with meaning; its domain is that of concrete discourse as field of the subject's transindividual reality; its operations are those of history insofar as the latter constitutes the emergence of truth within the real."[6] While the import of linguistics is obvious, and Kristeva draws on both Ferdinand de Saussure and Charles S. Peirce, the writings of Emile Benveniste are most significant. In a *Festschrift* published on the occasion of the linguist's retirement, she contributed an essay in which she noted the tendency of linguistics to "eliminate from its field of inquiry everything that cannot be systematized, structured, or logicized into a formal entity" and praised Benveniste who, although caught up in the same trend, "nevertheless opened this object called language to practices in which it realizes itself, which go beyond it, and on the basis of which its very existence as monolithic object is either made relative or appears as problematic."[7] Thus does Kristeva, in addition to affirming that a consideration of subject and history is necessary for a sound textual analysis, advocate breaking down the barriers that isolate related disciplines from one another.

Textual analysis is indeed a better phrase than "literary analysis" for the activity Kristeva engages in; it relegates esthetic and formalistic considerations to the background. Textual analysis also denies pertinence to "literary criticism" insofar as the latter evaluates a work by confronting it with one's preconceived or ideal notion of what that work should be. For the point is to give an account of what went into a work, how it affects readers, and why. The text that is analyzed is actually the effect of the dialectical interplay between semiotic and symbolic dispositions. Here it would be helpful to keep in mind the etymology of the word and think of it as a texture, a "disposition or connection of threads, filaments, or other slender bodies, interwoven" (*Webster* 2). The analogy stops there, however, for the text cannot be thought of as a finished, permanent piece of cloth; it is in a perpetual state of flux as different readers intervene, as their knowledge deepens, and as history moves on.

The nature of the "threads" thus interwoven will determine the presence or absence of poetic language. Those that are spun by drives and are woven within the semiotic disposition make up what Kristeva has defined as a genotext; they are actualized in poetic language. Those that issue from societal, cultural, syntactical, and other grammatical constraints constitute the phenotext; they insure communication. Seldom, however, does one encounter the one without the other. A mathematical demonstration is perhaps a pure phenotext; there are writings by Antonin Artaud that come close to being unblended genotext, those, in Susan Sontag's words, "in which language becomes partly unintelligible; that is, an unmediated physical presence."[8] For, as Kristeva's reader will soon discover, it is often the physical, material aspect of language (certain combinations of letters, certain sounds—regardless of the meaning of words in which they occur) that signals the presence of a genotext.

These and other theoretical concepts had previously been formulated separately in essays written as early as 1966–1967 before being brought together in more systematic fashion in *Revolution in Poetic Language*. They are roughly contemporaneous with some of the seminal works published by Roland Barthes, Jacques Derrida, Michel Foucault, Jacques Lacan, and others; she is indebted to some, just as they, in turn, have profited from her work. For, as Evelyn H. Zepp has noticed, specifically in the case of ideas presented by Barthes and Umberto Eco, Kristeva "had not only treated [such] concepts but had already gone beyond them in many ways."[9] With the possible exception of Barthes, none of these writers is a literary critic—and Barthes could hardly be restricted to that category (Kristeva's own department at the University of Paris-VII has been named "Science of Texts and Documents"). As is the case with other theoretical writers, what she has to say is of concern to "specialists" in several disciplines. All of these writers, just the same, have something to say to those whose principal affiliation is with "literary" research and she, perhaps more than others, has provided a conceptual foundation for significantly changing one's approach to whatever he or she chooses to include under that vague heading. As a "literary" scholar I shall now set forth those conclusions that I believe can be reached on the basis of Kristeva's theoretical work.

First, the need for interdisciplinary studies is tied to one's inability to provide a definition of literature that is both rigorous and generally accepted. The Russian Formalists tried, and so did others, but to no avail. The set of "literary" writings is a fuzzy set, in Lotfi Zadeh's sense of the term,[10] just as the set of "middle-aged" persons in society is a fuzzy set, dependent as both sets are on variable factual data as well as ideological constraints. As to factual data, I would mention life expectancy and the invention of movable type; among ideological constraints, cultural preconceptions and esthetic patterns of thought come to mind. While it is true that we usually have no hesitation in identifying a given person as being middle-aged (we would not think of calling him/her "young" or "elderly"), while we instinctively sense as we read a page in *Partisan Review*, for instance, that it belongs to the literary subset known as "short story" (we would never mistake it for a political essay, of which that review publishes many)—we also know that the criteria that enable us to come to such conclusions would not be acceptable at other times or in other places. François Villon was beyond middle age when he wrote his *Grand Testament*; Sylvia Plath was young when she died—and yet they were both thirty. Béranger's writings were considered "literary" when he was alive but they are no longer so valued today; the opposite has happened in the case of the Marquis de Sade. On account of that fuzziness, all we can conclude is that literature is whatever is called literature in a given society at a given moment in history.

As Kristeva had stated earlier, "literature" is an object that our culture consumes; it is viewed as a finished product and the process of its productivity is usually ignored.[11] When this process is taken into consideration, however, one realizes that what makes a work interesting or significant does not depend on its having been accepted in (or rejected from) the "literary" corpus; that latter judgment is both ethical and esthetic, hence a function of dominant ideology (in the Marxian sense of the phrase). What makes the work significant is a textual presence—poetic language. The mathematical demonstration I referred to earlier is significant from a scientific point of view; poetic language bears a more basic significance that has to do with our individual and collective being-in-the-world.

If one is to account for the production of a work, one needs to investigate the forces that brought it into being. Such forces are channeled through what shall be called a "writing subject" rather than an "author," for the latter term emphasizes the conscious intent of a writer who has author-ity over the meaning of his work. The notion of writing subject counters the illusions of Sartre, for instance, who asserted that no matter how far the reader might go, "the author has gone farther than he has. No matter how he connects various parts of the book . . . . , he can rest assured that those connections have been expressly intended."[12] This does not mean denying all intentionality or refusing to give a role to the conscious person who writes the work; rather, it means emphasizing that consciousness is far from dominating the process and that the writing subject is a complex, heterogeneous force (see *infra* part I, sections 5 and 10, and part III, section 4).

The writing subject, then, includes not only the consciousness of the writer but also his or her unconscious. The important thing here is to avoid repeating the mistakes of a few decades ago when misguided critics thought they could psychoanalyze a writer by studying his biography and then try to explain the work by means of what they had learned from the biography. The point of departure must be the text, the whole text, and nothing but the text. In a way, there is a resemblance (although one should be wary of pushing this too far) between this aspect of textual analysis and the manner in which Freud studied dream narratives. An important difference is that textual analysis involves more than this one aspect; narrating one's dreams does not necessarily make one a poet. Kristeva's examination of Céline's writings, in *Powers of Horror*, provides a good illustration of all this.

The subject of writing also includes the non-conscious, that is, the domain not subject to repression but not within the reach of consciousness either. This is an area covered by the notion of dominant ideology: the whole system of myths and prejudices that gives our view of society and of our place in it a specific orientation. It includes all those things that we take for granted, that we do not question because we assume they are true—not realizing that instead of being truths they are elaborate constructions that serve whatever group, class, or party is holding power. The process is a complex one, for the writer is also conscious of being situated in a moment of history, acted upon and reacting to (and perhaps against) historical forces or currents. All such aspects of the writing process are covered by Kristeva in the instances of Mallarmé and Lautréamont. Their impact could also be shown in the case of a modern American text such as Faulkner's *Absalom, Absalom!* That novel is the result of a process undergone by a writer who, in addition to whatever personal dialectic between his conscious and unconscious he was struggling through, was himself a Southerner living in Mississippi, concerned by history (reacting to and against it), had a Southern family history of which he was aware, witnessed the hardships caused by the Great Depression, knew of the often violent labor unrest of the Thirties, saw Congress pass the first social reform bills, and perhaps noted with approval the government's inaction concerning the status of blacks. All of this germinates within the threads of the text.[13]

The writing subject is further impelled by someone who has chosen to become a writer and to do so in a certain manner. The decision may have been to compose essays, or verse, or prose poetry, or a diary, or fiction; it may also have been to write transitively or intransitively, to use Roland Barthes's terminology;[14] it may have been to emulate an admired poet or novelist or to the contrary to react against what others have published. In general terms, as Kristeva explains in a part of the essay not translated in this book, "the texts presuppose several categories of narratives, either of the same period or written earlier, they appropriate the latter to themselves either to confirm or to reject them and at any rate to possess them. . . . As if these other narratives were an incitement to perform a deed that is the text itself."[15]

That statement exemplifies what textual analysis must constantly take into account in order to reach an understanding of the signifying process. On the one hand, no text signifies without its context—its *total* context, be it conscious, unconscious, preconscious, linguistic, cultural, political, literary; on the other, it is the text alone that leads one to the various areas of that total context. Needless to say, the textual scholar, while he or she cannot be a universal expert, needs to have a working knowledge of the relevant disciplines.

I have just alluded to a lack: part of the original version of this book has not been translated. Actually, only about a third of it now appears in English. *La Révolution du langage poétique* is a weighty 646-page tome that Kristeva presented for her State Doctorate in Paris in July 1973. The defense of such a doctoral dissertation, which has no real equivalent in this country, is an impressive ritual to which the public is invited. The newspaper *Le Monde* sent a reporter to cover the ceremony; he wrote that Roland Barthes, who was one of the examiners, pointedly refrained from asking any questions. He was quoted as saying, "Several times you have helped me to change, particularly in shifting away from a semiology of products to a semiotics of production."[16] In that context, Barthes's attitude was a manner of praise and his remarks an unusual acknowledgment of indebtedness. This might lead one to regret that the entire work has not been translated.

There is, however, a good reason for that—in addition to the prohibitive expense of publishing (and, for the eventual reader, of purchasing) such a volume. In the remaining four hundred and some odd pages of *La Révolution du langage poétique* Kristeva analyzes, often in great detail, French passages from Lautréamont and Mallarmé. But this translation is intended for persons who are not specialists in French literature and who perhaps read French with some difficulty or not at all. In all likelihood, an argument frequently based on the material shape and sound of French words would hardly be comprehensible. What has been translated constitutes the theoretical section of the book, which requires no special knowledge of either French or French literature other than what one assumes to be at the disposal of most scholars; it does, on the other hand, require some familiarity with (or interest in) philosophy, historical materialism, linguistics, and psychoanalysis, to the extent that those disciplines have provided the intellectual underpinnings of our time. Specialists in such fields will find much that is challenging here; "literary" scholars will discover new paths open to their investigations of those "simple" acts of our existence—reading and writing.

Leon S. Roudiez

What, therefore, is important in the *study* of *Science*, is that one should take on oneself the strenuous effort of the Notion.

Hegel, *Phenomenology of Spirit*

Prolegomenon

OUR PHILOSOPHIES of language, embodiments of the Idea, are nothing more than the thoughts of archivists, archaeologists, and necrophiliacs. Fascinated by the remains of a process which is partly discursive, they substitute this fetish for what actually produced it. Egypt, Babylon, Mycenae: we see their pyramids, their carved tablets, and fragmented codes in the discourse of our contemporaries, and think that by codifying them we can possess them.

These static thoughts, products of a leisurely cogitation removed from historical turmoil, persist in seeking the truth of language by formalizing utterances that hang in midair, and the truth of the subject by listening to the narrative of a sleeping body—a body in repose, withdrawn from its socio-historical imbrication, removed from direct experience: "To be or not to be . . . To die, to sleep . . . To sleep—perchance to dream."

And yet, this thinking points to a truth, namely, that the kind of activity encouraged and privileged by (capitalist) society represses the *process* pervading the body and the subject, and that we must therefore break out of our interpersonal and intersocial experience if we are to gain access to what is repressed in the social mechanism: the generating of signifiance.

The archivistic, archaeological, and necrophilic methods on which the scientific imperative was founded—the building of arguments on the basis of empirical evidence, a systematizable given, and an observable object—in this case, language—are an embarrassment when applied to modern or contemporary phenomena. These methods show that the capitalist mode of production has statified language into idiolects and divided it into self-contained, isolated islands—heteroclite spaces existing in different temporal modes (as relics or projections), and oblivious of one another.

These random discursive instances have yet to be assigned a typology corresponding to the subjective and socioeconomic typologies in society as a whole. Instead, as agents of totality, in positions of control, science and theory intervene to make such discursive instances intelligible, each within their separate domain, even though they may lose them and have to start unifying them over and over again, if only provisionally—for that is their Long March. Linguistics, semiotics, anthropology, and psychoanalysis reveal that the thinking subject, the Cartesian subject who defines his being through thought or language, subsumes within that being and the operations which supposedly structure it, all trans-linguistic practice—a practice in which language and the subject are merely moments. From this perspective, the philosophy of language and the "human sciences" that stem from it emerge as reflections on moments. Whether they are viewed as simply linguistic, subjective, or more largely socioeconomic—depending on the "discipline"—such moments are nevertheless fragments, remains; their individual articulation is often examined, but rarely their interdependence or inception.

The critical question is not whether one can do otherwise. One clearly cannot if the object chosen is a human universe of full subjects who simply make systematic combinations in language and are themselves implicated in communication. Nor is it a question of calculating the pyramid's base and slant height and miming traces on Babylonian tablets or letters in Cretan linear writing. Such refinements in economics, phenomenology, and psychoanalysis de-structure finite systems and show that they are produced by a random albeit necessary causality. But one must still posit an "outside" that is in fact internal to each closed set, since otherwise the set would remain enclosed, even if internal differentiation could be extended indefinitely. One must, then, de-center the closed set and elaborate the dialectic of a process within plural and heterogeneous universes.

We will make constant use of notions and concepts borrowed from Freudian psychoanalytic theory and its various recent developments in order to give the advances of *dialectical logic* a *materialist foundation*—a theory of signification based on the subject, his formation, and his corporeal, linguistic, and social dialectic. Our purpose is not to adhere to the orthodoxy of any particular school, but rather to select those aspects of analytic theory capable of rationalizing the signifying process as it is practiced within texts. Does this dialectic itself avoid archivism? At least it indicates its own position, and renounces both the totalizing fragmentation characteristic of positivist discourse, which reduces all signifying practices to a formalism, and a reductive identification with other (discursive, ideological, economic) islands of the social aggregate.

From this position, it seems possible to perceive a signifying practice which, although produced in language, is only intelligible *through* it. By exploding the phonetic, lexical, and syntactic object of linguistics, this practice not only escapes the attempted hold of all anthropomorphic sciences, it also refuses to identify with the recumbent body subjected to transference onto the analyser. Ultimately, it exhausts the ever tenacious ideological institutions and apparatuses, thereby demonstrating the limits of formalist and psychoanalytic devices.[1] This signifying practice—a particular type of modern literature—attests to a "crisis" of social structures and their ideological, coercive, and necrophilic manifestations. To be sure, such crises have occurred at the dawn and decline of every mode of production: the Pindaric obscurity that followed Homeric clarity and community is one of many examples. However, with Lautréamont, Mallarmé, Joyce, and Artaud, to name only a few, this crisis represents a new phenomenon. For the capitalist mode of production produces and marginalizes, but simultaneously exploits for its own regeneration, one of the most spectacular shatterings of discourse. By exploding the subject and his ideological limits, this phenomenon has a triple effect, and raises three sets of questions:

1. Because of its specific isolation within the discursive totality of our time, this shattering of discourse reveals that linguistic changes constitute changes in the *status of the subject*—his relation to the body, to others, and to objects; it also reveals that

Foucault

normalized language is just one of the ways of articulating the signifying process that encompasses the body, the material referent, and language itself. How are these strata linked? What is their interrelation within signifying practice?

2. The shattering further reveals that the capitalist mode of production, having attained a highly developed means of production through science and technology, no longer need remain strictly within linguistic and ideological *norms*, but can also integrate their *process qua process*. As art, this shattering can display the productive basis of subjective and ideological signifying formations—a foundation that primitive societies call "sacred" and modernity has rejected as "schizophrenia." What is the extent of this integration? Under what conditions does it become indispensable, censured, repressed, or marginal?

3. Finally, in the history of signifying systems and notably that of the arts, religion, and rites, there emerge, in retrospect, fragmentary phenomena which have been kept in the background or rapidly integrated into more communal signifying systems but point to the very process of significance. Magic, shamanism, esoterism, the carnival, and "incomprehensible" poetry all underscore the limits of socially useful discourse and attest to what it represses: the *process* that exceeds the subject and his communicative structures. But at what historical moment does social exchange tolerate or necessitate the manifestation of the signifying process in its "poetic" or "esoteric" form? Under what conditions does this "esoterism," in displacing the boundaries of socially established signifying practices, correspond to socioeconomic change, and, ultimately, even to revolution? And under what conditions does it remain a blind alley, a harmless bonus offered by a social order which uses this "esoterism" to expand, become flexible, and thrive?

If there exists a "discourse" which is not a mere depository of thin linguistic layers, an archive of structures, or the testimony of a withdrawn body, and is, instead, the essential element of a practice involving the sum of unconscious, subjective, and social relations in gestures of confrontation and appropriation, destruction and construction—productive violence, in short—it is "literature," or, more specifically, the *text*. Although simply sketched out, this notion of the text (to which we shall return) already takes us far from the realm of "discourse" and "art." The text is a practice that could be compared to political revolution: the one brings about in the subject what the other introduces into society. The history and political experience of the twentieth century have demonstrated that one cannot be transformed without the other—but could there be any doubt after the overturning [*renversement*] of the Hegelian dialectic[2] and especially after the Freudian revolution? Hence, the questions we will ask about literary practice will be aimed at the political horizon from which this practice is inseparable, despite the efforts of aestheticizing esoterism and repressive sociologizing or formalist dogmatics to keep them apart. We shall call this heterogeneous practice *signifiance* to indicate, on the one hand, that biological urges are socially controlled, directed, and organized, producing an excess with regard to social apparatuses; and, on the other, that this instinctual operation becomes a *practice*—a transformation of natural and social resistances, limitations, and stagnations—if and only if it enters into the code of linguistic and social communication. Laing and Cooper, like Deleuze and Guattari, are right to stress the de-structuring and a-signifying machine of the unconscious.[3] Compared with the ideologies of communication and normativeness, which largely inspire anthropology and psychoanalysis, their approach is liberating. What is readily apparent, however, is that their examples of "schizophrenic flow" are usually drawn from modern literature, in which the "flow" itself exists only through language, appropriating and displacing the signifier to practice *within it* the heterogeneous generating of the "desiring machine."

What we call *signifiance*, then, is precisely this unlimited and unbounded generating process, this unceasing operation of the drives toward, in, and through language; toward, in, and through the exchange system and its protagonists—the subject and his institutions. This heterogeneous process, neither anarchic, fragmented foundation nor schizophrenic blockage, is a structuring and de-structuring *practice*, a passage to the outer *boundaries* of the subject and society. Then—and only then—can it be jouissance and revolution.

I.

The Semiotic and the Symbolic

Further determine [the] object for itself,
[a] logic behind consciousness

Hegel, Autumn 1831

1.

The Phenomenological Subject of Enunciation

WE MUST specify, first and foremost, what we mean by the *signifying process* vis-à-vis general theories of meaning, theories of language, and theories of the subject.

Despite their variations, all modern linguistic theories consider language a strictly "formal" object—one that involves syntax or mathematicization. Within this perspective, such theories generally accept the following notion of language. For Zellig Harris, language is defined by: (1) the arbitrary relation between signifier and signified, (2) the acceptance of the sign as a substitute for the extra-linguistic, (3) its discrete elements, and (4) its denumerable, or even finite, nature.[1] But with the development of Chomskyan generative grammar and the logico-semantic research that was articulated around and in response to it, problems arose that were generally believed to fall within the province of "semantics" or even "pragmatics," and raised the awkward question of the *extra-linguistic*. But language [*langage*]—modern linguistics' self-assigned object[2]—lacks a subject or tolerates one only as a *transcendental ego* (in Husserl's sense or in Benveniste's more specifically linguistic sense),[3] and defers any interrogation of its (always already dialectical because trans-linguistic) "externality."

Two trends in current linguistic research do attend to this "externality" in the belief that failure to elucidate it will hinder the development of linguistic theory itself. Although such a lacuna poses problems (which we will later specify) for "formal" linguistics, it has always been a particular problem for semiotics, which is concerned with specifying the functioning of signifying practices such as art, poetry, and myth that are irreducible to the "language" object.

1. The first of these two trends addresses the question of the so-called "arbitrary" relation between signifier and signified by examining signifying systems in which this relation is presented as "motivated." It seeks the principle of this motivation in the Freudian notion of the unconscious insofar as the theories of drives [*pulsions*] and primary processes (displacement and condensation) can connect "empty signifiers" to psychosomatic functionings, or can at least link them in a sequence of metaphors and metonymies; though undecidable, such a sequence replaces "arbitrariness" with "articulation." The discourse of analysands, language "pathologies," and artistic, particularly poetic, systems are especially suited to such an exploration.[4] Formal linguistic relations are thus connected to an "externality" in the psychosomatic realm, which is ultimately reduced to a fragmented substance [*substance morcelée*] (the body divided into erogenous zones) and articulated by the developing ego's connections to the three points of the family triangle. Such a linguistic theory, clearly indebted to the positions of the psychoanalytic school of London and Melanie Klein in particular, restores to formal linguistic relations the dimensions (instinctual drives) and operations (displacement, condensation, vocalic and intonational differentiation) that formalistic theory excludes. Yet for want of a dialectical notion of the *signifying process* as a whole, in which signifiance puts the subject in process/on trial [*en procès*], such considerations, no matter how astute, fail to take into account the syntactico-semantic functioning of language. Although they rehabilitate the notion of the fragmented body—pre-Oedipal but always already invested with semiosis—these linguistic theories fail to articulate its transitional link to the post-Oedipal subject and his always symbolic and/or syntactic language. (We shall return to this point.)

2. The second trend, more recent and widespread, introduces within theory's own formalism a "layer" of *semiosis*, which had been strictly relegated to pragmatics and semantics. By positing a *subject of enunciation* (in the sense of Benveniste, Culioli, etc.), this theory places logical modal relations, relations of presuppo-

sition, and other relations between interlocutors within the speech act, in a very deep "deep structure." This *subject of enunciation*, which comes directly from Husserl and Benveniste (see n. 3), introduces, through categorial intuition, both *semantic fields* and *logical*—but also *intersubjective—relations*, which prove to be both intra- and trans-linguistic.[5]

To the extent it is assumed by a subject who "means" (*bedeuten*), language has "deep structures" that articulate *categories*. These categories are semantic (as in the semantic fields introduced by recent developments in generative grammar), logical (modality relations, etc.), and intercommunicational (those which Searle called "speech acts" seen as bestowers of meaning).[6] But they may also be related to historical linguistic changes, thereby joining diachrony with synchrony.[7] In this way, through the subject who "means," linguistics is opened up to all possible categories and thus to philosophy, which linguistics had thought it would be able to escape.

In a similar perspective, certain linguists, interested in explaining semantic constraints, distinguish between different types of *styles* depending on the speaking subject's position vis-à-vis the utterance. Even when such research thereby introduces stylistics into semantics, its aim is to study the workings of signification, taking into account the subject of enunciation, which always proves to be the phenomenological subject.[8] Some linguistic research goes even further: starting from the subject of enunciation/ transcendental ego, and prompted by the opening of linguistics onto semantics and logic, it views signification as an ideological and therefore historical production.[9]

We shall not be able to discuss the various advantages and drawbacks of this second trend in modern linguistics except to say that it is still evolving, and that although its conclusions are only tentative, its epistemological bases lead us to the heart of the debate on phenomenology which we can only touch on here— and only insofar as the specific research we are presently undertaking allows.[10]

To summarize briefly what we shall elucidate later, the two trends just mentioned designate *two modalities* of what is, for us, the same signifying process. We shall call the first "*the semiotic*" and the second "*the symbolic.*" These two modalities are inseparable within the *signifying process* that constitutes language, and the dialectic between them determines the type of discourse (narrative, metalanguage, theory, poetry, etc.) involved; in other words, so-called "natural" language allows for different modes of articulation of the semiotic and the symbolic. On the other hand, there are nonverbal signifying systems that are constructed exclusively on the basis of the semiotic (music, for example). But, as we shall see, this exclusivity is relative, precisely because of the necessary dialectic between the two modalities of the signifying process, which is constitutive of the subject. Because the subject is always *both* semiotic *and* symbolic, no signifying system he produces can be either "exclusively" semiotic or "exclusively" symbolic, and is instead necessarily marked by an indebtedness to both.

2.

The Semiotic *Chora*
Ordering the Drives

WE UNDERSTAND the term "semiotic" in its Greek sense: σημεῖον=distinctive mark, trace, index, precursory sign, proof, engraved or written sign, imprint, trace, figuration. This etymological reminder would be a mere archaeological embellishment (and an unconvincing one at that, since the term ultimately encompasses such disparate meanings), were it not for the fact that the preponderant etymological use of the word, the one that implies a *distinctiveness*, allows us to connect it to a precise modality in the signifying process. This modality is the one Freudian psychoanalysis points to in postulating not only the *facilitation* and the structuring *disposition* of drives, but also the so-called *primary processes* which displace and condense both energies and their inscription. Discrete quantities of energy move through the body of the subject who is not yet constituted as such and, in the course of his development, they are arranged according to the various constraints imposed on this body—always already involved in a semiotic process—by family and social structures. In this way the drives, which are "energy" charges as well as "psychical" marks, articulate what we call a *chora*: a nonexpressive totality formed by the drives and their stases in a motility that is as full of movement as it is regulated.

We borrow the term *chora*[11] from Plato's *Timaeus* to denote an essentially mobile and extremely provisional articulation constituted by movements and their ephemeral stases. We differentiate this uncertain and indeterminate *articulation* from a *disposition* that already depends on representation, lends itself to phenom-

enological, spatial intuition, and gives rise to a geometry. Although our theoretical description of the *chora* is itself part of the
discourse of representation that offers it as evidence, the *chora*, as
rupture and articulations (rhythm), precedes evidence, verisimilitude, spatiality, and temporality. Our discourse—all discourse—
moves with and against the *chora* in the sense that it simultaneously depends upon and refuses it. Although the *chora* can be
designated and regulated, it can never be definitively posited: as
a result, one can situate the *chora* and, if necessary, lend it a topology, but one can never give it axiomatic form.[12]

The *chora* is not yet a position that represents something
for someone (i.e., it is not a sign); nor is it a *position* that represents someone for another position (i.e., it is not yet a signifier
either); it is, however, generated in order to attain to this signifying position. Neither model nor copy, the *chora* precedes and
underlies figuration and thus specularization, and is analogous only
to vocal or kinetic rhythm. We must restore this motility's gestural and vocal play (to mention only the aspect relevant to language) on the level of the socialized body in order to remove motility from ontology and amorphousness[13] where Plato confines it
in an apparent attempt to conceal it from Democritean rhythm.
The theory of the subject proposed by the theory of the unconscious will allow us to read in this rhythmic space, which has no
thesis and no position, the process by which signifiance is constituted. Plato himself leads us to such a process when he calls
this receptacle or *chora* nourishing and maternal,[14] not yet unified
in an ordered whole because deity is absent from it. Though deprived of unity, identity, or deity, the *chora* is nevertheless subject
to a regulating process [*réglementation*], which is different from that
of symbolic law but nevertheless effectuates discontinuities by
temporarily articulating them and then starting over, again and
again.

The *chora* is a modality of signifiance in which the linguistic sign is not yet articulated as the absence of an object and as
the distinction between real and symbolic. We emphasize the regulated aspect of the *chora*: its vocal and gestural organization is
subject to what we shall call an objective *ordering* [*ordonnancement*],

which is dictated by natural or socio-historical constraints such as the biological difference between the sexes or family structure. We may therefore posit that social organization, always already symbolic, imprints its constraint in a mediated form which organizes the *chora* not according to a *law* (a term we reserve for the symbolic) but through an *ordering*.[15] What is this mediation?

According to a number of psycholinguists, "concrete operations" precede the acquisition of language, and organize preverbal semiotic space according to logical categories, which are thereby shown to precede or transcend language. From their research we shall retain not the principle of an operational state[16] but that of a preverbal functional state that governs the connections between the body (in the process of constituting itself as a body proper), objects, and the protagonists of family structure.[17] But we shall distinguish this functioning from symbolic operations that depend on language as a sign system—whether the language [*langue*] is vocalized or gestural (as with deaf-mutes). The kinetic functional stage of the *semiotic* precedes the establishment of the sign; it is not, therefore, cognitive in the sense of being assumed by a knowing, already constituted subject. The genesis of the *functions*[18] organizing the semiotic process can be accurately elucidated only within a theory of the subject that does not reduce the subject to one of understanding, but instead opens up within the subject this other scene of pre-symbolic functions. The Kleinian theory expanding upon Freud's positions on the drives will momentarily serve as a guide.

Drives involve pre-Oedipal semiotic functions and energy discharges that connect and orient the body to the mother. We must emphasize that "drives" are always already ambiguous, simultaneously assimilating and destructive; this dualism, which has been represented as a tetrad[19] or as a double helix, as in the configuration of the DNA and RNA molecule,[20] makes the semiotized body a place of permanent scission. The oral and anal drives, both of which are oriented and structured around the mother's body,[21] dominate this sensorimotor organization. The mother's body is therefore what mediates the symbolic law organizing social relations and becomes the ordering principle of the semiotic *chora*,[22] which is on the path of destruction, aggressivity, and death. For although drives have been described as disunited or contradictory structures, simultaneously "positive" and "negative," this doubling is said to generate a dominant "destructive wave" that is drive's most characteristic trait: Freud notes that the most instinctual drive is the death drive.[23] In this way, the term "drive" denotes waves of attack against stases, which are themselves constituted by the repetition of these charges; together, charges and stases lead to no identity (not even that of the "body proper") that could be seen as a result of their functioning. This is to say that the semiotic *chora* is no more than the place where the subject is both generated and negated, the place where his unity succumbs before the process of charges and stases that produce him. We shall call this process of charges and stases a *negativity* to distinguish it from negation, which is the act of a judging subject (see below, part II).

Checked by the constraints of biological and social structures, the drive charge thus undergoes stases. Drive facilitation, temporarily arrested, marks *discontinuities* in what may be called the various material supports [*matériaux*] susceptible to semiotization: voice, gesture, colors. Phonic (later phonemic), kinetic, or chromatic units and differences are the marks of these stases in the drives. Connections or *functions* are thereby established between these discrete marks which are based on drives and articulated according to their resemblance or opposition, either by slippage or by condensation. Here we find the principles of metonymy and metaphor indissociable from the drive economy underlying them.

Although we recognize the vital role played by the processes of displacement and condensation in the organization of the semiotic, we must also add to these processes the relations (eventually representable as topological spaces) that connect the zones of the fragmented body to each other and also to "external" "objects" and "subjects," which are not yet constituted as such. This type of relation makes it possible to specify the *semiotic* as a psychosomatic modality of the signifying process; in other words, not a symbolic modality but one articulating (in the largest sense of the word) a continuum: the connections between the (glottal and anal) sphincters in (rhythmic and intonational) vocal modulations, or those between the sphincters and family protagonists, for example.

All these various processes and relations, anterior to sign and syntax, have just been identified from a genetic perspective as previous and necessary to the acquisition of language, but not identical to language. Theory can "situate" such processes and relations diachronically within the process of the constitution of the subject precisely because *they function synchronically within the signifying process of the subject himself*, i.e., the subject of *cogitatio*. Only in *dream* logic, however, have they attracted attention, and only in certain signifying practices, such as the *text*, do they dominate the signifying process.

It may be hypothesized that certain semiotic articulations are transmitted through the biological code or physiological "memory" and thus form the inborn bases of the symbolic function. Indeed, one branch of generative linguistics asserts the principle of innate language universals. As it will become apparent in what follows, however, the *symbolic*—and therefore syntax and all linguistic categories—is a social effect of the relation to the other, established through the objective constraints of biological (including sexual) differences and concrete, historical family structures. Genetic programmings are necessarily semiotic: they include the primary processes such as displacement and condensation, absorption and repulsion, rejection and stasis, all of which function as innate preconditions, "memorizable" by the species, for language acquisition.

Mallarmé calls attention to the semiotic rhythm within language when he speaks of "The Mystery in Literature" ["Le Mystère dans les lettres"]. Indifferent to language, enigmatic and feminine, this space underlying the written is rhythmic, unfettered, irreducible to its intelligible verbal translation; it is musical, anterior to judgment, but restrained by a single guarantee: syntax. As evidence, we could cite "The Mystery in Literature" in its entirety.[24] For now, however, we shall quote only those passages that ally the functioning of that "air or song beneath the text" with woman:

And the instrument of Darkness, whom they have designated, will not set down a word from then on except to deny that she must have been the enigma; lest she settle matters with a wisk of her skirts: 'I don't get it!''
. . . .

—They [the critics] play their parts disinterestedly or for a minor gain: leaving our Lady and Patroness exposed to show her dehiscence or lacuna, with respect to certain dreams, as though this were the standard to which everything is reduced.[25]

To these passages we add others that point to the "mysterious" functioning of literature as a rhythm made intelligible by syntax: "Following the instinct for rhythms that has chosen him, the poet does not deny seeing a lack of proportion between the means let loose and the result." "I know that there are those who would restrict Mystery to Music's domain; when writing aspires to it."[26]

What pivot is there, I mean within these contrasts, for intelligibility? a guarantee is needed—
     Syntax—
     . . .an extraordinary appropriation of structure, limpid, to the primitive lightning bolts of logic. A stammering, what the sentence seems, here repressed [. . .]
. . . .

The debate—whether necessary average clarity deviates in a detail—remains one for grammarians.[27]

     Our positing of the semiotic is obviously inseparable from a theory of the subject that takes into account the Freudian positing of the unconscious. We view the subject in language as decentering the transcendental ego, cutting through it, and opening it up to a dialectic in which its syntactic and categorical understanding is merely the liminary moment of the process, which is itself always acted upon by the relation to the other dominanted by the death drive and its productive reiteration of the "signifier." We will be attempting to formulate the distinction between *semiotic* and *symbolic* within this perspective, which was introduced by Lacanian analysis, but also within the constraints of a practice— the *text*—which is only of secondary interest to psychoanalysis.

3.

Husserl's Hyletic Meaning:
A Natural Thesis Commanded
by the Judging Subject

IT SHOULD now be clear that our point of view is very different from that of an immanent semiotics, anterior to language, which explores a meaning that is always already there, as in Hjelmslev. Equally apparent is our epistemological divergence from a Cartesian notion of language, which views thought as *preconditioned* by or even *identical* to natural factual data, and gradually considers it innate. Now, however, we would like to stress another phase of epistemological justification, which modern theory on the semantico-syntactic function has recently taken up: indeed, more and more, Husserlian phenomenology seems to be taking the place of Cartesianism in modern elucidations of the language act.

Husserlian phenomenology will concern us here only insofar as it intersects current linguistic preoccupations, which is to say at two points:

On the one hand, drawing its inspiration from phenomenological considerations, one trend in generative grammar tends to consider syntactic competence not simply as a natural precondition of actual syntactic activity, but as a product of the conscious or intentional transcendental ego, which judges or speaks and, simultaneously, brackets all that is heterogeneous to its consciousness. This bracketing [*Einklammerung*] is presented as an *objectivity* which is always already present in linguistic activity in the form of a *nominal* category referring to a "thing" always/already meant and apprehended.[28] This slide from Cartesianism to a more phenomenological vision points out the limitations inherent in thinking of the linguistic universe as transcendental. It also shows that "perception" or linguistic "experience," conceived as logical acts, can never be proof of formal syntactico-semantic theory since they are always posited by that very theory, which is to say, by its thetic (naming) and synthesizing (predicating) transcendental ego. From our own perspective, however, recourse to phenomenology is useful nevertheless for demonstrating the insurmountable necessity of *positing* an ego as the single, unique constraint which is constitutive of all linguistic acts as well as all trans-linguistic practice. In this sense, in light of modern language theory, we see that Husserlian phenomenology might serve as the bridge leading to an interrogation of the very positionality of the speaking subject—from his permutations to his negativity: in short, an interrogation to be used hereafter on another—dialectical and psychoanalytic—horizon.

On the other hand, one moment of Husserlian phenomenology may seem to deviate from syntactic or predicative closure, from omnipresent Meaning or Intention. This "moment" finds its most radical presentation in the *hyle* [ὕλη], which, like the Platonic *chora* or the Hegelian *Force* (to which we shall return), is apprehended through difficult reasoning; though it is lost as soon as it is posited, it is nonexistent without this positing. We shall recall in what follows—without claiming that such a demonstration is original since it is inherent in the very path followed by Husserl: 1) that the *hyle*, which is always functional (in the Husserlian sense) since it is signifiable, apprehended, or named, appears directly to thetic consciousness, 2) that it is the projection of consciousness' positionality, and 3) that the same is true for everything that may appear heterogeneous to the noematic network of phenomenology—from "perception" to the phenomenological "drives" making up the ante-predicative sphere. Thus it seems to us that, in the framework of the Cartesian subject as in that of the transcendental ego, no heterogeneity vis-à-vis predicative articulation is possible which is not already the projection of the subject's positionality. At a later point in our argument we

shall therefore attempt to see how one might think this heterogeneity through the movement of negativity as the "fourth term"
of the Hegelian dialectic, and, especially, through Freud's discovery of the unconscious and its drives.

Hence what we call *the semiotic* [*le sémiotique*] is not Husserlian Meaning. The latter is constituted by the bracketing (*Einklammerung*) of the real object so that "intentional experience" with its
"intentional object [*Objekt*]" may be formed for the Ego: "To have
a meaning, or to have something 'in mind' [*etwas in Sinne zu ha-
ben*]," writes Husserl, "is the cardinal feature of all consciousness,
that on account of which it is not only experience generally but
meaningful, 'noetic.' "[29] Although Husserl's theory of meaning
undergoes modifications between his *Logical Investigations*[30] and *Ideas*,
and varies even within the latter, here we shall take up only those
aspects of the theory relevant to our discussion and, in particular,
to the distinction between our notion of *the semiotic* and the Husserlian phenomenological notion of meaning [*sens: Sinn*] and signification [*signification: Bedeutung*].[31]

Although, in the beginning of the phenomenological argument, meaning constitutes only the nucleus of the noema surrounded by "noematic phases," these other phases (doxy, syntactic forms, expressions, etc.) derive from the same positing of the
Ego that brings out meaning. But in some ways this meaning already appears in the *hyle* before any intentionality: the *hyle* is the
"matter" of meaning which is always already there; its noesis and
then noema will be the "form" of meaning. This "matter of noematic meaning" is a "universal medium which in the last resort
includes within itself all experiences, even those that are not
characterized as intentional" but which "resemble" intentionality.
Within the *hyle* Husserl classifies "sensory contents" which even
include "impulses" (*Triebe*).[32] In this way, matter-*hyle* is capable of
meaning only to the degree that it "resembles" the intentional;
thus, Husserlian "impulses," like all experience, "bear the specific
qualities of intentionality," which means that they are presented
to and by the same unified Ego. Here we see the fundamental
divergence separating phenomenological "experience" and its

"impulses" from Freudian drives [Triebe], which produce and/or destroy the semiotic and *precede* the distinction between "subject" and "object."

The superposition of the functional *hyle* (with the noesis) and the noema does not in any way introduce a break within the Ego since the same "directed glance," oriented toward the object (which is therefore apprehended as an object of consciousness) passes through both the *hyle* and the noema, and since that apprehension is the "*most inward* phrase of the noema," the " 'bearer' of the noematic peculiarities." Although "matter" and the "what" that intuition draws out from it correspond to the noematic nuclei, the "meant as such" constitutes its "bearer"; their conjunction is always realized within the ray of the apprehending glance; together they articulate "meaning" (*Sinn*) and "signification" (*Bedeutung*). A correlation is made between the *hyle* ("matter") and the noema: the latter consists of an "object," a "what," a *Meaning*, and a "content," a "development and conceptual apprehension" forming "a definite system of *predicates*—either formal or material, determined . . . or left 'indeterminate' " but always determinable—of a *Signification*. The positing of the glance never loses for a second its grasp [*visée, Meinung*] on the always already detached object for an always already present subject. Thus, even the apparent multiplicity of hyletic data and their corresponding noeses are always centered on the position of the "essentially possible individual consciousness," which is the consciousness of the *cogito*.[33] It will be all the more logical to rediscover this unity in the noemas, which, although woven out of an indefinite ideal multiplicity corresponding to the infinity of the human mind, always turn out to be centered on the unicity of the *thing*, which has been promoted to the rank of given.

To justify itself, an unshakable consciousness rests its position on transcendental laws, which it places outside itself in the natural sphere. As such, the concept of the "natural thesis" (the "thesis of the natural standpoint") epitomizes this circle. For it is, first, a positing of the natural, but as a result *any positing* in the natural realm and thus any positing of the object or meaning in a proposition that has signification. The positing of the subject of understanding as subject of the sign and of syntax (of meaning and signification, which is that of a proposition [Satz], in Husserl's terms) determines the positing of a *hyle* or a noesis, and hence of a nature which has been set aside but returns as "such" in what has been posited. The Ego and the object's evasion of each other, which then unfolds on the terrain of this meaning as matter, nucleus, or content, is preserved within *projection's specular enclosure* but does not in any sense represent a gap in the actual or collective unified individual and implies no eventual loss of object or Ego. Moreover, as Husserl demonstrates, this meaning and its Ego have a real basis in *seeing* and *judging*. Although they intervene at different levels in phenomenological reflection, *seeing* and *judging* prove to be at one in positing the transcending Ego, which will posit transcendental intention and intuition. A *posited* Ego is articulated in and by *representation* (which we shall call the sign) and *judgment* (which we shall call syntax) so that, on the basis of this position it can endow with meaning a space posited as previous to its advent. Meaning—which includes meaning as noematic nucleus or as bestowal of noetic meaning, and even the *hyle* upon which it rests—is thus nothing other than a projection of signification (*Bedeutung*) as it is presented by judgment. The proposition states or expresses a thesis of belief, a *doxa*, which, in the modality of certainty, is a protodoxa: "*All thetic characters harbour doxic modalities of this kind*, and when the modus is that of certainty, doxic primary theses which, on lines of noematic meaning, *coincide with* the thetic characters." This is to say that all *cogito*, because it is *thetic*, can be objectified or at least can make its objects plausible [*vraisemblables*]. "No one doubts that 'belief' and 'judgment' in the logical sense belong closely to each other (even if one does not propose to consider them identical), and that syntheses of belief [*Glaubens-synthesen*] find their 'expression' in the forms of stated meaning."[34] The fundamental protodoxa is obviously *Being*, the irreducible archontic position;[35] but when this protodoxa is presented as intimately linked to the judgment which expresses it because and to the extent that the latter is thetic, the question can be reversed: isn't that which posits the doxa of Being logically and practically a positing of judgment or of cogitation which is always thetic *to the extent that what it posits is an* "I"?

In other words, before being a "natural thesis" or a "thetic function" of judgment, isn't *thesis* above all a thesis of the "I"? Therefore, shouldn't the question be what the "I" produces rather than the operations of that "I"? Far from positing the judging "I" as origin, for us such a question merely places the thetic and doxic *within the signifying process* that goes beyond them, and it raises a new question: How is the thetic, which is a *positing* of the subject, produced?[36] In this reversal we are not eliminating the question of Signification (Bedeutung) as the utterance of a posited (thetic) subject with regard to an object. Instead we are showing that Bedeutung, the Thetic, and the Subject are *producible* in order to open up research on the semiotic conditions that produce them while remaining foreign to them. The semiotic can thus be understood as pre-thetic, preceding the positing of the subject. Previous to the ego thinking within a proposition, no Meaning exists, but there *do* exist articulations heterogeneous to signification and to the sign: the semiotic *chora*. Though discrete and disposed, the *chora* cannot be unified by a Meaning, which, by contrast, is initiated by a thesis, constituting, as we shall see, a break.

Returning now to generative grammar, we see that its semantic categories, which are capable of lexicalization, or the logical categories capable of specifying its connections, correspond, epistemologically, if not point by point, to the Husserlian noemas or noeses—to those nuclei or clouds of meaning deriving from a protodoxa (Being), itself given by and to the thetic consciousness of the judging subject. Moreover, because it had based itself on the judging thetic consciousness displayed in sentences, generative grammar was subsequently able to discover semantico-logical categories to saturate that epistemological space of thetic consciousness. Although these categories may be naive and empirical, at least they are *explicitly* dependent on the consciousness that posits categories and on the protodoxa that hides in it. It is obviously not the role of linguistics to demonstrate that any sentence may be converted into a protodoxa. But as a result of this qualification, language is understood as *eidos*, and is examined in its phenomenological purity rather than in the way it is carried out starting from the *hyle*. Consequently, the aim of linguistic metalanguage is a normativeness and/or a grammaticality given in its phenomenological purity as a synthesis of nuclei of meaning or of signification. But one can foresee that, having engaged on this course, all modern linguistics (and psycholinguistics) will do is rediscover all the old phenomenological—noetic, noematic, and hyletic—devices, while still avoiding the question of the corruption of Meaning (*Being* and judgment). Indeed such a question would lead it to review and revise its doctrine on the subject and hence its own problematic position.

Today when generative grammar attempts to resolve the semantic problems posed by discourse usage, it maintains that certain aspects of the *surface structure* are pertinent to semantic interpretation (presupposition, for example); "extended standard theory" even introduces *lexical entries* into the deep structure, but specifies that the positing of these entries is dominated by lexical *categories*.[37] In both these extensions of generative grammar theory, the major determiner remains the *deep structure* and *categories*, both of which, as we have demonstrated, depend on the thetic positing of the subject. Even multiple semantic choice and polysemy ultimately come down to this, since the same Cartesian-doxic subject underlies them both. From the point of view of this subject, Chomsky is quite correct when he writes:

Thus it seems to me that deep structure is a well-defined level which meets the phrase structure conditions of the base rules, defines the proper contexts for lexical insertion, and provides the appropriate grammatical relations for interpretation in terms of 'semantic relations' or 'conceptual structures.'[38]

We shall see that when the speaking subject is no longer considered a phenomenological transcendental ego nor the Cartesian ego but rather a *subject in process/on trial* [*sujet en procès*], as is the case in the practice of the *text*, deep structure or at least transformational rules are disturbed and, with them, the possibility of semantic and/or grammatical categorial interpretation.

4.

Hjelmslev's Presupposed Meaning

LINGUISTIC SEMIOLOGY generally shares the thesis that meaning is a "substance" preexisting its "formation" in an expression—either a sentence or a sign (morpheme, lexeme, etc.)—assumed by the thinking subject. Hjelmslev writes:

Thus we find that the chains
    jeg véd det ikke   (Danish)
    I do not know   (English)
    je ne sais pas   (French)
    . . .

despite all their differences, have a factor in common, namely the meaning, the thought itself. This meaning, so considered, exists provisionally as an amorphous mass, an unanalyzed entity, which is defined only by its external functions, namely its function to each of the linguistic sentences we have quoted. . . . Just as the same sand can be put into different molds, and the same cloud take on ever new shapes, so also the same meaning is formed or structured differently in different languages.[39]

Linguistic functions, and notably the semiotic function, in Hjelmslev's sense, determine the form of this amorphous meaning; only through the intervention of this function and form does meaning become *possible*. Yet the presupposition of an expressible meaning situated beyond content-form and expression-form, beyond content-substance and expression-substance, remains no less fundamental.

    Moreover the semiotic functions of *expression* and *content* refer to the phenomenological universe. In both instances they are relays between a presupposed meaning, hence one always al-

ready posited in some fashion, and its linguistic or more generally semiological enunciation. In both cases, the semiological involves a sign insofar as it is the sign of an object posited as
existing: "It seems to be true that a sign is a sign for something,
and that this something in a certain sense lies outside the sign
itself." Hjelmslev objects to the distinctions between morphology, vocabulary, and syntax; yet the meaning he posits as coming
to existence through form and substance, content and expression, is the meaning of an unavowed thetic consciousness which
reveals its transcendence even while concealing it under its substitute: the always already existing *object*. For us, glossematic substantialism is bound up with the phenomenological edifice, which
includes and goes beyond it, for even though Hjelmslev claims to
be unwilling to take part in the debate between "physicalism" and
"phenomenologism," he seems to opt for physicalism when he
declares that linguistic form may be physical and that "metase-
miology is in practice identical with the so-called description of
substance." Nevertheless, to the extent that Hjelmslevian semiology has to do with language, its semantic fields (content-form and
content-substance), which admit a kinship with Husserlian noemas and noeses, encounter *expression*, which this theory considers
the second constraint constitutive of meaning. Expression is defined with regard to language as a "phonetico-physiological sphere
of movement, which can of course be represented as spatialized
in several dimensions, and which can be presented as an unanalyzed but analyzable continuum . . ."[40] But the relations that divide this continuum and allow a signifier specific to each language to be articulated are not defined.[41] Nor does Hjelmslev
define the difference between the two functions of *expression* and
content in the semiological universe's process of production—indeed, the Hjelmslevian "process" is not a process of heterogeneous production, but an *eidos*, pure phenomenality. The notion
of process is put forward and then immediately presented as "a
limited number of elements that constantly recur in new combinations";[42] each one of these elements has the same status because they each depend on the same (unstated) positing of thetic
consciousness.

In fact, this failure to distinguish between qualitatively different stages in the unfolding of the signifying process would seem to stem from the imprecise place glossematics assigns to language within this process. Hjelmslev considers the functions of expression and content on the basis of meaning's functioning in verbal language, and then rediscovers these functions in all signifying systems (chromatic, vocalic, and so forth), although in different combinations. By contrast, in our own view, one must distinguish language from other signifying systems and consider the linguistic sign (and the dichotomies it can give rise to: expression/content, etc.) as only one stage of the signifying process, qualitatively different from the others and dependent on or produced by the position of the subject of understanding.[43]

To do so and maintain a metalinguistic description as well, we will obviously have to make use of concepts and *categories* to account for pre-sign functioning, which is internal to language but also capable of autonomy, giving rise to other signifying systems. Nevertheless, within this categorizing, an inevitable step in theoretical discourse, we are designating a new object—the *semiotic*—which is irreducible to the noetico-neomatic layers on which phenomenology and its semiological or semantic derivatives operate. It thereby becomes possible to disclose a fundamental stage—or region—in the process of the subject, a stage that is hidden by the arrival of signification, in other words, by the *symbolic*. Investigating the field of the semiotic as we have just defined it should enable us to designate more clearly the operations of that which becomes a *signifier* (in the Stoic and Saussurean sense) for the symbolic.[44]

The semiotic is articulated by flow and marks: facilitation, energy transfers, the cutting up of the corporeal and social continuum as well as that of signifying material, the establishment of a distinctiveness and its ordering in a pulsating *chora*, in a rhythmic but nonexpressive totality. The functioning of writing [*écriture*], the trace, and the grammè, introduced by Derrida in his critique of phenomenology and its linguistic substitutes, points to an essential aspect of the semiotic: *Of Grammatology* specifies that which escapes Bedeutung. We shall nevertheless keep the term semiotic to designate the operation that logically and chronologically precedes the establishment of the symbolic and its subject: the term will in fact allow us to envisage a heterogeneous functioning, which Freud called "psychosomatic." Despite their metaphysical connotations, this word's lexemes objectively indicate a double organizing constraint—both biological and social—which we view as the fundamental precondition of this functioning. As a result, the term "semiotic" can simultaneously be seen as part of a larger process that englobes it: the *signifying process*. The etymological kinship between the terms *semiotic, symbolic,* and *significance* clearly points to this differentiated unity, which is ultimately that of the process of the subject. The semiotic is thus a modality of the signifying process with an eye to the subject posited (but posited as absent) by the symbolic. In our view, structuralist linguistic theories come closer to the semiotic than to what we shall call the symbolic, which, dependent as it is on a punctual ego, appears in propositions. Structural linguistics, operating on phonological oppositions or on the two axes of metaphor and metonymy, accounts for some (though not all) of the articulations operating in what we have called the semiotic.[45]

Admittedly, structural linguistics often eliminates from the semiotic the drives that underly it and the role they play in establishing the subject. But when linguistic structuralism becomes a method of structural anthropology, the drives that form the foundation of structural dichotomies command the investigator's attention. Yet, even then, they are removed once again, and structuralism retains only the image of the unconscious as a depository of laws and thus a discourse.[46] Since they are considered solely from the point of view of their relationship to language, and deprived of their drive bases, these structural operations depend on the phenomenological reduction, just as they depend on what this reduction is able to make visible: thetic symbolic functioning (see Section 5, following). It has therefore been necessary to see these operations as similar to Freud's "primary processes," fill them with drives or even dissolve them in the undecidable grammè in order to remove them from their phenomenological refuge and define them, specifically, as processes forming the signifier, logically anterior to the grammatical sequences the Cartesian subject generates, but synchronous with their unfolding.

5.

The Thetic:
Rupture and/or Boundary

WE SHALL distinguish the semiotic (drives and their articulations) from the realm of signification, which is always that of a proposition or judgment, in other words, a realm of *positions*. This positionality, which Husserlian phenomenology orchestrates through the concepts of *doxa, position,* and *thesis,* is structured as a break in the signifying process, establishing the *identification* of the subject and its object as preconditions of propositionality. We shall call this break, which produces the positing of signification, a *thetic* phase. All enunciation, whether of a word or of a sentence, is thetic. It requires an identification; in other words, the subject must separate from and through his image, from and through his objects. This image and objects must first be posited in a space that becomes symbolic because it connects the two separated positions, recording them or redistributing them in an open combinatorial system.

The child's first so-called holophrastic enunciations include gesture, the object, and vocal emission. Because they are perhaps not yet sentences (NP-VP), generative grammar is not readily equipped to account for them. Nevertheless, they are already thetic in the sense that they separate an object from the subject, and attribute to it a semiotic fragment, which thereby becomes a signifier. That this attribution is either metaphoric or metonymic ("woof-woof" says the dog, and all animals become "woof-woof") is logically secondary to the fact that it constitutes an *attribution*, which is to say, a positing of identity or difference, and that it represents the nucleus of judgment or proposition.

We shall say that the thetic phase of the signifying process is the "deepest structure" of the possibility of enunciation, in other words, of signification and the proposition. Husserl theologizes this deep logic of signification by making it a productive *origin* of the "free spontaneity" of the Ego:

Its *free spontaneity and activity* consists in positing, positing on the strength of this or that, positing as an antecedent or a consequent, and so forth; it does not live within the theses as a passive indweller; the theses radiate from it as from a primary source of generation [*Erzeugungen*]. Every thesis begins with a *point of insertion* [*Einsatzpunkt*] with a point at which *the positing has its origin* [*Ursprungssetzung*]; so it is with the first thesis and with each further one in the synthetic nexus. This 'inserting' even belongs to the thesis as such, as a remarkable modus of original actuality. It somewhat resembles the *fiat*, the point of insertion of will and action.[47]

In this sense, *there exists only one signification*, that of the thetic phase, which contains the object as well as the proposition, and the complicity between them.[48] There is no sign that is not thetic and every sign is already the germ of a "sentence," attributing a signifier to an object through a "copula" that will function as a signified.[49] Stoic semiology, which was the first to formulate the matrix of the sign, had already established *this complicity between sign and sentence*, making them proofs of each other.

Modern philosophy recognizes that the right to represent the founding *thesis* of signification (sign and/or proposition) devolves upon the transcendental ego. But only since Freud have we been able to raise the question not of the origin of this thesis but rather of the process of its production. To brand the thetic as the foundation of metaphysics is to risk serving as an antechamber for metaphysics—unless, that is, we specify the way the thetic is produced. In our view, the Freudian theory of the unconscious and its Lacanian development show, precisely, that thetic signification is a stage attained under certain precise conditions during the signifying process, and that it constitutes the subject without being reduced to his process precisely because it is the threshold of language. Such a standpoint constitutes neither a reduction of the subject to the transcendental ego, nor a denial [*dénégation*] of the thetic phase that establishes signification.

6.

The Mirror and Castration
Positing the Subject
as Absent from the Signifier

IN THE development of the subject, such as it has been reconstituted by the theory of the unconscious, we find the thetic phase of the signifying process, around which signification is organized, at two points: the mirror stage and the "discovery" of castration.

The first, the mirror stage, produces the "spatial intuition" which is found at the heart of the functioning of signification—in signs and in sentences. From that point on, in order to capture his image unified in a mirror, the child must remain separate from it, his body agitated by the semiotic motility we discussed above, which fragments him more than it unifies him in a representation. According to Lacan, human physiological immaturity, which is due to premature birth, is thus what permits any permanent positing whatsoever and, first and foremost, that of the image itself, as separate, heterogeneous, dehiscent.[50] Captation of the image and the drive investment in this image, which institute primary narcissism, permit the constitution of objects detached from the semiotic *chora*. Lacan maintains, moreover, that the specular image is the "prototype" for the "world of objects."[51] Positing the imaged ego leads to the positing of the object, which is, likewise, separate and signifiable.

Thus the two separations that prepare the way for the sign are set in place. The sign can be conceived as the voice that is projected from the agitated body (from the semiotic *chora*) onto the facing *imago* or onto the object, which simultaneously detach from the surrounding continuity. Indeed, a child's first holophrastic utterances occur at this time, within what are considered the boundaries of the mirror stage (six to eighteen months). On the basis of this positing, which constitutes a *break*, signification becomes established as a digital system with a double articulation combining discrete elements. Language learning can therefore be thought of as an acute and dramatic confrontation between positing-separating-identifying and the motility of the semiotic *chora*. Separation from the mother's body, the *fort-da* game, anality and orality (see parts II and III below), all act as a permanent negativity that destroys the image and the isolated object even as it facilitates the articulation of the semiotic network, which will afterwards be necessary in the system of language where it will be more or less integrated as a *signifier*.

Castration puts the finishing touches on the process of separation that posits the subject as signifiable, which is to say, separate, always confronted by an other: *imago* in the mirror (signified) and semiotic process (signifier). As the addressee of every demand, the mother occupies the place of alterity. Her replete body, the receptacle and guarantor of demands, takes the place of all narcissistic, hence imaginary, effects and gratifications; she is, in other words, the phallus. The discovery of castration, however, detaches the subject from his dependence on the mother, and the perception of this lack |*manque*| makes the phallic function a symbolic function—*the* symbolic function. This is a decisive moment fraught with consequences: the subject, finding his identity in the symbolic, *separates* from his fusion with the mother, *confines* his jouissance to the genital, and transfers semiotic motility onto the symbolic order. Thus ends the formation of the thetic phase, which posits the gap between the signifier and the signified as an opening up toward every desire but also every act, including the very jouissance that exceeds them.[52]

At this point we would like to emphasize, without going into the details of Lacan's argument, that the phallus totalizes the effects of signifieds as having been produced by the signifier: the phallus is itself a signifier. In other words, the phallus is not given in the utterance but instead refers outside itself to a precondition that makes enunciation possible. For there to be enunciation, the *ego* must be posited in the signified, but it must do so as a function of the *subject* lacking in the signifier; a system of finite positions (signification) can only function when it is supported by a subject and on the condition that this subject is a want-to-be [*manque à être*].[53] Signification exists precisely because there is no subject in signification. The gap between the imaged ego and drive motility, between the mother and the demand made on her, is precisely the break that establishes what Lacan calls the place of the Other as the place of the "signifier." The subject is hidden "by an ever purer signifier,"[54] this want-to-be confers on an *other* the role of containing the possibility of signification; and this other, who is no longer the mother (from whom the child ultimately separates through the mirror stage and castration), presents itself as the place of the signifier that Lacan will call "the Other."

Is this to say, then, that such a theoretical undertaking transcendentalizes semiotic motility, setting it up as a transcendental Signifier? In our view, this transformation of semiotic motility serves to remove it from its autoerotic and maternal enclosure and, by introducing the signifier/signified break, allows it to produce signification. By the same token, signification itself appears as a stage of the signifying process—not so much its base as its boundary. Signification is placed "under the sign of the preconscious."[55] Ultimately, this signifier/signified transformation, constitutive of language, is seen as being indebted to, induced, and imposed by the social realm. Dependence on the mother is severed, and transformed into a symbolic relation to an other; the constitution of the Other is indispensable for communicating with an other. In this way, the signifier/signified break is synonymous with social sanction: "the first social censorship."

Thus we view the thetic phase—the positing of the *imago*, castration, and the positing of semiotic motility—as the place of the Other, as the precondition for signification, i.e., the precondition for the positing of language. The thetic phase marks a threshold between two heterogeneous realms: the semiotic and the symbolic. The second includes part of the first and their scission is thereafter marked by the break between signifier and signified. Symbolic would seem an appropriate term for this always split unification that is produced by a rupture and is impossible without it. Its etymology makes it particularly pertinent. The σύμβολον is a sign of recognition: an "object" split in two and the parts separated, but, as eyelids do, σύμβολον brings together the two edges of that fissure. As a result, the "symbol" is any joining, any bringing together that is a contract—one that either follows hostilities or presupposes them—and, finally, any exchange, including an exchange of hostility.

Not only is symbolic, thetic unity divided (into signifier and signified), but this division is itself the result of a break that put a heterogeneous functioning in the position of signifier. This functioning is the instinctual semiotic, preceding meaning and signification, mobile, amorphous, but already regulated, which we have attempted to represent through references to child psychoanalysis (particularly at the pre-Oedipal stage) and the theory of drives. In the speaking subject, fantasies articulate this irruption of drives within the realm of the signifier; they disrupt the signifier and shift the metonymy of desire, which acts within the place of the Other, onto a jouissance that divests the object and turns back toward the autoerotic body. That language is a defensive construction reveals its ambiguity—the death drive underlying it. If language, constituted as symbolic through narcissistic, specular, imaginary investment, protects the body from the attack of drives by making it a place—the place of the signifier—in which the body can signify itself through positions; and if, therefore, language, in the service of the death drive, is a pocket of narcissism toward which this drive may be directed, then fantasies remind us, if we had ever forgotten, of the insistent presence of drive heterogeneity.[56]

All poetic "distortions" of the signifying chain and the structure of signification may be considered in this light: they yield under the attack of the "residues of first symbolizations" (Lacan), in other words, those drives that the thetic phase was not able to sublate [relever, aufheben] by linking them into signifier and signified. As a consequence, any disturbance of the "social censorship"—that of the signifier/signified break—attests, perhaps first and foremost, to an influx of the death drive, which no signifier, no mirror, no other, and no mother could ever contain. In "artistic" practices the semiotic—the precondition of the symbolic—is revealed as that which also destroys the symbolic, and this revelation allows us to presume something about its functioning.

Psychoanalysts acknowledge that the pre-Oedipal stages Melanie Klein discusses are "analytically unthinkable" but not inoperative; and, furthermore, that the relation of the subject to the signifier is established and language learning is completed only in the pregenital stages that are set in place by the retroaction of the Oedipus complex (which itself brings about initial genital maturation).[57] Thereafter, the supposedly characteristic functioning of the pre-Oedipal stages appears only in the complete, postgenital handling of language, which presupposes, as we have seen, a decisive imposition of the phallic. In other words, the subject must be firmly posited by castration so that drive attacks against the thetic will not give way to fantasy or to psychosis but will instead lead to a "second-degree thetic," i.e., a resumption of the functioning characteristic of the semiotic *chora* within the signifying device of language. This is precisely what artistic practices, and notably poetic language, demonstrate.

Starting from and (logically and chronologically) after the phallic position and the castration that underlies it—in other words, after the Oedipus complex and especially after the regulation of genitality by the retroactive effect of the Oedipus complex in puberty—the semiotic *chora* can be read not as a failure of the thetic but instead as its very precondition. Neurotics and psychotics are defined as such by their relationship to what we are calling the thetic. We now see why, in treating them, psychoanalysis can only conceive of semiotic motility as a disturbance of language and/or of the order of the signifier. Conversely, the refusal of the thetic phase and an attempt to hypostasize semiotic motility as autonomous from the thetic—capable of doing without it or unaware of it—can be seen as a resistance to psychoanalysis. Some therefore even contend that one can find in poetry the unfolding of this refusal of the thetic, something like a direct transcription of the genetic code—as if practice were possible without the thetic and as if a text, in order to hold together as a text, did not require a completion [finition], a structuration, a kind of totalization of semiotic motility. This completion constitutes a synthesis that requires the thesis of language in order to come about, and the semiotic pulverizes it only to make it a new device—for us, this is precisely what distinguishes a text as *signifying practice* from the "drifting-into-non-sense" [dérive] that characterizes neurotic discourse. The distinction cannot be erased unless one puts oneself outside "monumental history" in a transcendence which often proves to be one of the reactionary forces combining that history's discrete blocks.[58]

In this way, only the subject, for whom the thetic is not a repression of the semiotic *chora* but instead a position either taken on or undergone, can call into question the thetic so that a new disposition may be articulated. Castration must have been a problem, a trauma, a drama, so that the semiotic can return through the symbolic position it brings about. This is the crux of the matter: both the completion of the Oedipus complex and its reactivation in puberty are needed for the Aufhebung of the semiotic in the symbolic to give rise to a signifying *practice* that has a socio-historical function (and is not just a self-analytical discourse, a substitute for the analyst's couch). At the same time, however, this completion of the Oedipal stage and the genitality it gives rise to should not repress the semiotic, for such a repression is what sets up metalanguage and the "pure signifier." No pure signifier can effect the Aufhebung (in the Hegelian sense) of the semiotic without leaving a remainder, and anyone who would believe this myth need only question his fascination or boredom with a given poem, painting, or piece of music. As a traversable boundary, the thetic is completely different from an imaginary castration that must be evaded in order to return to the maternal *chora*. It is clearly distinct as well from a castration imposed once and for all, perpetuating the well-ordered signifier and positing it as sacred and unalterable within the enclosure of the Other.[59]

7.

Frege's Notion of Signification: Enunciation and Denotation

WHAT BECOMES of signification once the signifier has been posited?

We have seen that, according to Husserl, signification is a predication that necessitates the fundamental thesis of a Dasein, which is essentially that of the transcendental ego. Whether this predication, or more accurately, this judgment, is existential or attributive is—as Freud seemed to believe in his article on *Verneinung*—secondary to its being, first and foremost, a positing. But *what* does it posit, since the semiotic *chora* has been separated from the "subject"-"object" continuum? It posits an *object* or a *denotatum*. Frege calls the utterance of this *denotatum* a *Bedeutung* (signification), which in this case is denotation. But Frege's departure from Husserl is only apparent.

For Husserl, the isolation of an object as such is, as we have seen, the inseparable and concomitant precondition for the positing of the judging Ego, since that Ego's enunciation refers to an object. So much so that, as Frege shows, signs can be attributed the same signification by the same denotation. But Frege goes further: Doesn't the immense profusion of signs, even before denoting objects, imply the very *precondition of denotation*, which is the *positing of an object*, of the object, of object-ness? In other words, denotation would be understood as the subject's ability to separate himself from the ecosystem into which he was fused, so that, as a result of this separation, he may designate it. Frege writes: "If now the truth value of a sentence is its denotation, then on the one hand all true sentences have the same denotation and so, on the other hand, do all false sentences. *From this we see that in the denotation of the sentence all that is specific is obliterated.*"[60] According to Frege, sentences are able to have an object and be true or false solely on the basis of that object by virtue of their relation to "concept" and to "thought"; however, although he does not enter into this labyrinth, Frege maintains that the stated *predication* is the logical matrix of *Bedeutung*, which is nevertheless not identical to it. Judgment produces *Bedeutung* but does not enclose it, referring it instead elsewhere, to a heterogeneous domain, which is to say, within the existing object.[61]

By straddling these two "levels," Frege's *Bedeutung*, in our view, designates, precisely, the break that simultaneously sets up the symbolic thesis and an object; as an externality within judgment, it has a truth value only by virtue of this scission. We may conclude, therefore, that *the thetic is the precondition for both enunciation and denotation.*[62] If the very possibility of such an internal externality is that which founds signification's truth capacity, we can understand why Frege suggests that there is in fact only one denotation.[63] But denotation is not equivalent to the Saussurean referent: Frege posits the existence of signs, "artistic" signs, for example, that have no *denotation*, only *meaning*, because they do not refer to a real object. Therefore one should not be concerned with the denotation of a thought or a part of a thought taken as a work of art. Yet it must be supposed that the desire to do so exists, even with works of art, whenever they include thoughts in the form of propositions. The specific status of signification in art thus results from a constantly maintained ambiguity between the possibility of a *meaning* that amounts to grammaticality[64] and a *denotation* that is, likewise, given in the very structure of the judgment or proposition but is realized only under certain conditions—notably when predication achieves an existential value.[65] But under what conditions does predication cease being a copula that is indifferent to the existence of an object and obtain instead a denotative value referring to that object? Frege does not specify the economy of the signifying act that makes enunciation a denotation; but when he speaks of the "same denotation" for all true propositions, he lets us see that the subject's ability to separate from the semiotic *chora* and to designate an object as real lies in the thetic function of symbolism.

The thetic posits the signifiable object: it posits signification as both a *denotation* (of an object) and an *enunciation* (of a displaced subject, absent from the signified and signifying position). From then on, the thetic prepares and contains within itself the very possibility of making this division explicit through an opposition and a juxtaposition of syntagms: the proposition, and judgment as well—to the extent that the latter is coexistensive with the proposition—unfold or *linearize* (by concatenation or application) the signification (enunciation + denotation) opened up by the thetic. Even if it is presented as a simple act of naming, we maintain that the thetic is already *propositional* (or syntactic) and that syntax is the ex-position of the thetic. The subject and predicate represent the division inherent in the thetic; they make it plain and actual. But if theory persists in regarding them as independent entities, notions of the subject and predicate may end up obscuring not only the link between (thetic) signification and syntactic structure, but also the complicity and opposition between denotation (given in the subject) and enunciation (given in the predicate).

Therefore we could consider that which has been relegated to the terms "subject" and "predicate" or, more narrowly, "noun" and "verb," as two modalities of the thetic, representing the posited and positing, linked and linking elements—denotation and enunciation—that are indissociable from the thetic process and, consequently, permutable or reversible. The positing, linking, assertive, cohesive element, the one that completes the utterance and makes it finite (a sentence), in short, the element in which the spatio-temporal and communicational positing of the speaking subject is marked, is the element with the predicative *function*. It may be, but is not necessarily, what morphology identifies as a "verb." But at the same time, as Benveniste shows, variable predication itself is the "seat of an invariant" which simultaneously posits an extra-linguistic reality [*réel*] and phrastic completion and ensures the relation between the two orders. This is, in fact, what we have called a thetic function, demonstrating that assertion and intra-syntactic completion are inseparable.

Conceiving the signifying process as a thetic negativity thus leads us to relativize the classic terms "subject" and "predicate" and see them as mere "subsets" (characteristic of certain languages or linguistic theories) of a more general relation which is actually in play between two indissociable modalities of the thetic (posited-positing, linked-linking, modified-modifier, etc.) The relations between Kuryłowicz's "modifier" and "modified," Strawson's "feature concepts" or "feature-placing statements" or Shaumyan's "applicational generative model"[66] on a technical linguistic level would also seem to corroborate the inseparability of the thetic and syntax. Their indivisibility implies that signification (*Bedeutung*) is a process in which opposable "terms" are posited as phenomena but can be identified as the two faces (denotation-enunciation) of the thetic break.[67]

Syntax registers the thetic break as an opposition of discrete and permutable elements but whose concrete position nevertheless indicates that each one has a definite signification. Syntax displaces and represents, within the homogeneous element of language, the thetic break separating the signifier from what was heterogeneous to it. The *transformation* [from drive to signifier] produced by the thetic is registered only as an inter-syntactical *division* (modified-modifier, "feature-placing" or subject-predicate). This transformation, which produced the speaking subject, comes about only if it leaves that subject out, within the heterogeneous. Indeed, although he is the bearer of syntax, the speaking subject is absent from it.

But when this subject reemerges, when the semiotic *chora* disturbs the thetic position by redistributing the signifying order, we note that the denoted object and the syntactic relation are disturbed as well. The denoted object proliferates in a series of connoted objects produced by the *transposition* of the semiotic *chora*[68] and the syntactic division (modified-modifer, NP-VP, or the placement of semantic features) is disrupted. In the latter aspect of the signifying process—syntax—we note that the division of the grammatical sequence (which we have called the transposition of the thetic break into a homogeneous sign system) is maintained; this means that syntactic categories, which ensure the possibility of both verisimilar denotation and communication, are also preserved. But the *completion* of the grammatical sequence does not take place because the division is not completely rejoined in a NP-VP, modified-modifier, etc. whole. This ellipsis or syntactic *noncompletion* can be interpreted as the thetic break's inability to remain simply intra-syntactic—a division within a signifying homogeneity. A heterogeneous division, an irruption of the semiotic *chora*, marks each "category" of the syntactic sequence and prevents the "other" from being posited as an identifiable syntactic term (subject or predicate, modifed or modifier, etc.). In this realization of the signifier, particularly as it is seen in poetic texts, alterity is maintained within the pure signifier and/or in the simply syntactic element only with difficulty. For the Other has become heterogeneous and will not remain fixed in place: it negativizes all terms, all posited elements, and thus syntax, threatening them with possible dissolution.

It should be understood that the path completed by the *text* is not a simple return, as in the Hegelian dialectic, from the "predicate" to the "subject," from the "general" to the "particular"; it does not constitute a Hegelian synthesis operating in judgment and realized in the syllogism. Instead it involves both shattering and maintaining *position* within the heterogeneous *process*: the proof can be found in the phonetic, lexical, and syntactic disturbance visible in the *semiotic device* of the text.[69] The disturbance of sentential completion or syntactic ellipsis lead to an infinitization of logical (syntactic) applications. Terms are linked together but, as a consequence of nonrecoverable deletion,[70] they are linked ad infinitum. The sentence is not suppressed, it is infinitized. Similarly, the denoted object does not disappear, it proliferates in mimetic, fictional, connoted objects.

8.

Breaching[71] the Thetic: Mimesis

SIGNIFICATION IN literature implies the possibility of denotation. But instead of following denotative sequences, which would lead, from one judgment to another, to the knowledge of a real object, literary signification tends toward the exploration of grammaticality and/or toward enunciation. Mimesis is, precisely, the construction of an object, not according to truth but to *verisimilitude*, to the extent that the object is posited as such (hence separate, noted but not denoted); it is, however, internally dependent on a subject of enunciation who is unlike the transcendental ego in that he does not suppress the semiotic *chora* but instead raises the *chora* to the status of a signifier, which may or may not obey the norms of grammatical locution. Such is the *connoted* mimetic object.

Although mimesis partakes of the symbolic order, it does so only to re-produce some of its constitutive rules, in other words, grammaticality. By the same token, it must posit an object, but this "object" is merely a result of the drive economy of enunciation; its true position is inconsequential.[72] What is more, when poetic language—especially modern poetic language—transgresses grammatical rules, the *positing* of the symbolic (which mimesis has always explored) finds itself subverted, not only in its possibilities of *Bedeutung* or denotation (which mimesis has always contested), but also as a possessor of *meaning* (which is always grammatical, indeed more precisely, syntactic). In imitating the constitution of the symbolic as *meaning*, poetic mimesis is led to dissolve not only the denotative function but also the specifically thetic function of *positing* the subject. In this respect, modern poetic language goes further than any classical mimesis—whether theatrical or novelistic—because it attacks not only denotation (the positing of the object) but meaning (the positing of the enunciating subject) as well.

In thus eroding the verisimilitude that inevitably underlaid classical mimesis and, more importantly, the very position of enunciation (i.e., the positing of the subject as absent from the signifier), poetic language puts the subject in process/on trial through a network of marks and semiotic facilitations. But the moment it stops being mere instinctual glossolalia and becomes part of the linguistic order, poetry meets up with denotation and enunciation—verisimilitude and the subject—and, through them, the social.

We now understand how the thetic conditions the possibilities of truth specific to language: all transgressions of the thetic are a crossing of the boundary between true and false—maintained, inevitably, whenever signification is maintained, and shaken, irremediably, by the flow of the semiotic into the symbolic. Mimesis, in our view, is a transgression of the thetic when truth is no longer a reference to an object that is identifiable outside of language; it refers instead to an object that can be constructed through the semiotic network but is nevertheless posited in the symbolic and is, from then on, always verisimilar.

Mimetic verisimilitude does not, therefore, eliminate the unique break Frege saw presiding over signification. Instead it maintains that break because it preserves meaning and, with it, a certain object. But neither true nor false, the very status of this verisimilar object throws into question the absoluteness of the break that establishes truth. Mimesis does not actually call into question the unicity of the thetic; indeed it could not, since mimetic discourse takes on the structure of language and, through narrative sentences, posits a signified and signifying object. Mimesis and the poetic language inseparable from it tend, rather, to prevent the thetic from becoming theological; in other words, they prevent the imposition of the thetic from hiding the semiotic process that produces it, and they bar it from inducing the subject, reified as a transcendental ego, to function solely within the systems of science and monotheistic religion.

To note that there can be no language without a thetic phase that establishes the possibility of truth, and to draw consequences from this discovery is quite a different matter from insisting that every signifying practice operate uniquely out of the thetic phase. For this would mean that the thetic, as origin and transcendence, could only produce (in the Husserlian sense) a tautological discourse, which, having originated in a thesis, can only be a synthesis of theses. We maintain therefore that science and theological dogma are doxic. By repressing the *production* of doxy, they make the thetic a belief from which the quest for truth departs; but the path thus programmed is circular and merely returns to its thetic point of departure.[73] If mimesis, by contrast, pluralizes denotation, and if poetic language undermines meaning, by what specific operations are these corruptions of the symbolic carried out?

As we know, Freud specifies two fundamental "processes" in the work of the unconscious: *displacement* and *condensation*. Kruszewski and Jakobson[74] introduced them, in a different way, during the early stages of structural linguistics, through the concepts of *metonymy* and *metaphor*, which have since been interpreted in light of psychoanalysis.[75]

To these we must add a third "process"—the *passage from one sign system to another*. To be sure, this process comes about through a combination of displacement and condensation, but this does not account for its total operation. It also involves an altering of the thetic *position*—the destruction of the old position and the formation of a new one. The new signifying system may be produced with the same signifying material; in language, for example, the passage may be made from narrative to text. Or it may be borrowed from different signifying materials: the transposition from a carnival scene to the written text, for instance. In this connection we examined the formation of a specific signifying system—the novel—as the result of a redistribution of several different sign systems: carnival, courtly poetry, scholastic discourse.[76] The term *inter-textuality* denotes this transposition of one (or several) sign system(s) into another; but since this term has often been understood in the banal sense of "study of sources," we prefer the term *transposition* because it specifies that the passage from one signifying system to another demands a new articulation of the thetic—of enunciative and denotative positionality. If one grants that every signifying practice is a field of transpositions of various signifying systems (an inter-textuality), one then understands that its "place" of enunciation and its denoted "object" are never single, complete, and identical to themselves, but always plural, shattered, capable of being tabulated. In this way polysemy can also be seen as the result of a semiotic polyvalence—an adherence to different sign systems.

Along with condensation (*Verdichtung*) and displacement (*Verschiebung*), Freud also speaks of *considerations of representability* (*die Rücksicht auf Darstellbarkeit*), which are essential to dream-work (*die Traumarbeit*). Representability comes about through a process, closely related to displacement but appreciably different from it, that Freud calls "ein Vertauschung des sprachlichen Ausdruckes." We shall call *transposition* the signifying process' ability to pass from one sign system to another, to exchange and permutate them; and *representability* the specific articulation of the semiotic and the thetic for a sign system. Transposition plays an essential role here inasmuch as it implies the abandonment of a former sign system, the passage to a second via an instinctual intermediary common to the two systems, and the articulation of the new system with its new representability.[77]

Poetic mimesis maintains and transgresses thetic unicity by making it undergo a kind of anamnesis, by introducing into the thetic position the stream of semiotic drives and making it signify.[78] This telescoping of the symbolic and the semiotic pluralizes signification or denotation: it pluralizes the thetic doxy. Mimesis and poetic language do not therefore disavow the thetic, instead they go through its truth (signification, denotation) to tell the "truth" about it. To be sure, the latter use of the term "truth" is inappropriate, since it no longer refers to denotative truth in Frege's sense. This "second truth" reproduces the path which was cleared by the first truth (that of *Bedeutung*) in order to posit itself.

Both mimesis and poetic language with its connotations assume the right to enter into the social debate, which is an ideological debate, on the strength of their confrontation with *Bedeutung* (signification and denotation) but also with all meaning, and hence all enunciation produced by a posited subject.

But mimesis and poetic language do more than engage in an intra-ideological debate; they question the very principle of the ideological because they unfold the *unicity* of the thetic (the precondition for meaning and signification) and prevent its theologization. As the place of production for a subject who transgresses the thetic by using it as a necessary boundary—but not as an absolute or as an origin—poetic language and the mimesis from which it is inseparable, are profoundly a-theological. They are not critics of theology but rather the enemy within and without, recognizing both its necessity and its pretensions. In other words, poetic language and mimesis may appear as an argument complicitous with dogma—we are familiar with religion's use of them—but they may also set in motion what dogma represses. In so doing, they no longer act as instinctual floodgates within the enclosure of the sacred and become instead protestors against its posturing. And thus, its complexity unfolded by its practices, the signifying process joins social revolution.

9.

The Unstable Symbolic.
Substitutions in the Symbolic:
Fetishism

THE THETIC permits the constitution of the symbolic with its vertical stratification (referent, signified, signifier) and all the subsequent modalities of logico-semantic articulation. The thetic originates in the "mirror stage" and is completed, through the phallic stage, by the reactivation of the Oedipus complex in puberty; no signifying practice can be without it. Though absolutely necessary, the thetic is not exclusive: the semiotic, which also precedes it, constantly tears it open, and this transgression brings about all the various transformations of the signifying practice that are called "creation." Whether in the realm of metalanguage (mathematics, for example) or literature, what remodels the symbolic order is always the influx of the semiotic. This is particularly evident in poetic language since, for there to be a transgression of the symbolic, there must be an irruption of the drives in the universal signifying order, that of "natural" language which binds together the social unit. That the subject does not vanish into psychosis when this transgression takes place poses a problem for metaphysics, both the kind that sets up the signifier as an untransgressable law and the kind for which there exists no thetic and therefore no subject.

The semiotic's breach of the symbolic in so-called poetic practice can probably be ascribed to the very unstable yet forceful positing of the thetic. In our view, the analysis of texts shows that thetic lability is ultimately a problem with imaginary captation (disorders in the mirror stage that become marked scopophilia, the need for a mirror or an identifying addressee, etc.) and a resistance to the discovery of castration (thereby maintaining the phallic mother who usurps the place of the Other). These problems and resistances obstruct the thetic phase of the signifying process. When they fail to prevent the constitution of the symbolic (which would result in psychosis), they return in and through its position. In so doing, they give rise to "fantasies"; more importantly, they attempt to dissolve the first social censorship—the bar between signifier and signified—and, simultaneously, the first guarantee of the subject's position—signification, then meaning (the sentence and its syntax). Language thus tends to be drawn out of its symbolic function (sign-syntax) and is opened out within a semiotic articulation; with a material support such as the voice, this semiotic network gives "music" to literature.

But the irruption of the semiotic within the symbolic is only relative. Though permeable, the thetic continues to ensure the position of the subject put in process/on trial. As a consequence, musicality is not without signification; indeed it is deployed within it. Logical syntheses and all ideologies are present, but they are pulverized within their own logic before being displaced toward something that is no longer within the realm of the idea, sign, syntax, and thus Logos, but is instead simply semiotic functioning. The precondition for such a heterogeneity that alone posits and removes historical meaning is the thetic phase: we cannot overemphasize this point.

Without the completion of the thetic phase, we repeat, no signifying practice is possible; the negation/denial [*dénégation*] of this phase leads the subject to shift the thetic, even though he is determined by it, onto one of the places that the signifying process must cross on its way to fulfillment. Negating or denying the symbolic, without which he would be incapable of doing anything, the subject may imagine the thetic at the place of an object or a partner. This is a fetishist mechanism, which consists in denying the mother's castration, but perhaps goes back even further to a problem in separating an image of the ego in the mirror from the bodily organs invested with semiotic motility. Negation-as-denial (*Verneinung*) or disavowal (*Verleugung*) in perversion, which may go so far as the foreclosure (*Verwerfung*) of the thetic phase, represent different modalities capable of obscuring castration and the sexual difference underlying it as well as genital sexuality. Further on we shall see how a marked investment in anal eroticism leads to this rejection of the thetic because it allows a questioning of the symbolic order; but by this very process it shifts the *thesis* onto *objects*. The prototype of such objects is excrement since it is midway between an autoerotic body, which is not yet autonomous from its eroticized sphincters, and the pleasure the mother's body or her supposed phallus would procure—a belief that is disclaimed but maintained, behind, as a compromise.

Since there can be no signifying practice without a thetic phase, the thetic that does not manage to posit itself in the symbolic order necessarily places itself in the objects surrounding the body and instinctually linked to it. Fetishism is a compromise with the thetic; although erased from the symbolic and displaced onto the drives, a "thesis" is nevertheless maintained so that signifying practice can take place. Therefore we shall contend that it is the thetic, and not fetishism, that is inherent in every cultural production, because fetishism is a displacement of the thetic onto the realm of drives. The instinctual *chora* articulates facilitations and stases, but fetishism is a telescoping of the symbolic's characteristic thetic moment and of one of those instinctually invested stases (bodies, parts of bodies, orifices, containing objects, and so forth). This stasis thus becomes the ersatz of the sign. Fetishism is a stasis that acts as a thesis.

We might then wonder whether the semiotic's dismantling of the symbolic in poetry necessarily implies that the thetic phase is shifted toward the stases of the semiotic *chora*. Doesn't poetry lead to the establishment of an object as a substitute for the symbolic order under attack, an object that is never clearly *posited* but always "in perspective."[79] The object may be either the body proper or the apparatuses erotized during vocal utterance (the glottis, the lungs), objects that are either linked to the addressee of desire or to the very material of language as the predominant object of pleasure. Moreover, since the symbolic is corrupted so that an object—the book, the work—will result, isn't this object a substitute for the thetic phase? Doesn't it take the thetic's place by making its symbolicity opaque, by filling the thetic with its presence whose pretension to universality is matched only by its very finite limits? In short, isn't art the fetish par excellence, one that badly camouflages its archaeology? At its base, isn't there a belief, ultimately maintained, that the mother is phallic, that the ego—never precisely identified—will never separate from her, and that no symbol is strong enough to sever this dependence? In this symbiosis with the supposedly phallic mother, what can the subject do but occupy her place, thus navigating the path from fetishism to autoeroticism? That indeed is the question.

In order to keep the process signifying, to avoid foundering in an "unsayable" without limits, and thus posit the subject of a practice, the subject of poetic language clings to the help fetishism offers. And so, according to psychoanalysis, poets as individuals fall under the category of fetishism; the very practice of art necessitates reinvesting the maternal *chora* so that it transgresses the symbolic order; and, as a result, this practice easily lends itself to so-called perverse subjective structures. For all these reasons, the poetic function therefore converges with fetishism; it is not, however, identical to it. What distinguishes the poetic function from the fetishist mechanism is that it maintains a *signification* (Bedeutung). All its paths into, indeed valorizations of, presymbolic semiotic stases, not only require the ensured maintenance of this signification but also serve signification, even when they dislocate it. No text, no matter how "musicalized," is devoid of meaning or signification; on the contrary, musicalization pluralizes meanings. We may say therefore that the text is not a fetish. It is, moreover, just like "natural" language in this regard, if the abstract word is thought of as a correlate for the fetish in primitive societies. The text is completely different from a fetish because it *signifies*; in other words, it is not a *substitute* but a *sign* (signifier/signified), and its semantics is unfurled in sentences.[80] The text signifies the un-signifying: it assumes [relève] within a signifying practice this functioning (the semiotic), which ignores meaning and operates before meaning or despite it. Therefore it cannot be said that everything signifies, nor that everything is "mechanistic." In opposition to such dichotomies, whether "materialist" or "metaphysical," the text offers itself as the dialectic of two heterogeneous operations that are, reciprocally and inseparably, preconditions for each other.[81]

We understand, then, that this heterogeneity between the semiotic and the symbolic cannot be reduced to computer theory's well-known distinction between "analog" and "digital."[82] "An analog computer is defined as any device that 'computes' by means of an analog between real, physical, *continuous* quantities and some other set of variables," whereas the digital computer presupposes "*discrete* elements and discontinuous scales."[83] Certain linguists have wanted to transpose this distinction—which arose with the development of computers and perhaps applies to "natural" codes (nerve cell codes or animal communication, for example)—onto the functioning of language. But in making this transposition, one quickly forgets not only that language is simultaneously "analog" and "digital" but that it is, above all, a doubly articulated system (signifier and signified), which is precisely what distinguishes it from *codes*. We therefore maintain that what we call the semiotic can be described as both analog and digital: the functioning of the semiotic *chora* is made up of continuities that are segmented in order to organize a digital system as the *chora*'s guarantee of survival (just as digitality is the means of survival both for the living cell and society);[84] the stases marked by the facilitation of the drives are the discrete elements in this digital system, indispensable for maintaining the semiotic *chora*.

Yet this description (which itself is possible only on the basis of a highly developed symbolic system) does not account for what produces the *qualitative leap* between a code and a double articulation.[85] But this essential phase is precisely what we are examining when we distinguish between the semiotic and the symbolic, and when we assign the thetic phase the role of boundary between the two heterogeneous domains. Because of the human being's prematurity, his semiotic "code" is cut off from any possible identification unless it is assumed by the other (first the mother, then the symbolic and/or the social group). Making the analog digital is thus not enough to ensure our bodily survival because it cannot check the drives' endless facilitations. An *alteration* must be made, making the *other* the regulator between the semiotic *chora* and the totality called the *ecosystem*. This alteration makes it possible to gather together the analog and digital "code" and, through a break prepared by the mirror stage, posit it as unified, mastered, dominated, and in another space—imaginary, representational, symbolic. Through this alteration, the "code" leaves the place of the body and the ecosystem and, freed from their constraints, acquires the variability characteristic of a system of "arbitrary" signs—human language—the later development of which forms the immense edifice of signifying practices.

The *semiotic* (analog and digital) thereby assumes the role of a linguistic signifier signifying an *object* for an *ego*, thus constituting them both as thetic. Through its thetic, altering aspect, the signifier *represents* the subject—not the thetic ego but the very process by which it is posited. A signifier indebted in this manner to semiotic functioning tends to return to it. In all its various vacillations, the thetic is displaced toward the stages previous to its positing or within the very stases of the semiotic—in a particular element of the digital code or in a particular continuous portion of the analog code. These movements, which can be designated as fetishism, show (human) language's characteristic tendency to return to the (animal) code, thereby breaching what Freud calls a "primal repression." The thetic—that crucial place on the basis of which the human being constitutes himself as signifying and/or social—is the very place textual experience aims toward. In this sense, textual experience represents one of the most daring explorations the subject can allow himself, one that delves into his constitutive process. But at the same time and as a result, textual experience reaches the very foundation of the social—that which is exploited by sociality but which elaborates and can go beyond it, either destroying or transforming it.

10.

The Signifying Process

ONCE THE break instituting the symbolic has been established, what we have called the semiotic *chora* acquires a more precise status. Although originally a precondition of the symbolic, the semiotic functions within signifying practices as the result of a transgression of the symbolic. Therefore the semiotic that "precedes" symbolization is only a *theoretical supposition* justified by the need for description. It exists in practice only within the symbolic and requires the symbolic break to obtain the complex articulation we associate with it in musical and poetic practices. In other words, symbolization makes possible the complexity of this semiotic combinatorial system, which only theory can isolate as "preliminary" in order to specify its functioning. Nevertheless, the semiotic is not solely an abstract object produced for the needs of theory.

As a precondition of the symbolic, semiotic functioning is a fairly rudimentary combinatorial system, which will become more complex only after the break in the symbolic. It is, however, already put in place by a biological setup and is always already social and therefore historical. This semiotic functioning is discernible before the mirror stage, before the first suggestion of the thetic. But the semiotic we find in signifying practices always comes to us after the symbolic thesis, after the symbolic break, and can be analyzed in psychoanalytic discourse as well as in so-called "artistic" practice. One could not, then, limit oneself to representing this semiotic functioning as simply "analog" or "digital" or as a mere scattering of traces. The thetic gathers up these facilitations and instinctual semiotic stases within the positing of signifiers, then opens them out in the three-part cluster of referent, signified, and signifier, which alone makes the enunciation of a truth possible. In taking the thetic into account, we shall have to represent the semiotic (which is produced recursively on the basis of that break) as a "second" return of instinctual functioning within the symbolic, as a negativity introduced into the symbolic order, and as the transgression of that order.

This transgression appears as a breach [*effraction*] subsequent to the thetic phase, which makes that phase negative and tends to fuse the layers of signifier/signified/referent into a network of traces, following the facilitation of the drives. Such a breach does not constitute a positing. It is not at all thetic, nor is it an *Aufhebung* of "original doxy" through a synthesizing spiral movement and within the pursuit of the exhaustion of truth undertaken by Hegelian absolute knowledge. On the contrary, the transgression breaks up the thetic, splits it, fills it with empty spaces, and uses its device only to remove the "residues of first symbolizations" and make them "reason" [*"raisonner"*] within the symbolic chain. This explosion of the semiotic in the symbolic is far from a negation of negation, an *Aufhebung* that would suppress the contradiction generated by the thetic and establish in its place an ideal positivity, the restorer of pre-symbolic immediacy.[86] It is, instead, a *transgression* of position, a reversed reactivation of the contradiction that instituted this very position.

The proof is that this negativity has a tendency to suppress the thetic phase, to de-syn-thesize it. In the extreme, negativity aims to foreclose the thetic phase, which, after a period of explosive semiotic motility, may result in the loss of the symbolic function, as seen in schizophrenia.

"Art," on the other hand, by definition, does not relinquish the thetic even while pulverizing it through the negativity of transgression. Indeed, this is the only means of transgressing the thetic, and the difficulty of maintaining the symbolic function under the assault of negativity indicates the risk that textual practice represents for the subject. What had seemed to be a process of fetishizing inherent in the way the text functions now seems a structurally necessary protection, one that serves to check negativity, confine it within stases, and prevent it from sweeping away the symbolic position.

The regulation of the semiotic in the symbolic through the thetic break, which is inherent in the operation of language, is also found on the various levels of a society's signifying edifice. In all known archaic societies, this founding break of the symbolic order is represented by murder—the killing of a man, a slave, a prisoner, an animal. Freud reveals this founding break and generalizes from it when he emphasizes that society is founded on a complicity in the common crime.[87] We indicated earlier how language, already as a semiotic *chora* but above all as a symbolic system, is at the service of the death drive, diverts it, and confines it as if within an isolated pocket of narcissism. The social order, for its part, reveals this confinement of the death drive, whose endless course conditions and moves through every stasis and thus every structure, in an act of murder. Religions, as we know, have set themselves up as specialists on the discourse concerning this radical, unique, thetic event.

Opposite religion or alongside it, "art" takes on murder and moves through it. It assumes murder insofar as artistic practice considers death the inner boundary of the signifying process. Crossing that boundary is precisely what constitutes "art." In other words, it is as if death becomes interiorized by the subject of such a practice; in order to function, he must make himself the bearer of death. In this sense, the artist is comparable to all other figures of the "scapegoat." But he is not just a scapegoat; in fact, what makes him an artist radically distinguishes him from all other sacrificial murderers and victims.[88]

In returning, through the event of death, toward that which produces its break; in exporting semiotic motility across the border on which the symbolic is established, the artist sketches out a kind of second birth. Subject to death but also to rebirth, his function becomes harnessed, immobilized, represented, and idealized by religious systems (most explicitly by Christianity), which shelter him in their temples, pagodas, mosques, and churches. Through themes, ideologies, and social meanings, the artist introduces into the symbolic order an asocial drive, one not yet harnessed by the thetic. When this practice, challenging any stoppage, comes up, in its turn, against the produced object, it sets itself up as a substitute for the initially contested thetic, thus giving rise to the aesthetic fetishism and narcissism supplanting theology.

11.

Poetry That Is Not a Form of Murder

LET US now examine the social implications of the structural fact we have just established, that there can be no language without a thetic phase. If one accepts, as we do, the viewpoint of contemporary anthropology, which has given up the search for a sociological theory of symbolism that would state the symbolic "origin" of society, one may say that, since "the social" and "the symbolic" are synonymous, they both depend on what we call the thetic. From Mauss to Lévi-Strauss, social anthropology continually reconfirms this equivalence between the symbolic and the social when it considers society's various means of self-regulation—the exchange of women, different kinds of magic, myths, etc.—as languages. In reading the parallels or equivalencies that anthropology establishes between social symbolism and language, it becomes clear that the latter converge in a single place, which we have called the thetic, where positions and their syntheses (i.e., their relations) are set up. This is what Lévi-Strauss seems to be saying when he maintains that the common ground between kinship structure and language is a *symbolic* commonality:

Because they are symbolic systems, kinship systems offer the anthropologist a rich field, where his efforts can almost (and we emphasize the "almost") converge with those of the most highly developed of the social sciences, namely, linguistics. But to achieve this convergence, from which it is hoped a better understanding of man will result, we must never lose sight of the fact that, *in both sociological and linguistic research, we are dealing strictly with* symbolism [*nous sommes en plein symbolisme*]. And although it may be legitimate or even inevitable to fall back upon a naturalistic interpretation in order to understand the emergence of symbolic thinking, once the latter is given, the nature of the explanation must change as radically as the newly appeared phenomena differs from those which have preceded and prepared it.[89]

On this basis, what structural anthropology is *allowed* to study are thetic productions (in Husserl's sense): positions, dispositions, syntheses, i.e., structural relations. The social order, like the linguistic order (in the Saussurean sense), is just such a device, presented by the always already thetic symbolic. Whether we consider the social order from the point of view of structural or generative linguistics does not change the fundamental postulate according to which social relations are symbolic, which is to say thetic.

The question that remains is: what becomes of the semiotic in this symbolic arrangement? What about the semiotic motility preceding the break that establishes both language and the social? Does the course of the "human mind" consist uniquely in learning how to absorb the "integrity of the signifier" that is constituted once and for all, by finding corresponding signifieds? The anthropologist would seem to suppose so when he views culture as entirely symbolic, programmed by symbolism, and destined to carry out a certain continuity starting from symbolism's discontinuous and inaugural irruption:

Whatever the moment or circumstances of its appearance on the evolutionary scale, language must have arisen all at once. Things could not have begun signifying in stages. Instead, after a transformation—one that is studied not by the social sciences but by biology and psychology—there was a sudden transition from one stage in which nothing had meaning to the next in which everything did. This apparently banal remark is important because such a radical change has no counterpart within the realm of knowledge, which, by contrast, develops slowly and progressively. In other words, at the moment when—suddenly—the entire Universe became *meaningful*, it did not, for all that, become better *known*, even though the appearance of language must have accelerated the rate at which knowledge developed. Hence, there exists a fundamental opposition, in the history of human thought, between symbolism, which is discontinuous, and knowledge, which is marked by continuity. As a consequence, although the two categories, signifier and signified, came into existence simultaneously and interdependently as two complementary units, knowledge, which is to say the intellectual capacity to identify certain aspects of the signifier with certain aspects of the signified, . . . got under way only very slowly. . . . from the outset, man has at his disposal a whole signifier which he is uncomfortable allocating to a signified, given as such yet still unknown. There is always a lack of proportion between the two which can be absorbed [résorbable] only by divine understanding, and which results in the existence of an overabundance of signifier with respect to the signifieds it may settle on. . . . this *floating signifier* enslaves all finite thought (but is also the guarantee of all art, poetry, mythic and esthetic invention); scientific knowledge may not be capable of damming it up, but at least it can partially control it.[90]

We would like to emphasize three points in the preceding passage: (1) Social anthropology is to be constituted as a linguistics of language [langue], seeking out structures or relations subsequent to the imposition of symbolism; it will not question symbolism's emergence and eventual corruption since any splitting of the social and/or symbolic chain is relegated outside the scientific field as it is defined here. (2) All things stemming from social symbolism, hence kinship structures and myth itself, are symbolic devices, made possible by the thetic, which has taken on social symbolism as such. They neither question nor challenge the thetic but rather function as a result of it, and tend to discipline the signifier which is thus set free. (But only science actually manages to do so, albeit partially.) (3) Finally, it would appear that nothing in the symbolic order can be considered a counterpart to the symbolic break.

We believe, however, that two types of "events" in the social order may be viewed as the counterpart of the thetic moment instituting symbolism, even though they do not unfold according to the logic of the signifier's depletion, which structural anthropology detects in social symbolism.

The first is sacrifice: this violent act puts an end to previous (semiotic, presymbolic) violence, and, by focusing violence on a victim, displaces it onto the symbolic order *at the very moment* this order is being founded. Sacrifice sets up the symbol and the symbolic order at the same time, and this "first" symbol, the victim of a murder, merely represents the structural violence of language's irruption as the murder of soma, the transformation of the body, the captation of drives.

Sacrifice has been viewed as an unleashing of animal violence, a commemoration of prehuman bestiality.[91] But, in our opinion, classical anthropological sociology has a more accurate view, assigning sacrifice an ambiguous function, simultaneously violent and regulatory. For sacrifice designates, precisely, the watershed on the basis of which the social and the symbolic are instituted: the thetic that confines violence to a single place, making it a signifier. Far from unleashing violence, sacrifice shows how representing that violence is enough to stop it and to concatenate an order. Conversely, it indicates that all order is based on representation: what is violent is the irruption of the symbol, killing substance to make it signify.

Murder itself is only *one* of the phantasmatic and mythic realizations of the logical phase inherent in any socio-symbolic order. Indeed, human sacrifice would seem to be logically, if not chronologically, posterior to animal and vegetable sacrifice, and the sacrifice of a god merely a very late form, a very recent semantic cover for the thetic moment celebrated in rites.[92] Within the diversity of sacrificial forms, Hubert and Mauss reveal what unites them. All of them reiterate the structure of the symbol: the reserving of substance, of the self, or of the "referent"; the setting up of a contract; a "play of images"; the establishment of an ideal community; the introduction of the object of jouissance into the "social norm."

The following definitions, taken from their conclusion, will illustrate: "The sacrificer gives up something of himself but he does not give himself. Prudently, he sets himself aside." "Fundamentally there is perhaps no sacrifice that has not some contractual element." "The whole system is merely a play of images." "Here everything occurs in the world of ideas, and it is mental and moral energies that are in question. . . . Individuals . . . confer upon each other, upon themselves, and upon those things they hold dear, the whole strength of society." "The social norm is thus maintained without danger to themselves, without dimunition for the group."[93] And yet, although sacrifice exemplifies the structural law of symbolism, it simultaneously ensures the concrete relation of this logical phase to social history: this is why the *same* sacrificial structure takes *different forms* depending on the development of the relations of production and productive forces. The "sacrificial objects" that are charged with representing the thetic moment founding the symbolic and/or social contract may be an animal, a crop, a slave, a warrior, or a god representing the subject as pure signifier, depending on the demands dictated by the society's degree of economic development.

Social anthropology does not yet seem to have systematically studied the history of the different forms and internal changes of the structure of sacrifice. But it does take a big step forward by associating the sacrificial with the social.[94] It is only from this position bordering on the social that sacrifice can be viewed not only as an imposition of social coherence but also as its outer limit. On the other side of this boundary is the a-symbolic, the dissolution of order, the erasing of differences, and finally the disappearance of the human in animality. In this light one might well reread Robertson Smith, who ascribes to rites the function of maintaining the community between man and animal.[95] Pierre Vidal-Naquet has recently shown the close structural, functional, and historical imbrications of the hunt and sacrifice in Greek myth and tragedy, so close that they are expressed in the same vocabulary and give rise to figures of transition such as hunters, the ephebi, and the Furies.[96]

Lévi-Strauss has shown that totemism and sacrifice are contrasting and even incompatible.[97] Totemism is constructed as a language, as a system of differential spaces between discontinuous terms—the natural series (plants or animals) understood as globally homomorphic to the social series. Sacrifice, by contrast, is the reign of substitution, metonymy, and ordered continuity (one victim may be used for another but not vice-versa). This second operation merits closer examination.

In sacrifice, the two series, sacrificer and "deity," far from being homomorphic, must, precisely, establish their relation within sacrifice, making sacrifice not a posited relation but its elaboration. On the one hand, a contiguity is established between the two poles of the relation "by means of a series of successive identifications": each victim or sacrificial substance is analogous to another (the cucumber for the egg, for example, but not the reverse). Evans-Pritchard calls this relation an analogy but does not go into further detail,[98] whereas Lévi-Strauss speaks of metonymy.[99] On the other hand, in order to establish a relation (between the sacrificer and the deity), the metonymic chain must nevertheless break: hence the destruction of the victim. Metonymy and rupture, such is the logic of this "relation" which is not yet an "is," but prepares the way for it to be posited. The outcome of this positing is that disrupted metonymy, having set a divinity in place, expects, as a reward, an answer from it; furthermore, a "compensatory continuity"—prayer—follows the rupture that is murder. In this way, the entire circuit of symbolic communication between two hierarchized discursive agencies [instances] is established (gift—reward—symbolic praise), a circuit on which symbolic economy is based. In this way, sacrifice stages the *advent* of this economy, its *emergence* from the ecological continuum, and the *socialization of this ecology*. Totemism, by contrast, is already an interpretative system for this continuum, encoding it and classifying it according to social devices; like myth and, later, like science, it is symbolism in action.

It cannot be said, however, that totemism is true and sacrifice false. Sacrifice would be false only if its role were to classify; it occupies, instead, the other side of symbolism. Rather than present symbolic functioning as an already existing system, it reproduces the process of its production. In its metonymic logic, its broken continuity, and its symbolic relation to a dominant agency, sacrifice resembles not language but the unconscious, which is the unspoken precondition of linguistic systematization. This explains why sacrifice, like incest and bestiality, is found at the extreme end of the social code: it reproduces both the foundation of that code and what it represses. In this way, we can say that the relation between sacrifice and totem is not accidental since they both articulate relations between society and the continuum of nature. But these relations are clearly distinct: sacrifice reminds us that the symbolic emerges out of material continuity through a violent and unmotivated leap; whereas totemism is already an appropriation of this continuum based on the symbolic that has already been set in place.

The sacred—sacrifice—which is found in every society, is, then, a theologization of the thetic, itself structurally indispensable to the positing of language. This theologization takes on different forms depending on the degree of development of the society's productive forces. It represents either the signifying process' dependence on natural forces and the surrounding ecological system, or its subordination to the social relations between subjects caught in kinship relations. In this way, the parricide at the origin of the social contract, which Freud evokes in *Totem and Taboo*, can be thought of as one of the forms assumed by the thetic phase, and undoubtedly the one best indicating that the establishment of symbolism tends to prohibit jouissance, but at the same time, permits it. Indeed this prohibition proves impossible: brothers do take possession of women, although not any and all women, and above all not their mothers or sisters. Jouissance is thus not so much forbidden as regulated; it slips in through the rules of that language which is kinship structure.

Sacrifice presents only the legislating aspect of the thetic phase: sacred murder merely points to the violence that was *confined* within sacrifice so as to found social order. Sacrifice represents the thetic only as the *exclusion* establishing social order, *positing* the violence that was caught and lodged within murder as within an inaugural break. This positing—"a boundary to the infinite" (Mallarmé)—is the basis on which socio-symbolic sets are structured. All violence can do is to filter into the symbolic order and explode, transforming or shattering it. The sacred does not, therefore, celebrate pure violence; it celebrates instead the *positing* of violence, the "boundary to the infinite" which, though fragile under the attack of violence, violates and calls on violence, thus constituting a precarious but indispensable guarantor of its accomplishment.[100]

Nevertheless—and this is the second point we would like to stress—a certain practice accompanies sacrifice. Through, with, and despite the positing of sacrifice, this practice deploys the expenditure [*dépense*][101] of semiotic violence, breaks through the symbolic border, and tends to dissolve the logical order, which is, in short, the outer limit founding the human and the social. This practice is the representation that generally precedes sacrifice; it is the laboratory for, among other things, theater, poetry, song, dance—art. That the combat it mimes precedes the sacrificial slaying is less important than the fact that it *mimes* in the full sense of the term: it repeats not a detached object but the movement of the symbolic economy. By *reproducing signifiers*—vocal, gestural, verbal—the subject crosses the border of the symbolic and reaches the semiotic *chora*, which is on the other side of the social frontier. The reenacting of the signifying path taken from the symbolic unfolds the symbolic itself and—through the border that sacrifice is about to present or has already presented on stage—opens it up to the motility where all meaning is erased. There exist a number of sacred "representations," including those of the Dinka, which precede the sacrificial slaying or offering, and which are considered more exalting than the sacrifice that follows them.[102] The Dionysian festivals in Greece are the most striking example of this deluge of the signifier, which so inundates the symbolic order that it portends the latter's dissolution in a dancing, singing, and poetic animality.

Art—this semiotization of the symbolic—thus represents the flow of jouissance into language. Whereas sacrifice assigns jouissance its productive limit in the social and symbolic order, art specifies the means—the only means—that jouissance harbors for infiltrating that order. In cracking the socio-symbolic order, splitting it open, changing vocabulary, syntax, the word itself, and releasing from beneath them the drives borne by vocalic or kinetic differences, jouissance works its way into the social and symbolic. In contrast to sacrifice, poetry shows us that language lends itself to the penetration of the socio-symbolic by jouissance, and that the thetic does not necessarily imply theological sacrifice.

We thus find sacrifice and art, face to face, representing the two aspects of the thetic function: the prohibition of jouissance by language and the introduction of jouissance into and through language. Religion seizes this first aspect, necessary to the institution of the symbolic order. First myth and then science seek to justify it by elaborating a complex system of relations and mediations, even though the very fact that the latter are produced, vary, and change, refutes their claim that language prohibits jouissance. On the other hand, poetry, music, dance, theater—"art"—point *at once* to a pole opposite that of religious prohibition. One may say, in this sense, that they know more about it than it does. Far from denying the thetic, which through the ages religion has assigned itself the privilege of celebrating—though only as a prohibition—art accepts the thetic break to the extent that it resists becoming either delirium or a fusion with nature. Nevertheless, through this break, art takes from ritual space what theology conceals: trans-symbolic jouissance, the irruption of the motility threatening the unity of the social realm and the subject.

In this way poetry (though we could also speak of dance and music since they are always more or less linked) confronts, through time, the different "soma" that are sacrificed for the social group's survival—plants, totemic animals, kinsmen, and finally the man-god. After this last sacrifice, poetry meets up with what is no longer a mere soma-bearer of the thetic but the true "element" from which the thetic originated: *language* and social *structure*. Indeed, with the bourgeoisie, poetry confronts *order* at its most fundamental level: the logic of language and the principle of the State. From its roots in ritual, poetry retains the expenditure of the thetic, its opening onto semiotic vehemence and its capacity for letting jouissance come through. Faced with language and society, however, poetry no longer encounters a sacrifice that is suggestive of the thetic but rather thesis itself (logic—language—society). It can therefore no longer remain merely "poetry"; instead, through the positing of the thetic, poetry becomes an explicit confrontation between jouissance and the thetic, that is, a permanent struggle to show the facilitation of drives within the linguistic order itself. Since the social order favors the order of knowledge, the signifieds Lévi-Strauss spoke of tend to encounter the floating signifier, and the bourgeois technocratic era imagines itself to be the one carrying out this reunion. In such an era, in any case, no sacrifice is available for presenting a signified (or a referent—plant, animal, man, man-god) that has not yet met with its signifier but that remains nevertheless as the limit ensuring the functioning of the order. So within this saturated if not already closed socio-symbolic order, poetry—more precisely, poetic language—reminds us of its eternal function: to introduce through the symbolic that which works on, moves through, and threatens it. The theory of the unconscious seeks the very thing that poetic language practices within and against the social order: the ultimate means of its transformation or subversion, the precondition for its survival and revolution.

In what ways does this idea of the semiotic as inherent in the symbolic—but also going beyond it and threatening its position—modify the generally accepted notion of semantic functioning?

First, it requires us to consider semiotic functioning as part of a signifying *practice* that includes the agency of the symbolic. This means that a semiotic description would not merely reconstitute the analog or digital model of this functioning but must instead situate it *vis-à-vis the subject*, vis-à-vis the enunciation of a denotation, a truth, and finally an ideology.[103]

Consequently—and more specifically with respect to semiotic description in a strict sense—although semiotic functioning can be defined as the articulation of facilitations and stases that mean nothing, this mechanism must immediately be considered within the signifying chain instituted by the thetic. Without this new *dialectic*,[104] a description of this functioning might eventually be related to the semiotic *chora* preceding the mirror stage and the Oedipal stage, but not to a signifying practice that is anti-Oedipal to the extent that it is anti-thetic, para-doxical.

Ultimately, such a dialectic lets us view signifying practices as asymmetrically divided—neither absolutizing the thetic into a possible theological prohibition, nor negating the thetic in the fantasy of a pulverizing irrationalism: neither intransgressable and guilt-producing divine fiat nor "romantic" folly, pure madness, surrealist automatism, or pagan pluralism. Instead we see the condition of the subject of signifiance as a heterogeneous contradiction between two irreconcilable elements—separate but inseparable from the *process* in which they assume asymmetrical functions.

Literature has always been the most explicit realization of the signifying subject's condition. Indeed it was in literature, starting in the first half of the nineteenth century, that the dialectical condition of the subject was made explicit, beginning in France with the work of Nerval, but particularly with Lautréamont and Mallarmé. We shall attempt to show that poetic language changed at the end of the century precisely because it became a practice involving the subject's dialectical state in language. As such, this transformation inaugurates a new period in what has been called literature: the end of poetry as delirium, which is contemporaneous with its inseparable counterpart—literature as an attempted submission to the logical order. In the experience of a Joyce or a Bataille, for example, literature moves beyond madness and realism in a leap that maintains both "delirium" and "logic."

We take the names Joyce and Bataille as emblems of the most radical aspects of twentieth-century literature, which seem to have been heralded by the work of Lautréamont and Mallarmé. For these two late nineteenth-century writers, making literature a test of the subject's dialectic within the signifying process implied, above all, a refusal of poetry as a flight into madness and a struggle against poetry as fetishism (a play of language, a hypostasis of the work as material object, an acceptance of rhetoric as an imperative necessity). At the same time, this meant accepting the ineluctable constraint of logic, its positing, and the community it implies so that excess could be introduced into it—an excess that would be "more-than-logical." Lautréamont's *Poems* and Mallarmé's "*Livre*" were the first writings to reveal what Bataille would later point out: "The meaning of poetry . . . ends in its opposite, in a feeling of hatred for poetry." [105]

Poetry emerged alongside sacrifice as the expenditure of the thesis establishing the socio-symbolic order and as the bringing into play of the vehemence of drives through the positing of language. But starting with the Renaissance and the brief Romantic celebration of the sacrifices made in the French Revolution, poetry had become mere rhetoric, linguistic formalism, a fetishization, a surrogate for the thetic. The established bourgeois regime had been consuming this kind of poetry since the Restoration and especially during the Second Empire, which began in 1852, reducing it to a decorative uselessness that challenged none of the subjects of its time.

The problem, then, was one of finding practices of expenditure capable of confronting the machine, colonial expansion, banks, science, Parliament—those positions of mastery that conceal their violence and pretend to be mere neutral legality. Recovering the subject's vehemence required a descent into the most archaic stage of his positing, one contemporaneous with the positing of social order; it required a descent into the structural positing of the thetic in language so that violence, surging up through the phonetic, syntactic, and logical orders, could reach the symbolic order and the technocratic ideologies that had been built over this violence to ignore or repress it. To penetrate the era, poetry had to disturb the logic that dominated the social order and do so through that logic itself, by assuming and unraveling its position, its syntheses, and hence the ideologies it controls.

What one had to fight were all the possibilities in poetry that had been transgressive but were now encoded and thus categorized within the symbolic order as fetishes. Mallarmé's practice emerges, precisely, out of a compromise with Parnassian and Symbolist poetry whose stases he accepts in order to reject, bypass, and go beyond them. But having rejected the old poetry as a fetishistic guardian of meaning and the subject, one also had to shun the lie of unspeakable delirium, first by maintaining the difficult crossroad of heterogeneous contradiction with and in the symbolic order and then by signifying the violence of drives in and through codes—moral, scientific, everyday, journalistic, modern, familial, economic, . . . interminably. Witness the shattered unity of Lautréamont's *Maldoror* and *Poems*. In confronting the world of discourse in its constitutive laws, poetry ceased being poetry and opened a gap in every order where the dialectical experience of the subject in the signifying process might begin.

Although pre-Freudian, this practice violently and dangerously prefigures what Freud would listen for in his patients' discourse. But it constructs a realm that the psychoanalytic discovery was not able to encompass, though today it is still the only theory even preparing the way into that realm.[106] Indeed the Freudian position, which looks for the process of the subject through the positing of language, joins—at a distance but with an equivalent logical rigor—the combat led by Lautréamont and Mallarmé against fetishism and madness, thereby lifting the crushing social weight still masking them, which Bataille would herald:

I refuse, rebel, but why wander off. If I were delirious I'd simply be *natural.*

Poetic delirium has a place *within* nature, justifies it, agrees to embellish it. Refusal is the attitude of a clear conscience, measuring what is happening to it. . . .

Relaxation takes one out of play—so does excessive attentiveness. A cheerful fit of anger, a raving leap, and calm lucidity are required of the player until the day luck drops him—or life.

I get close to poetry—but end up failing it.[107]

By raising the veil of mystery the nineteenth century had held over sexuality, Freud's discovery designated sexuality as the nexus between language and society, drives and the socio-symbolic order. Thanks to this revelation, the practice of a Lautréamont or a Mallarmé could not only be made radical, but could also have the objective and social impact it was aiming for. This is to say that, on the threshold, yet still in the absence of this discovery, the poetic experience of the end of the century constitutes a breakthrough that was quickly concealed, or re-fetishized (Apollinaire), even academized (Valéry). Only after Freud has it had a future (Joyce, Bataille) and it is only starting with Freud that one may attempt to measure its significance.

12.

Genotext and Phenotext

IN LIGHT of the distinction we have made between the semiotic *chora* and the symbolic, we may now examine the way texts function. What we shall call a *genotext* will include semiotic processes but also the advent of the symbolic. The former includes drives, their disposition, and their division of the body, plus the ecological and social system surrounding the body, such as objects and pre-Oedipal relations with parents. The latter encompasses the emergence of object and subject, and the constitution of nuclei of meaning involving categories: semantic and categorial fields. Designating the genotext in a text requires pointing out the transfers of drive energy that can be detected in phonematic devices (such as the accumulation and repetition of phonemes or rhyme) and melodic devices (such as intonation or rhythm), in the way semantic and categorial fields are set out in syntactic and logical features, or in the economy of mimesis (fantasy, the deferment of denotation, narrative, etc.). The genotext is thus the only transfer of drive energies that organizes a space in which the subject is not *yet* a split unity that will become blurred, giving rise to the symbolic. Instead, the space it organizes is one in which the subject will be *generated* as such by a process of facilitations and marks within the constraints of the biological and social structure.

In other words, even though it can be seen in language, the genotext is not linguistic (in the sense understood by structural or generative linguistics). It is, rather, a *process*, which tends to articulate structures that are ephemeral (unstable, threatened by drive charges, "quanta" rather than "marks") and nonsignifying (devices that do not have a double articulation). It forms these

structures out of: a) instinctual dyads, b) the corporeal and ecological continuum, c) the social organism and family structures,
which convey the constraints imposed by the mode of production, and d) matrices of enunciation, which give rise to discursive
"genres" (according to literary history), "psychic structures" (according to psychiatry and psychoanalysis), or various arrangements of "the participants in the speech event" (in Jakobson's
notion of the linguistics of discourse).[108] We may posit that the
matrices of enunciation are the result of the repetition of drive
charges (a) within biological, ecological, and socio-familial constraints (b and c), and the stabilization of their facilitation into
stases whose surrounding structure accommodates and leaves its
mark on symbolization.

The genotext can thus be seen as language's underlying
foundation. We shall use the term *phenotext* to denote language
that serves to communicate, which linguistics describes in terms
of "competence" and "performance." The phenotext is constantly
split up and divided, and is irreducible to the semiotic process
that works through the genotext. The phenotext is a structure
(which can be generated, in generative grammar's sense); it obeys
rules of communication and presupposes a subject of enunciation and an addressee. The genotext, on the other hand, is a process; it moves through zones that have relative and transitory
borders and constitutes a *path* that is not restricted to the two
poles of univocal information between two full-fledged subjects.
If these two terms—genotext and phenotext—could be translated
into a metalanguage that would convey the difference between
them, one might say that the genotext is a matter of topology,
whereas the phenotext is one of algebra. This distinction may
be illustrated by a particular signifying system: written and
spoken Chinese, particularly classical Chinese. Writing represents-
articulates the signifying process into specific networks or spaces;
speech (which may correspond to that writing) restores the diacrit-
ical elements necessary for an exchange of meaning between two
subjects (temporality, aspect, specification of the protagonists,
morpho-semantic identifiers, and so forth).[109]

The signifying process therefore includes both the genotext and the phenotext; indeed it could not do otherwise. For it is in language that all signifying operations are realized (even when linguistic material is not used), and it is on the basis of language that a theoretical approach may attempt to perceive that operation.

In our view, the process we have just described accounts for the way all signifying practices are generated.[110] But every signifying practice does not encompass the infinite totality of that process. Multiple constraints—which are ultimately sociopolitical—stop the signifying process at one or another of the theses that it traverses; they knot it and lock it into a given surface or structure; they discard *practice* under fixed, fragmentary, symbolic *matrices*, the tracings of various social constraints that obliterate the infinity of the process: the phenotext is what conveys these obliterations. Among the capitalist mode of production's numerous signifying practices, only certain literary texts of the avant-garde (Mallarmé, Joyce) manage to cover the infinity of the process, that is, reach the semiotic *chora*, which modifies linguistic structures. It must be emphasized, however, that this total exploration of the signifying process generally leaves in abeyance the theses that are characteristic of the social organism, its structures, and their political transformation: the text has a tendency to dispense with political and social signifieds.

It has only been in very recent years or in revolutionary periods that signifying practice has inscribed within the phenotext the plural, heterogeneous, and contradictory process of signification encompassing the flow of drives, material discontinuity, political struggle, and the pulverization of language.

Lacan has delineated four types of discourse in our society: that of the hysteric, the academic, the master, and the analyst.[111] Within the perspective just set forth, we shall posit a different classification, which, in certain respects, intersects these four Lacanian categories, and in others, adds to them. We shall distinguish between the following signifying practices: narrative, metalanguage, contemplation, and text-practice.

Let us state from the outset that this distinction is only provisional and schematic, and that although it corresponds to actual practices, it interests us primarily as a didactic implement |*outil*|—one that will allow us to specify some of the modalities of signifying dispositions. The latter interest us to the extent that they give rise to different practices and are, as a consequence, more or less coded in modes of production. Of course narrative and contemplation could also be seen as devices stemming from (hysterical and obsessional) transference neurosis; and metalanguage and the text as practices allied with psychotic (paranoid and schizoid) economies.

13.

Four Signifying Practices

A. IN NARRATIVE, *instinctual dyads* (positive/negative, affirmation/negation, life drive/death drive) are articulated as a nondisjunction (-v̄-). In other words, the two "terms" are distinct, differentiated, and opposed but their opposition is later disavowed [*après coup*], and so the two are considered identical. Elsewhere we have studied this operation as one that founds psychology, the denial of sexual difference, and temporality.[112]

This instinctual nucleus, articulated as a nondisjunction, moves through the *corporeal and ecological continuum*, which forms a dichotomous structure; in it, material discontinuity is reduced to correlations between opposites (high/low, good/bad, outside/inside), which delineate narrative's geography, temporality, plot, etc. Although the flow of drives moves through innumerable zones of objective materiality, and although various sensations from different objects are imprinted on this signifying practice, such a diversity is poured into the rigid molds of a nondisjunctive structure.

In narrative, the social organism is dominated, ruled by, and finally reduced to or viewed through the structure of the family. The family or the clan (in primitive societies and up until feudalism), the exchange of women, conjugal relations, and those associated with conjugality and kinship are the prism through which the flow of drives invests social structures.

Clinical experience, moreover, seems to show that the subject's first elaboration-reconstruction of his past history takes the form of a narrative: "The first narrative, the individual's first true past, is elaborated during the Oedipal phase. In other words, in a phase when all the previous stages are taken up again, but this time within the framework of a desire (henceforth constantly mediated) and the problematic of castration." In analysis, this narrative structure is characterized by a repetition with a "momentary resumption of a free circulation of energy in the higher systems, rapidly followed by the binding of that energy with unconscious representations," which are overdetermined by the family triangle.[113]

The *matrix of enunciation* in narrative tends to center on an axial position that is explicitly or implicitly called "I" or "author"—a projection of the paternal role in the family. Although axial, this position is mobile; it takes on all the possible roles in intra- and inter-familial relations, and is as changeable as a mask. Correlatively, this axial position presupposes an addressee who is required to recognize himself in the multiple "I" 's of the author. We could say that the matrix of enunciation structures a subjectal space in which, strictly speaking, there is no unique and fixed subject; but in this space, the signifying process is organized, that is, provided with meaning, as soon as it encounters the two ends of the communicative chain and, in between, the various crystallizations of "masks" or "protagonists" corresponding to the signifying process' abutments against parental and social structures. The subjectal structure thus appears as a series of entities, which are infinite to the extent that material discontinuity is projected there, but locked in place to the extent that the parental and social network is applied to it. Within this framework, One is all, and all (multiple addressees, the crowd, the community) are a structuration of entities.

Strictly linguistic structures (the phenotext) remain normative in narrative. They obey grammatical rules, which remain intact since drive charges barely cross the thetic that imposes language.[114] The drive charges were seized and absorbed by the structuring borders of the preceding strata, obtained a meaning there, became a sign and, in turn, were replaced by the sign. Language may thus function without reintroducing within the sign the instinctual nucleus that would have disarticulated it, pluralized it, and imbued it with non-sense. Limited drive discharges filter through this skeleton to produce a mimesis that calls into question *Bedeutung* as denotation but not as enunciation. Thus subordinated to the broad outlines of narrativity, the semiotic drive flow gives only a faint indication of the signifying process.

Mythic narratives, the epic, its theatrical substitutes, and even the novel (including its stage or screen adaptations), news reporting, newspaper columns, and other journalistic genres fall within the province of the signifying system—narrative—we have just described. Differences between these "genres" are due to variations in the social organism and hence the latter's constraints, as well as to certain transformations of the matrices of enunciation. But these variations do not fundamentally disturb the enunciation's disposition; they merely indicate that *meaning* has been constituted and has taken shape at different levels of the same system. Lévi-Strauss showed that myth semanticizes kinship and social relations by using elements of material continuity as a semantic cover. According to Lukàcs, the novel, by contrast, subjects this continuity to the quest undertaken by a hero anxious to appropriate the truth of social and kinship relations (the primal scene)—a "problematic hero" whose psychology is never complete.

In his study of *Les Formes simples*, André Jolles examines exclusively narrative forms—legends, sagas, myths, riddles, idioms, cases, memoirs, tales, jokes—and finds the family construct [*la disposition familiale*] only in the *sagas*.[115] Whatever their national or ethnic origin, the sagas treat great ethnic migrations as a family matter—the *Iliad*, the Icelandic *Saga*, the *Niebelungenlied*, and the Old Testament are the most notable examples.[116] Although he presents Christianity as the destroyer of this familial "mental construct," Jolles recognizes that Christianity has retained this heritage to such an extent that even "high-culture forms," like the naturalist novel, show its effects.

It should be recalled that the distinction we are attempting to make between different signifying systems is not based on Jolles's "mental construct." In fact, because we are examining signifying operations before and at the very moment that enunciation devices are constituted, we can see that "familialism" is not unique to the saga except in its "content-forms" (as Hjelmslev would say) or in the substance of its content. On the contrary, in our view, all the "simple forms" reproduce various aspects of the way in which the subject positions himself within the family triangle when he identifies with it. For example: the objective, historical, or personal quest of the saint in a *legend*, and of the sportsman in *news reports*, who test their phallic endurance; *mythic* knowledge in which a single unit (of the self or the community) longs to grasp a unique phenomenon through an unlimited variation in which oppositions are posited but also become erased or confused, either resolving themselves or foundering definitively in the question of sexual difference;[117] the test to which the subject is submitted in the *riddle*; the "understood" nature of *idioms* (understood by the population, the clan, "our kind"—the family); the suspense (always ultimately sexual and/or a threat to legality) in the *case*; the marital or childish story of the *tale*, which anyone can grasp; and even the *joke* with its double meanings and word plays "untying the bonds, undoing the knots" of the superego.

And, finally, it was in narrative that psychoanalysis recognized the display of neurosis and, through it, found in family members its unconscious foundation, which is said to articulate *one* of the levels of the narrative system, but which in fact dominates the entire system and concentrates in it its complex functioning. Indeed, this is not surprising since narrative itself is capable of dismantling only the *topoi* of narrative. What remains to be seen is whether narrative is the only signifying practice that mimes the process of the subject in signifiance or is, as we believe, only one among many. In the latter case, narrative's truths would be valid only for itself and for the historical moment from which it emerges, and narrative would constitute an essential but not exhaustive construct of the signifying process.

B. *Metalanguage* may be said to suture the signifying process by eliminating the negative charge, by subordinating negativity to affirmation, and by *reducing instinctual dyads to positivity*. Once it has helped constitute the real object as such and, hence, symbolism, the negative charge seems to withdraw into this symbolism and become subsumed by the *Bejahung* Freud speaks of.[118] The object is thus posited as real only if it is forever dissociated from the positivity directly observing it, hovering over it, *meta-*; overhanging it, raising it, as in a meta-physics, meta-body, meta-logic, and meta-language. The object is forever cast out, and made inaccessible as such; though it has no existence of its own, it can be constructed, deduced, and known from a position in front and above. *Material discontinuity* is thus posited as the predicate of a syllogism and assimilated within it as a *complement* to be constructed in utterances; metaphysics is indissociable from a meta-logos.

In this signifying device—metalanguage—the social organism is a hierarchy that subsumes family zones and, especially, individuals *directly*, without the intermediary of the clan. The Greek city-state, Royalty, and the Republic are, each in its own way, hierarchies, structures in dominance,[119] which more or less directly, in more or less mediated fashion, subordinate human entities. Even when this mediation passes through the family (as in feudalism), the family as social function operates within a totality that dominates and represses it: its autonomy as a unit of production is relativized within the State, which has the last—in fact the only—word.

The *matrix of enunciation* that lies within this *topos* is centered on an *entity* Descartes called a *subject*. The subject draws its position, its isolation within the signifying process, from the reduction of the negative, from the absorption of material discontinuity into affirmation and symbolism—from its abutment against the constraint of state control. Checked on all sides, the signifying process can only be realized within the enclosure these obstructions allow it. The process then becomes thought. From the Stoics to Descartes and after,[120] metalanguage has found its bearings in the various manifestations of this cogitation: the subject-predicate clause, syllogisms, and deductive logic, all supported by the matrix of the sign and the system.

Since the subject articulated in this way is an axial position, he is not included, dissolved, or implicated in the system; instead he hovers above it, subdues it, and is absent from it. Signifying systems alone allow us to deduce that the subject is a fixed point and, conversely, this fact is the sole guarantee of the symbolic system and its logical laws. Therefore the subject calls himself "we" or "anonymous" when he links the terms of his logical argument. He is incapable of talking about the time of invention—the one in which the object emerged out of material discontinuity—because this emergence is produced by the very same negativity that the logos of the subject represses. The subject speaks instead of the systematization of this emergence—one should say, "we are speaking of the systematization of this emergence."

The addressee of metalanguage is made in the image of its "we"—an indifferent subject, supposedly everyone, since symbolic systematicity eliminated heterogeneity by eliminating the negative and unfolds, purporting to be transparent, eternally communicable, omnivalent. The addressee is thus an undifferentiated totality which is not in process; the addressee is a "them" and, following "our" example, has become a mere *term*, an element of the system with which it is identified because it has no existence as a subject apart from the system.

In our view, positivist philosophy, all explanation, and science come out of this *topos*. They give this *topos* its most radical ramification in the form of specific signifying systems that fall within the domain of epistemology.

C. *Contemplation*, what Pythagoras calls Θεωρία [*theoria*], is a signifying system that includes "genres" as diverse in appearance as religions, philosophy, and the deconstruction of philosophy (which is aided by psychoanalysis): spaces of transformation, of law, and of law's transgression, which is immediately designated as impossible.

In this signifying system, *instinctual dyads* are knotted in a nonsynthetic combination in which "plus" and "minus" interpenetrate like the ends of a magnetized chain; they close up a ring that has no outside but can be endlessly dissected, split, deeper and deeper, ever boundless and without origin, eternally returning, perpetually trapped. For this ring, materiality is a hole, a lack [*manque*], whose existence it suspects and covets but never reaches. It is as if, once it posits the real, rejection (see part II, below) folds back in upon itself, never to touch the real again, returning instead to attack its (own) corollary—the affirmative, the "positing." Nostalgic for a lack that would allow it to close in on itself and function as a circle, to alternate the + and the −, and even pulverize them, this *Aufhebung* of the instinctual *chora* is always already inevitably and inseparably symbolic. The *chora's* closure within contemplation condemns contemplation to meaning, disarticulating it, only to return to it, disenchanted.

The *social organism* that sustains and fosters this sealing off of instinctual rhythm is a "phratry." This hierarchized community is itself subject to the archaic or state-controlled social hierarchy, but enjoys an apparent autonomy because it is not implicated in social materiality: these are "ideological apparatuses." A symbolic cog in a hierarchical totality, a hierarchy within a hierarchy, the social cell that shelters or stimulates this sealing off of drives may be a caste, an elite, a clergy, or an initiatory cell. It constitutes a symbolic, not blood-related family, which is unreal in the sense that it is not a unit of (sexual) reproduction and (social) production. The symbolic cell reproduces productive and reproductive family structures, but having "swallowed" negativity only to experience it as symbolic, it proceeds to dismantle them. The family triangle supports this symbolic cell only to be attacked and dissolved by it.

In certain societies, a member of such a caste is a parricide, matricide, fratricide—but endlessly so. He plays the role of a "pretend relative" [*parent à plaisanterie*], the equivalent of a twin of the opposite sex, whose sexuality is the opposite of the one officially constituting us. He represents the sexuality that must be repressed in order for the social being to constitute itself, marry, and participate in the work and exchanges of the clan.[121] He is a sexual but also a social negative who must be renounced so that society may be formed and social harmony introduced. He is the tamed negative, represented and held in subordination by the potlatch, receiving gifts or committing thefts, humiliated and sublime. The most striking examples of this phenomenon are the *griots,* the singer-poets, the manipulators of language. They force society to lend them goods and thus recognize their poverty and negativity, but these gifts are useless surplus, worthless refuse. Although they are the negative that authorizes and maintains exchange, members of castes do not participate in it; their system operates outside exchange, outside the social; it is a symbolic surplus. Through them, the negative is sublimated; waste and anality are acknowledged only to be put aside. Society protects itself from negativity precisely by producing such social groups—the "specialists of the negative," the contemplatives, "theoretical" and "intellectual" types—which represent negativity as sublimated and set apart. Through them, society purges itself of negativity and endlessly calls itself into question so as to avoid breaking apart.

If, in certain modes of production, social structure protects itself in this way, by circumscribing a represented, assumed, encased negativity, the following question remains: How does this closed place function generally, logically, outside the caste system? The product of an ambiguous social attitude, the "theoretical" subject sets himself up with even more power in this situation inasmuch as he will mime the dissolution of all positions. The empty, hollow space he represents, by the very fact of its representation, acts as a magnetic pole and experiences itself as such. This subject of enunciation either says nothing or else dissects his speech for the sole purpose of becoming the focal point where all the other signifying systems converge. One could say that his discourse becomes hysteric only to position itself better within the place of impregnable transference—dominating, capturing, and monopolizing everything within the discourse's obsessive retreat, which is haunted by power/impotence. There is nothing that does not refer to it (because) it is never there. In other words, blocked in this way, the signifying process cannot come about without the presence of an addressee who will be required to recognize as his own the desires (and language) of this focal point, and submit to it—first to be split, then to introduce the negative as lack [*manque*] and become entwined in the infinite circle of its being put in question—an involvement that leads to death. Hegel's notion of totality probably gives the best account of this device: the identity and difference of opposites, implying the endless excavation of the Idea on the path of self-consciousness.

In a different way, institutionalized psychoanalysis, by destroying the very presence of the Idea and Meaning, summons, through the signifier, the active reintroduction of lack into narrative so that interlocutors and masks will dissolve and all that will remain is the eternal loop of a knotted signifier within the transference relation, which in fact offers no way out. Similarly, if, while remaining within the trajectory of the symbolic enclosure, we take pains to cut up the loop by making it a loop of loops and so on, we shall be perpetrating an act of subtle violence against this same signifier, rejecting it and rediscovering, beneath this rejection, the arch-rejection, the jetting motion that is posited, the atom, the trace, the void in its mobility. At this stage there is no longer anything to dissect: the loop is an empty point, the trajectory is reduced to its seed, which has no future because it has neither beginning nor end—no identity, no outside, no sociality.

One might think that here we have reached and unmasked the very "core" of the signifying process, far from any obstruction. But this is an illusion, for, emptied of its heterogeneous contradiction, withdrawn from material discontinuity and social imbrication, the flow of drives is merely mimed within a simulacrum and its unfolding, a sidestepping. The enunciation of this hollowing out of drives constitutes a drifting [dérive] of the signifier within the boundaries of the symbolic. This drifting shows up in the subject who had set himself up as the subject of metalanguage. It unbridles him, makes him deplore his fixed position and reveal the lack that constitutes him, i.e., his doubling and his loss of materiality and sociality. This drifting bypasses the subject but takes him as its point of departure and destination; it makes him an impassable boundary to the degree that the subject is bound up with the sign, the signifier, and that which is semantic. This drifting of the signifier thus disavows the subjective (the signifier), but does not decenter it, transferring it instead toward ideal neutrality where, for lack of contradiction, everything slips away.

Strictly linguistic materiality thus undergoes modifications which, without breaking the communicative function of the signifying chain, alter it through an always mimetic, simulating, signifying play. Contemplative discourse is strewn with shifts in style: plays on phonic similarities, obsolete turns of phrase, ellipses, parables. Archaic and mannered, borrowed from the textual practices of bygone eras, and following the traces but not the facilitation of previous collapsings of signifiance, the various devices of the signifier's drifting oscillate, depending on the era, between the baroque and the esoteric.

D. What we call the *text* differs radically from its contemplative simulation, for in the text the *instinctual binominal* consists of two opposing terms that alternate in an endless rhythm. Although the negative, aggressivity, anality, and death predominate, they nevertheless pass through all the theses capable of giving them meaning, go beyond them, and in so doing convey positivity in their path. The entire gamut of partial drives is triggered within the *chora* underlying the text, endlessly "swallowing"/rejecting, appropriating/expelling, inside/outside. The real object is never posited as lost, lacking. As a provocation for the subject, instinctual rhythm simultaneously posits and passes through the object. Material discontinuity is in fact both continuous and discontinuous, but "quantum" rather than "atomic," because drives pass through the body as well as the surrounding natural and social configuration. Although rejection posits them as elements, the reactivation of rejection traverses these elements and knots them in a dynamic interdependence. Negativity is not reified directly as lack or as the impossible real: it is reintroduced into every reality |*réel*| already posited to expose it to other realities, make it dynamic, and effect its *Aufhebung* in an endless mobility—positing elements (time of rest), reactivating the whirlwind (time of the crossing).

To facilitate the imperious, dynamic passage of this alternating, instinctual rhythm, a *hierarchically fluctuating*[122] social system is necessary. Although such a social group is governed by the code or authority |*instance*| supporting it, its members are relatively independent of that code or authority. Hence, between this authority and individual freedom, relatively small autonomous groups are formed: small communities of socialized work. As a result, this society has a "head," but the entities it regulates have the same legal status it does.[123] To govern this centralized dispersion, its units of production also include families, but they are subjected to the rules of the group's production, not to those of the clan's reproduction.

In general, societies characterized by the Asiatic mode of production, such as ancient Chinese society, have this type of social organization. In such social systems, relations of reproduction—kinship exchanges and structures—are not distinguished from relations of production, but rather merge with them or are subordinated to them. (In Chinese, 生, the character for "to be born" is phonetically and graphically identical to the one for "to produce"; it is said to derive from the ancient 生, meaning a "plant that keeps growing.") Trans-familial groups in these societies include family protagonists in a process of production whose mobility displaces but does not threaten the code or authority governing the whole, thus ensuring the harmonious dynamic of the social process. This kind of organization makes the drive process flexible by "topologizing" it without bringing it into conflict with insurmountable repression. But only members of certain social categories (those outside production: literati or warriors) can enjoy the structural possibilities offered by the social system and, from them, produce the text.

The text's semiotic distribution is set out in the following manner: when instinctual rhythm passes through ephemeral but specific theses, meaning is constituted but is then immediately exceeded by what seems outside meaning: materiality, the discontinuity of real objects. The process' matrix of enunciation is in fact *anaphoric* since it designates an elsewhere: the *chora* that generates what signifies. To have access to the process would therefore be to break through any given *sign* for the subject, and reconstitute the heterogeneous space of its formation. This practice, a continuous passing beyond the limit, which does not close off signifiance into a system but instead assumes the infinity of its process, can only come about when, simultaneously, it assumes the laws of this process: the biological-physiological and social laws which allow, first, for the discovery of their precedents and then for their free realization. That this practice assumes laws implies that it safeguards boundaries, that it seeks out theses, and that in the process of this search it transforms the law, boundaries, and constraints it meets. In this way such a practice takes on meanings that come under laws and subjects capable of thinking them; but it does not stop there or hypostasize them; it passes beyond, questioning and transforming them. The subject and meaning are only phases of such a practice, which does not reject narrative, metalanguage, or theory. It adopts them but then pushes them aside as the mere scaffolds of the process, exposing their productive eruption within the heterogeneous field of social practice.

Caught up within this dynamic, the human body is also a process. It is not a unity but a plural totality with separate members that have no identity but constitute the place where drives are applied. This dismembered body cannot fit together again, set itself in motion, or function biologically and physiologically, unless it is included within a practice that encompasses the signifying process.

Without such a practice, the body in process/on trial is disarticulated; its drives tear it up into stymied, motionless sectors and it constitutes a weighty mass. Outside the process, its only identity is inorganic, paralyzed, dead. Within the process, on the other hand, by confronting it, displacing its boundaries and laws, the subject in process/on trial discovers those boundaries and laws and makes them manifest in his practice of them.

The *linguistic structures* that attest to this practice of the process are radically transformed by it. These rhythmic, lexical, even syntactic changes disturb the transparency of the signifying chain and open it up to the material crucible of its production. We can read a Mallarmé or a Joyce only by starting from the signifier and moving toward the instinctual, material, and social process the text covers.

This practice has no addressee; no subject, even a split one, can understand it. Such a practice does not address itself at all; it sweeps along everything that belongs to the same space of practice: human "units" in process/on trial. Though it is made by one who is all, this practice does not claim all who would be One. It does not instigate the "process-of-becoming-a-subject" of the masses. Instead it includes them in an upsurge of transformation and subversion.

Since the violence of drive charges is not halted, blocked, or repressed, what takes the place of the bodily, natural, or social objects these charges pass through is not just a representation, a memory, or a sign. The instinctual *chora*, in its very displacement, transgresses representation, memory, the sign. In contrast to the hysteric, the subject in process/on trial does not suffer from reminiscences, but rather from obstacles that tend to transform the facilitation, the "affective charge," and the "excitation" into reminiscences. Unlike hysteria, where the subject visualizes past experience and represents those "memories . . . in vivid visual pictures,"[124] this process breaks up the totality of the envisioned object and invests it with fragments (colors, lines, forms). Such fragments are themselves linked to sounds, words, and significations, which the process rearranges in a new combination. This combinatory moment, which accompanies the destructive process and makes it a *practice*, is always produced with reference to a moment of stasis, a boundary, a symbolic barrier. Without this temporary resistance, which is viewed as if it were insurmountable, the process would never become a practice and would founder instead in an opaque and unconscious organicity.

The essential operation dominating the space of the subject in process/on trial, and to which schizophrenia bears painful testimony, is that of the *appending of territories*—corporeal, natural, social—invested by drives. It involves *combination*: fitting together, detaching, including, and building up "parts" into some kind of "totality." These parts may be forms, colors, sounds, organs, words, etc., so long as they have been invested with a drive and, to begin with, "represent" only that drive.[125] At the same time (though in schizophrenia this will happen at a second stage), this structuring of drive facilitations through invested objects becomes meaningful, represents, or signifies—by image or word—entities, experiences, subjects, and ideologies. But this *secondary* representation is itself *dynamited* for two reasons. On the one hand, a drive charge is inherent in it and underlies it; the simple repetition of the representation or words is not the equivalent of this charge. (This is unlike hysteria in which "language serves as a substitute for action; by its help, an affect can be 'abstracted' almost as effectively.")[126] On the other hand, signification is pulverized because the drive charge has always pre-altered representation and language (a painting by Giotto or, even more so, one by Rothko, represents, if anything, a *practice*, more than it represents *objectivity*). If, therefore, any representation or language were the equivalent of this practice, it would be the representation and language of "art"; it is only in their performance that the dynamic of drive charges bursts, pierces, deforms, reforms, and transforms the boundaries the subject and society set for themselves. To understand this practice we must therefore break through the sign, dissolve it, and analyze it in a semanalysis, tearing the veil of representation to find the material signifying process.

The drive process cannot be released and carried out in narrative, much less in metalanguage or theoretical drifting. It needs a text: a destruction of the sign and representation, and hence of narrative and metalanguage, with all their lock-step, univocal seriousness. To do this, however, the text must move through them; it cannot remain unaware of them but must instead seep into them, its violent rhythm unleashing them by alternating rejection and imposition.

This practice cannot be understood unless it is being carried out. To do so, the subject must abandon his "*meta-*" position, the series of masks or the semantic layer, and complete the complex path of significance.

Such a practice has been carried out in texts that have been accepted by our culture since the late nineteenth century. In the case of texts by Lautréamont, Mallarmé, Joyce, and Artaud, *reading* means giving up the lexical, syntactic, and semantic operation of deciphering, and instead retracing the path of their production. How many readers can do this? We read signifiers, weave traces, reproduce narratives, systems, and driftings, but never the dangerous and violent crucible of which these texts are only the evidence.

Going through the experience of this crucible exposes the subject to impossible dangers: relinquishing his identity in rhythm, dissolving the buffer of reality in a mobile discontinuity, leaving the shelter of the family, the state, or religion. The commotion the practice creates spares nothing: it destroys all constancy to produce another and then destroys that one as well.

Although modern texts are the most striking example of this unsatisfied process, equivalents can also be found fairly readily in nonverbal arts that are not necessarily modern. Music and dance, inasmuch as they defy the barrier of meaning, pass through sectors within the signifying process which, though fragmentary (since there is no signified, no language), obey the same lines of force as those induced by the productive device of signifiance seen in texts.

Work as process, whatever kind of work it may be—when it is being carried out (and not when it is reified according to the exchange structures of a particular society)—shares something with this signifying process. *Revolutionary practice,* the *political activity* whose aim is the radical transformation of social structures, is no doubt one of the most obvious manifestations of this process. In bypassing the very materiality of language, and therefore without disturbing the forms of linguistic exchange, revolutionary practice initially locates the signifying practice within the social realm, but the landslides it produces there completely change all signifying structures as well. We shall therefore say that the explosions set off by practice-process within the social field and the strictly linguistic field are logically (if not chronologically) contemporaneous, and respond to the same principle of unstoppable breakthrough; they differ only in their field of application.

The various modalities—"artistic" or "political"—the process takes on as infinite practice can be seen throughout history. Only the *textual,* literary realization of this practice has recently been accepted in all its "purity," without any justification of it as "insane," "sacred," etc., or blending with other types. The novelty of the text's status is due to two divergent but contemporaneous factors. The ramification of capitalist society makes it almost impossible for the signifying process to attack material and social obstacles, objective constraints, oppressive entities, and institutions directly. As a consequence, the signifying process comes to the fore in the matrix of enunciation, and, through it, radiates toward the other components of the space of production. At the same time, the development of imperialism's forces of production brings about a relative relaxation of the relations of production and reproduction, and helps process break through into the most stable cogs of signifiance, its untouchable mainsprings: linguistic structures. This not only guarantees the survival of men whom sociocultural shackles in other ages had condemned to schizophrenia, it also ensures that human experience will be *broadened* beyond the narrow boundaries assigned to it by old relations of production and yet still be *connected* to those relations, which will consequently be threatened by it. Marx believed that capitalism had produced its own gravedigger: the proletariat. Imperialism produces its true gravedigger in the non-subjected man, the man-process who sets ablaze and transforms all laws, including—and perhaps especially—those of signifying structures. The productive process of the text thus belongs not to this established society, but to the social change that is inseparable from instinctual and linguistic change.

Since, as Marx notes, it lies outside the sphere of material production per se, the signifying process, as it is practiced by texts—those "truly free works"—transforms the opaque and impenetrable subject of social relations and struggles into a subject in process/on trial. Within this apparent asociality, however, lies the social function of texts: the production of a different kind of subject, one capable of bringing about new social relations, and thus joining in the process of capitalism's subversion: "The realm of freedom actually begins only where labour which is determined by necessity and mundane considerations ceases; thus in the very nature of things it lies beyond the sphere of actual material production."[127] "Truly free works, musical composition for example . . ." "Free time—which is both leisure and higher activity—will have naturally transformed its possessor into a different subject, and it is as a new subject that he will enter into the process of immediate production."[128]

II.

Negativity: Rejection

The negative having been in all probability greatly strengthened by the "struggle," a decision between insanity and security is imminent.

                    Kafka, *Diaries* (February 2, 1922)

1.

The Fourth "Term" of the Dialectic

THE NOTION of *negativity* (*Negativität*), which may be thought of as both the cause and the organizing principle of the *process*, comes from Hegel[1] The concept of negativity, distinct from that of nothingness (*Nichts*) and negation (*Negation*), figures as the indissoluble relation between an "ineffable" mobility and its "particular determination." Negativity is the mediation, the supersession of the "pure abstractions" of being and nothingness in the concrete where they are both only moments. Although *negativity* is a concept and therefore belongs to a contemplative (theoretical) system, it reformulates the static *terms* of pure abstraction as a process, dissolving and binding them within a mobile law. Thus, while still maintaining their dualism, negativity recasts not only the theses of *being* and *nothingness*, but all categories used in the contemplative system: universal and particular, indeterminate and determinate, quality and quantity, negation and affirmation, etc. Negativity constitutes the logical impetus beneath the thesis of negation and that of the negation of negation, but is identical to neither since it is, instead, the logical functioning of the movement that produces the theses.

Lenin noted Hegel's statement that the "triplicity" of the dialectic is its "external, superficial side."[2] By contrast, negativity is the liquefying and dissolving agent that does not destroy but rather reactivates new organizations and, in that sense, affirms. As transition (*Übergang*), negativity constitutes an *enchaînement* in the choreographical sense, "the necessary connection" and "the immanent emergence of distinctions." Here Lenin writes:

Very important!! This is what it means, in my opinion:
1) *Necessary* connection, the objective connection of all the aspects, forces, tendencies, etc., of the given sphere of phenomena;
2) The "immanent *emergence* of distinctions"—the inner objective logic of evolution and of the struggle of the differences, polarity.

Lenin underscores and accepts the notion of "inherent negativity" as an *objective* principle—the principle of all physical and spiritual life—and not as a simple "subjective craving to shake and break down what is fixed and true."[3] In the final analysis, dialectical materialism will inherit from Hegel's dialectic this and only this founding principle; it will reinstate materialist dualism and see negativity at work in and through two differentiated and heterogeneous orders.

Before returning to this heteronomy, we would like to stress that the Hegelian conception of negativity already prepared the way for the very possibility of thinking a materialist *process*. While remaining an intra-speculative notion, Hegelian negativity bursts, as it were, from within its conceptual unity since it links |*enchaîne*|—unleashes |*déchaîne*|—the "real" and the "conceptual," the objective and the subjective, and, if one wished to find its representation, culminates in the ethical order: although it is *objectivity* itself, negativity is at the same time and for that very reason the "free subject." The *ethics* that develops in the process of negativity's unfolding is not the kind of "ethics" that consists in obedience to laws. It amounts instead to the corruption and absorption of laws by what Hegel calls the aesthetic. The subject of that Hegelian aesthetic—the free subject par excellence—reveals the diremption |*épuisement*| of the ethical subject and effects its *Aufhebung* in order to reintroduce him into a process of transformation of community relations and discursive strata.[4] The logical definition given to this negativity is freedom "for itself": "The highest form of nothingness |taken| for itself is *freedom*, but it is negativity to the extent that it goes as deep into itself as possible, and is itself affirmation."[5]

As the logical expression of the objective process, negativity can only produce a subject in process/on trial. In other words, the subject, constituted by the law of negativity and thus by the law of an objective reality, is necessarily suffused by negativity—opened onto and by objectivity, he is mobile, nonsubjected, free. A subject submerged in negativity is no longer "outside" objective negativity as a transcendant unity or a specifically regulated monad; instead he positions himself as the *"innermost* and *most objective* moment of Life and Spirit." This Hegelian principle is the ferment of dialectical materialism, where it becomes both the concept of *human activity* as revolutionary activity and that of the *social and natural laws* this activity shows to be objective. Hegel writes:

The negativity which has just been considered is the *turning-point* of the Notion. It is the simple point of negative self-relation, the internal source of all activity, vital and spiritual self-movement, the dialectic soul which all truth has in it and through which it alone is truth; for the transcendence of the opposition between the Notion and Reality, and that unity which is the truth, rest upon this subjectivity alone.—The second negative, the negative of the negative, which we have reached, is this transcendence of the contradiction but is no more the *activity* of *an* external reflection than the contradiction is; it is the *innermost* and *most objective* moment of Life and Spirit, by virtue of which a subject, the person, the free, has being.

Lenin notes in the margins of this passage: "the kernel of dialectics," "the criterion of truth (the unity of the concept and reality)."[6]

But the materialist dialectic will retain only one element of the subject's negativation: his subordination, as a unit, to the social and natural process. Inheriting the weak points of dialectical materialist logic, dogmatico-revisionism will either dismiss the very problem of the subject and retain only the process of substance in a Spinozistic sense or the process of modes of production (as in dogmatism); or else it will hypostasize a psychological "subject" that has no process and only an external negativity (as in revisionism).

Let us take a closer look at the vicissitudes and dead ends of Hegelian negativity. If "the truth is, not either Being or Nothing, but that Being—not passes—but *has passed over* into Nothing, and Nothing into Being" (emphasis added), and if "their truth is therefore this *movement*, this immediate disappearance of the one into the other, in a word, *Becoming*; a movement wherein both are distinct, but in virtue of a distinction which has equally immediately dissolved itself,"[7] then we see that this supersession amounts to the erasing of heterogeneity within the Hegelian dialectic. Nothing, posited as such or active as a *relation* in negativity, can only be a *Becoming* or an *abstract negation*: the "absolute void" in Oriental systems. When negativity is considered a logical operation, it becomes reified as a void, as an absolute zero—the zero used in logic and serving at its base—or else as a connective in the logical Becoming. Yet what the dialectic represents as negativity, indeed Nothing, is precisely that which remains outside logic (as the signifier of a subject), what remains heterogeneous to logic even while producing it through a movement of separation or rejection, something that has the necessary objectivity of a law and can be seen as the logic of matter. This notion is possible because of and in spite of Hegel because he maintains, in opposition to Spinoza, the inseparability, the interpenetration, indeed the contradiction of "Being" and "Nothing" even if only within the sphere of the Idea:

Those who assert the proposition that Nothing is just Nothing, and even grow heated in its defence, do not know that in so doing they are subscribing to the abstract Pantheism of the Eleatics and, in essentials, of Spinoza. That view in philosophy which takes for principle that Being is merely Being, and Nothing merely Nothing, deserves the name of system of identity: this abstract identity is the essence of Pantheism.[8]

To those surprised by this thesis of the inseparability of Being and Nothing, Hegel objected that such "wonderment . . . forgets that in this Science [philosophy] there occur determinations quite different from those of ordinary consciousness and so-called common-sense,—which is not exactly sound understanding, but understanding educated up to abstractions and the faith, or rather superstition, of abstractions."[9]

A *negativity* inseparable from the Hegelian notion of *Being* is thus precisely what splits and prevents the closing up of Being within an abstract and superstitious understanding. It points to an outside that Hegel could only think of as something inherent in belief, and which his phenomenological descendants would posit as a negative theology. We nevertheless maintain that Hegelian negativity prevents the immobilization of the thetic, unsettles doxy, and lets in all the semiotic motility that prepares and exceeds it. Hegel, moreover, defines this negativity as the *fourth term* of the true dialectic: triplicity is only an appearance in the realm of the Understanding.[10]

The logic exposed above will become materialist when, with the help of Freud's discovery, one dares think negativity as the *very movement of heterogeneous matter*, inseparable from its differentiation's symbolic function. Although in Kant this material movement of scission, of rejection (to which we shall return), remains a "negative" term for the understanding, it is conceived dialectically, *because it is considered inseparable from Being*, as a fundamental *positivity*: "In this respect therefore mere Unseparateness or Inseparability would be a good substitute for Unity; but these would not express the affirmative nature of the relation of the whole."[11]

Thus, even while maintaining Kantian oppositions, the Hegelian dialectic moves toward a fundamental reorganization of these oppositions—one that will establish an *affirmative negativity*, a *productive dissolution* in place of "Being" and "Nothing." The theology inherent in this reorganization will, however, leave its mark in an implicit teleology: namely, the *Becoming* that subordinates, indeed erases, the moment of rupture.

2.

Independent and Subjugated "Force" in Hegel

ALREADY IN the *Phenomenology of Spirit* negativity is presented under the rule of the One and the Understanding, even in those moments when it appears most material and independent—closest to what we have called a semiotic *chora* (energy discharges and their functioning)—in other words, when it appears as Force [*Kraft*]. As an object for the Understanding, Force is always already double in its movement: "One of its moments, *the dispersal of the independent 'matters' in their [immediate] being* [emphasis added], is the *expression* [*extériorisation*] of Force; but Force, taken as that in which they have disappeared, is Force *proper*, Force which has been *driven back into itself* [emphasis added] from its expression."[12] Although, as Notion, Force is driven back into itself, Force as reality is not, and constitutes a freedom from thought. It therefore acts in a space that is *other*, which (Hegelian) speculation, unable to situate it within a concrete signifying practice—in the materiality of the signifying process—ends up superseding not only under the unity of the Understanding, but also under that of reason—but not without first indicating its heterogeneity. This labyrinthian movement recognizes "another subsisting essence" of Force but represses its material negativity, free energy:

In order, then, that Force may in truth *be*, it must be completely set free from thought, it must be posited as the *substance* [emphasis added] of these differences, i.e., *first* the *substance*, as this whole Force, remaining essentially *in and for itself*, *and then* its *differences* as possessing *substantial being*, or as moments existing on their own account. Force as such, or as driven back into itself, thus exists on its own account as an *exclusive One*, for while the unfolding of the |different| "matters" is *another* subsisting essence; and thus two distinct independent aspects are set up.[13]

The movement between these two "moments" is that of the Force that will produce a *non-objective inner world*, a return of Forces as a Notion within the Understanding. A play of Forces, the "inner being" will be established as the "beyond of consciousness," a "void": "In order, then, that in this *complete void*, which is even called the *holy of holies*, there may yet be something, we must fill it up with reveries, *appearances*, produced by consciousness itself. It would have to be content with being treated so badly for it would not deserve anything better, since even reveries are better than its own emptiness."[14]

Driving *Force* back under the *Notion* leads Force to an inner world where it is depreciated for precisely that doubling, i.e., its persistence in "expressing" itself and in emptying this inner being, constituted by "Forces," of any possible knowledge. Although posited, the "material" expression of Force, when thought of within the framework of conceptual unity, remains an *opaque* expression and, in ideal totality, this cannot be otherwise. In conceiving radical negativity as an *expression*, the idealist dialectic deprives itself of negativity's powerful moment: the scission that exceeds and precedes the advent of thetic understanding. It closes itself off both to the primacy of the objective laws of material transformation (no longer "exterior" but *heterogeneous* to the zone of the Understanding) and to signifying practices in which material drives striate, displace, and sometimes attain the clarity of the Understanding. Artaud was to give this description: "In it we feel a grinding of sluices, a kind of horrible volcanic shock from which the light of day has been *dissociated*. And from this clash, from the tearing of two principles, all potential images are born in a thrust stronger than a ground swell."[15]

By contrast, for the idealist dialectic, the reality of Force is ultimately the *thought* of it, where Force supersedes itself as Force; conversely, its realization as Force is a loss of reality:

Force, as *actual*, exists simply and solely in its *expression*, which at the same time is nothing else than a supersession of itself. This *actual* Force, when thought of as free from its expression and as being for itself, is Force driven back into itself; but in fact this determinateness, as we have found, is itself only a moment of Force's expression. Thus the truth of Force remains only the *thought* of it; the moments of its actuality, their substances and their movement, collapse unresistingly into an undifferentiated unity, a unity which is not Force driven back into itself (for this is itself only such a moment), but is its *Notion qua Notion*. Thus the realization of Force is at the same time the loss of reality.[16]

This impeccable logic constitutes signifying unity on the basis of explosions—scissions, impulses, collisions, rejections—yet they remain driven back in the name of and in view of the subjective unity not only of the Understanding but also of reason, which is necessary because it ensures the assertion of reality.

We have seen the way in which Hegel's phenomenological and logical philosophical descendants (Husserl and Frege), in their concern with signifying formation and functioning, tend to bury the negativity that was sketched out albeit already repressed in Hegel. What made its materialist overturning possible, in our view, was the key notion of drives in Freudian theory.

3.

Negativity as Transversal to Thetic Judgment

WE MUST emphasize that our notion of *negativity* should not be confused with *negation* in judgment or with the "negative quantities" that Kant introduced in philosophy as a "polarity" or "opposition," and that modern philosophy has attempted to displace by substituting the notion of difference and repetition.[17] Hegelian negativity operates within the Hegelian Reason (*Vernunft*) and not within the Understanding (*Verstand*); although it moves within a non-Kantian Reason, it succeeds in synthesizing Kant's theoretical and practical orders.[18] Hegelian negativity, aiming for a place transversal to the *Verstand*, completely disrupts its position (*stand*) and points toward the space where its production is put in practice. Hegelian negativity is not a component of the Kantian Idea, nor an oppositional element within the Understanding; it constitutes, in short, neither a logical operation nor the boundary that has set up paired oppositions from Kant to linguistic and anthropological structuralism (Troubetskoï—Jakobson—Lévi-Strauss). Furthermore, a materialist reading of Hegel allows us to think this negativity as the trans-subjective, trans-ideal, and trans-symbolic movement found in the *separation of matter*, one of the preconditions of symbolicity, which generates the symbol as if through a leap—but never merges with it or with its opposite logical homologue.

"Negativity" is undoubtedly an inappropriate term for this semiotic movement, which moves through the symbolic, produces it, and continues to work on it from within. For the term "negativity" is still too closely associated with that of negation (in the sense of a real or logical opposition), as it was introduced by Kant twenty years before the *Critique of Pure Reason* in his *Attempt to Introduce the Notion of Negative Quantities Into Philosophy* (1763). (In his work, Kant strictly adheres to the unity of the Cartesian subject determining his own reasoning: although he rebels against the rationalism of Descartes and Wolff, he does not attack the notion of the judging subject as a fixed point. The notion of negative quantities serves only to posit the real and allow its systematic or scientific articulation; it does not involve the generating space which is the semiotic.)

Though marked by the indelible trace of the judging subject's presence, the concept of *negativity* leads this trace and presence elsewhere—to a place where they are produced by a struggle of heterogeneous antitheses. The concept of negativity registers a *conflictual state* which stresses the heterogeneity of the semiotic function and its determination, and which dialectical materialism, reading Hegel through Freud, will posit as instinctual (social and material). But in order to talk about the functioning of meaning and to analyze the signifying—semiotic and symbolic—function, we cannot lose sight of the present subject's unifying agency [instance] to which the function of negation appears as an intrasemiotic function. We shall therefore not reject this function of negation as if it were merely the mirage of an archaic difference, the shadow of a false problem. On the contrary, we shall see, first with Frege, the logical inconsistency of intra-logical negation, then with Freud, the movement that produces negation and of which negation is only an oblique mark in the presence of consciousness.

In its etymology and history, the notion of negativity can be seen as a crossroad that is set up in conjunction with the symbolic function inasmuch as the latter is the function of a subject. Our purpose here is to specify the production of this subject as a process, an intersection—an impossible unity. To dismiss the notion of negativity as a crossroad would lead us to abandon any materialist aim in our conception of signifying functioning. In place of the heterogeneous dialectic of its process, we would have to establish either the presence of the Idea, structured through multiple networks but never open to the outside, or the drifting [*dérive*] of neutral traces in which this Idea itself, deprived of its identity, shatters. Both these moves serve to unify the Platonic vision of being—the cynosure of the contemplative subject—even when they intend to pluralize it. In identifying meaning with nature or nature with meaning, metaphysics avoids thinking the *production of the symbolic function* as the *specific* formation of material contradictions within matter itself.

In our view, *expenditure* or *rejection* are better terms for the movement of material contradictions that generate the semiotic function. Certainly the terms' implications in drive theory and general analytic theory make them preferable to that of negativity. We must nevertheless stress that the concept of rejection owes a debt to the materialist transformation of the dialectic in its focus on the practice of the subject, in this case, the signifying practice which puts his (subjective and/or signifying) unity in process/on trial. *The sole function of our use of the term "negativity" is to designate the process that exceeds the signifying subject, binding him to the laws of objective struggles in nature and society.* In the following remarks we shall specify the kind of negativity implied by the notion of *rejection.*

It is undoubtedly Frege who most subtly elaborates the status of logical negation, concluding, we recall, that this operation is "useless" in the realm of "thought." Negation is a "chimerical construction" in thought because the realm of thought's very configuration is situated within the thetic moment of the signifying function: the moment of *stehen, meinen, fassen.* Thought does not include its own production: "In thinking we do not produce thoughts, we grasp [*fassen*] them." "The thinker does not create them [thoughts] but must take them as they are." If thought is what does not involve production, it can include no negation that is not already an affirmation, always already *positing* the indestructible presence of the unitary subject: "I." Negation is a part of being: "I cannot negate what is not there." Whether thinking is "grasping" or "judging"—two different but interdependent moments—it cannot be altered by negation. Instead thought absorbs negation within the thetic position of its bearer [porteur], the subject who is always identical to himself: "And by negation I cannot transform something that needs me as its bearer into something of which I am not the bearer, and which can be grasped by several people as one and the same thing."[19] Negative thought does not exist; thought is always already the indistinguishableness of positive and negative; the negative is merely one of its possible components.

Even more than thought, which has no subject (according to Frege), the act of judging (which is different from thought in that, as a "physical process," it requires a judging subject) does not allow any negation because one cannot deny through judgment the subject bearing it. Consequently, negation, which appears in judgment as "not," is a "chimerical construction." The source of this chimera is the hypothesis of a "thought" presumably preexisting "judgment," in which "another negation" would function—one that would be different from the negation of judgment because it would not need a bearer and would be situated outside the field of consciousness. This is a tempting hypothesis, which Frege momentarily accepts and then immediately rejects, for how can one think two kinds of negation and two kinds of judgment or two kinds of thought? Indeed, since for him all signifying functioning is reduced to judgment, to suppose another negation would imply another judgment, and the introduction of "another negation" into this "other judgment" would merely overload the logical apparatus. Refusal in judgment is also found to be complementary to affirmation, and is its necessary precondition. Negation cannot therefore be posited as the polar opposite of judgment.

In light of Frege's remarks, to think the specificity of negation vis-à-vis judgment, we must think of it in a no man's land, within a "thought" that "needs no bearer, [and] must not be regarded as a content of consciousness."[20] But even in thought that is outside the subject and outside consciousness, negation as destruction would be impossible because the philosopher considers thought itself to be indestructible:

How, indeed, could a thought be dissolved? How could the inter-connexion of its parts be split up? The world of thoughts has a model in the world of sentences, expression, words, signs. To the structure of the thought there corresponds the compounding of words into a sentence; and here the order is in general not indif-ferent. To the dissolution or destruction of the thought there must accordingly correspond a tearing apart of the words, such as happens, e.g., if a sentence written on paper is cut up with scissors, so that on each scrap of paper there stands the expres-sion for part of a thought. These scraps can be shuffled at will or carried away by the wind; the connexion is dissolved, the original order can no longer be recognized. Is this what happens when we negate a thought? No! The thought would undoubtedly survive even this execution of it in effigy.[21]

Hence the only place negation exists is outside the subject's con-sciousness, but this outside does not exist, since thought and consciousness are indestructible. At this point it is evident that only a theory of the unconscious can propose a logical device within which "negation" can be inscribed, not as something within judgment but as something economic—that which produces the signifying position itself. In his article on *Verneinung*, Freud pos-ited the movement of this other negation, this *negativity* that is both trans-logical and produces logic.[22]

Although Frege himself does not formulate this possibil-ity—the movement of the "other negation," *negativity*, rejection, operating on the border between "consciousness" and "uncon-sciousness"—the precision with which he posits the status of ne-gation in judgment brings him close to what would become the basis for the analytical concept of negativity. For Frege, the "other negation" inherent in impersonal thought is located in the lin-guistic *predicate*. It produces in language the predicative "not" and gives the illusion that it aims to destroy the predicate and thus judgment itself. Yet, as part of the predicate, "not" is part of judg-ment—which we call the thetic—and is merely a variant of the *positive predicate*. The latter, by contrast, has no special lexical sign, since it derives its value solely from the "affirmative sentence's form," in other words, its syntax.

This point is crucial: negation in judgment is a negation of the predicate; it is linked to the *predicate function* and can only occur within syntax, which simultaneously assimilates it. Negation thus serves as the supplementary and explicit mark of the predicate and/or of the syntactic and thetic function. In fact, certain languages, such as Chinese, go so far as to define the verb as an "element that can be denied" (in contrast with the noun which is "an element that can be counted").[23] Furthermore, it has been shown that all negative transformations, including lexical ones, already constitute a syntactic transformation, or can be interwoven into one.[24] It has been noted that, in the course of language acquisition, signified negation (the word "no" as opposed to simple kinetic refusal) appears around the age of fifteen months,[25] coinciding with the peak of the "mirror stage" and with holophrastic language acquisition. Although the latter includes certain syntactic sequences, it generally precedes true syntactic competence, which is exhibited in syntactically formed utterances. In other words, if the symbolic function is a syntactic function, and if the latter consists essentially in linking a subject (and elements relating to it) and a predicate (and its related elements), the formation of the *symbol of negation precedes this function or coincides with its development*. To say "no" is already to formulate syntactically oriented propositions that are more or less grammatical. In other words, negation in judgment is a mark of the symbolic and/or syntactic function and the first mark of sublimation or the thetic. These observations and linguistic analyses confirm Frege's position, which holds that negation is a variant of predication in judgment.

In order to understand that which operates in a developmental and logical stage prior to the constitution of the symbolic function which absorbs the negative within the predicate, we will have to direct our attention outside the confines of language. We must *leave the verbal function* and move toward what produces it, so as to understand the process of rejection which pulsates through the drives in a body that is caught within the network of nature and society.

Preverbal gestures mark the *"concrete operations"* that precede the positing of the static terms/symbols of language and syntax. Psycholinguists speak of "concrete operations" which involve the subject's practical relations to objects—their destruction, seriation, organization, and so forth. They are "forms of knowledge which modify the object to be known in order to bring about transformations and their results"; these "concrete operations" include "sensorimotor actions (though not imitation), the internalized actions prolonging them, and operations per se."[26] It is on this level of "concrete operations" preceding language acquisition, in the infant's "*fort-da*," that Freud perceives the drive of rejection. This *Ausstossung* or *Verwerfung* indicates a basic biological operation of scission, separation, and division; at the same time, it joins the always already splitting body to family structure and to the continuum of nature in a relation of rejection.

Within this specific space, which is corporeal and biological but already social since it is a link with others, there operates a nonsymbolized negativity that is neither arrested within the terms of judgment, nor predicated as negation in judgment. This negativity—this expenditure—posits an object as separate from the body proper and, at the very moment of separation, fixes it in place as *absent*, as a *sign*. In this way, rejection establishes the object as real and, at the same time, as signifiable (which is to say, already taken on as an object within the signifying system and as subordinate to the subject who posits it through the sign). The vertical dimension (speaking subject/outside) of the sign relation which rejection establishes ends up being projected within the signifying system in the horizontal dimension of language (syntactic subject/predicate). Both the outside, which has become a signifiable object, and the predicate function operate as checks on negativity—rejection—that are interdependent and indissociable. Negativity—rejection—is thus only a *functioning* that is discernible through the *positions* that absorb and camouflage it: the real, the sign, and the predicate appear as differential moments, steps in the process of rejection. Rejection exists only in the transsymbolic materiality of this process, in the material drives of the body subject to the biological operations of the division of matter, and to its social relations. Ready-made verbalization [language] can register rejection only as a series of differences, thus fixing it in place, and losing sight of its dynamic process. True negativity is a dialectical notion specific to the signifying process, on the crossroads between the biological and social order on the one hand, and the thetic and signifying phase of the social order on the other.

Both negation and the predicate it is part of thus witness the passage of rejection, which constitutes them inasmuch as rejection constitutes the real and the sign designating reality. Both negation in judgment and predication harness, stop, and knot the mobility specific to rejection. But when rejection refuses to be stopped by specular identification and the concomitant symbolic function, negation and predication bear the brunt of its attacks. In schizophrenia and in the poetic language of the modern text, negation and syntactic structure find their status transformed and their normativeness disturbed: they become textual phenomena that bespeak a specific economy of drives, an expenditure or a shattering of the "drive vector," and hence a modification of the relation between the subject and the outside. Negativity, stopped and absorbed within the negation of judgment, therefore shows through only *in modifications of the function of negation or in syntactic and lexical modifications*, which are characteristic of psychotic discourse and poetry. It is not the cut made by a pair of scissors that destroys what Frege had considered thought's indestructibility, but rather the return of rejection, discernible in various modifications of the phenotext. Frege undoubtedly suspected as much since he excluded poetry from "thought." For him, "thought" does "not belong to poetry [Dichtung]."[27]

Negation in judgment, like strictly linguistic (morphological or lexical) negation, puts the subject in a position of *mastery* over the statement as a structured whole, and in a position to generate language, which in turn implies, among other things, competence in selection and an ability to grasp infinity through a recursive movement. Negation is a symptom of syntactic capacity: indeed, Mallarmé's statement that "a guarantee is needed: syntax," could be read as "a guarantee is needed: negation." Negation serves, along with syntax, as the strongest breakwater for protecting the unity of the subject and offers the most tenacious resistance to the shattering of the verbal function in the psychotic process.

The frequency of negation in schizophrenic discourse has often been noted.[28] Although such "research" is based on presuppositions of linguistic "normativeness" and "normalcy," it nevertheless accentuates certain elements of the phenotext that have two important implications for the economy of negativity in the schizophrenic process. On the one hand, this negation goes outside the framework of the utterance and/or language and involves the subject's relation to the unobjectifiable outside: it constitutes a negativity rather than a negation—rejection rediscovered through linguistic and logical negation. On the other hand, this negativity "disturbs" the normative rules of lexical oppositions by replacing them with the trajectory of "primary processes" (displacements, condensations) which operate in the formation of these lexical units as signs. Instead of the "normal" antonyms, the "patient" will give, for example, the most contrasting and "stylistically marked" "negative" ("*minus*" for "big")[29] or a semi-homophone ("*ne pas être*" for "*naître*") ["not to be" for "to be born"]. This occurs because rejection brings pressure to bear against the *locking* of signifiance into *units* of meaning, which is also the precondition for their arrangement in oppositional pairs. The lexical discrepancy between the term given by the schizophrenic and the "normal" antonym opens up an abyss within the basic signified, and unsettles it by attributing complementary sememes to it. (When "*minus*" is given for "big," the latter acquires other sememes: "more," "*magis*," "important," and so forth.[30]) Rejection may, on the other hand, refer the basic signified to a basic absence, in other words, to phonemes and to their constitutive drive bases which form the only connection—"concrete operation"—to the other signified. (When the schizophrenic gives "*ne pas être*" as its opposite, "*naître*" dissolves into "*n'être*" [its homophone]. No longer the "sign" of a real, compact event, "*naître*" refers instead to a play of signifying differentials within the trans-sign, semiotic signifying process.)[31]

Rejection—negativity—ultimately leads to a "fading" of negation: a surplus of negativity destroys the pairing of opposites and replaces opposition with an *infinitesimal differentiation within the phenotext*. This negativity is *insistent*, as can be seen in the *frequency* of negation's morphological devices (*ne . . . pas*), which tend to connote it as "active," "marked," and "abrupt."[32] In this sense, negativity affirms the position of the subject—the thetic, positivizing phase of a subject mastering the verbal function. In psychosis, this insistence on negation indicates the struggle, constitutive of symbolicity, between thesis and rejection, which, if lost, may result in the extinction of all symbolic capacity. Negativism is then followed by a shattering of syntactic sequences, and a simultaneous loss of the immobilizing sign and of corresponding reality.

Although, as an "experience of limits,"[33] the text conveys this struggle constitutive of symbolicity and the verbal function, it also establishes a *new, real device*, called the "author's" "universe." Rejection, whether inscribed in an abundance of negative statements as in *Maldoror* or in syntactic distortions as in A *Throw of the Dice*,[34] is characteristic of the subject in process/on trial who succeeds—for biographical and historical reasons—in remodeling the historically accepted *signifying device* by proposing the representation of a different relation to natural objects, social apparatuses, and the body proper. This subject moves through the linguistic network and uses it to indicate—as in anaphora or in a hieroglyph—that the linguistic network does not represent something real posited in advance and forever detached from instinctual process, but rather that it experiments with or practices the objective process by submerging in it and emerging from it through the drives. This subject of expenditure is not a fixed point—a "subject of enunciation"—but instead acts *through* the text's organization (structure and completion) where the *chora* of the process is represented. The best metaphor for this transversal rhythmicity would not be the grammatical categories it redistributes, but rather a piece of music or a work of architecture.

4.

"Kinesis," "Cura," "Desire"

HAVING DEFINED what we mean by *negativity* in the wake of Hegel, we shall now call to mind certain fundamental philosophical trends which we see as indebted to his philosophy, even though they deny its import, criticize its abstractness, or seek a new domain that would be capable of specifying, and thus transforming, the way it functions.

Phenomenological doctrines tend to preserve the notion of the subject's characteristic motricity, but they isolate it from the natural and social process. The only "dialectic" phenomenology acknowledges seeking is an ethical one. What interests Kierkegaard is the mobility characteristic of the empirical subject, and it is in connection with this ethical empiricism that, over against Hegel, he conceives of an empirical form of negativity—*kinesis*—which is intended to unite abstract thought and *being* and cut short Hegel's logical and categorial "excess."[35]

Such a critique of Hegelian idealism necessarily attempts to break through its circular reasoning and reach both the concrete materiality of "existence" and a notion of the practice of the subject as more than mere logical abstraction (theoretical contemplation). It is nevertheless unlikely—and Kierkegaard's failure to found his theory of *kinesis* proves it—that this can be done *within* theory without the categorial apparatus of abstraction. For the desire to *think* this breakthrough demands a theoretical construction; otherwise, the choice is one between pre-Hegelian philosophy (subjectivity or substantiality) and (textual or political) practice, but the latter already requires a subject in process/on trial, which Kierkegaard called for but was actually realized by Nietzsche, following in the footsteps of Hölderlin.

As for contemplative signifying systems per se, the Heideggerean notions of *cura* [care], "existential care," and "Dasein as care" probably best reveal the merely ethical and finally conformist stasis of the dialectic's notion of negativity as rupture, transformation, and freedom. Heidegger recognizes "the very 'emptiness' and 'generality' which obtrude themselves ontically in existential structures"; in other words, in contrast with the essayical Kierkegaard, he claims a logical status for the ontic level and for his philosophy in general. Heidegger nevertheless psychologizes the movement of negativity when he considers these structures to "have an ontological definiteness and fulness of their *own*. Thus Dasein's whole constitution itself is not simple in its unity, but shows a structural articulation; in the existential conception of care, this articulation becomes expressed." *Care* thus becomes the "basis on which *every* interpretation of Dasein which is ontical and belongs to a world-view [*Weltanschaulich*] must move." Care, which raises to the level of the concept "what has already been disclosed in an ontico-existentiell manner," is aimed at an *ontological a priori* and thus proves to be the basis of all ontological constitution.[36] As a result, care constitutes the primordial mortar in the phenomenological edifice and its structural *articulation*, its impetus or ferment, and the logic governing its development and structure. It even brings together existential metaphysics' most cherished division, "body" and "mind," unifying them in "man."

The semantic purport of this key notion—man, the agent of structural articulation in phenomenology—is crucial: Heidegger borrows it from a Latin fable representing Jupiter, Earth, and Saturn creating man, and a fragment from Seneca's last letter.[37] The boldness of phenomenology's structural articulation is thereby cloaked in semantic anthropomorphism and mythic ideology and, what is more, a myth dating from this signifying system's waning period, the pre-Christian Roman era. We have already seen that when the objective movement of Hegelian negativity took on semantic form, it found the *free* subject, which Hegel saw emerging in a continuous movement from comedy, inherent in Greek democracy, up to the advent of revealed religion. In addition, the French Revolution afforded Hegel a contemporary, objective, and historical realization of the free subject. Phenomenological *care*, by contrast, is the logically and chronologically regressive mythological travesty of the process whose logical totality is traced by the Hegelian dialectic. In short-circuiting history and the history of knowledge, in crushing them both between the three poles of pre-Christian mythology, Plato, and prewar capitalist anxiety—Heidegger's text dates from 1935—Heideggerean *cura*, like all phenomenology, is only falsely logical, and stops logical formulation itself at a mythic, narrative—existential—stasis in which the unitary subject takes cover as if in a religion. Obsessed by what is lying in wait for him outside, this subject decides not to get involved unless he does so with "devotedness," "carefulness," and "anxious exertion." Negativity is thereby tamed in a subject who is posited there only as a subject anguished by an inaccessible sociality or transcendence.

The Heideggerean subject strives toward an other to reduce it to the same; he creates a community that is always lacking [*manquante*]; he aims for a closure that is never achieved. *Care* is a metaphor for the wet-nurse, the mother, or the nurse. Reassuring and promising something beyond the eternal frustration that it simultaneously proclaims, Heideggerean *cura* breaks off the logical flight of negativity and replaces it with a narrow domain that starts out being simply ethical but turns out to belong to a mere medical ethic that has a kind of patching-up or first-aid function. The free subject that Hegelian phenomenology saw *emerging* from the artisan, through the actor, up to the abnegation for the crowd (from which the materialists drew the revolutionary principle), is here reduced to anxiety and social work.

As Karel Kosík shows, *care* is a way of unifying and subjectifying the shattering of the individual within the capitalist mode of production.[38] As "a system made up of apparatuses and installations," fragmented, no longer demanding a producer or a "creative" worker but rather a manipulator, capitalism eliminates the free subject unified in his process, which Hegel was the last philosopher to summon. At the same time, on the basis of its own state and juridical unification, capitalism gathers up this subject—manipulator and subordinate—into a hypostasized subjectivity, but one that is worried because it is cut off from the signifying and socio-historical process. This subjectivity then appears as an opaque unity which is represented as the concentration and immobilization of the contradictions of social practice and, for this reason, as forever separate from it.

"Care" is the repression of social practice as *objective* practice, and its replacement by the resigned expectation of a meaning—social or transcendental—always anticipated, never attained, but one that presupposes in any case its existential (thetic) subject—slave of his own mastery. This subject then attributes meaning to the world, which he thereafter considers a corollary to himself, a kind of system of signification. "Care" "represents the reified moment of praxis, as does the 'economic factor' and the 'homo œconomicus.' "[39]

The post-phenomenological concept of *desire*, which is based on psychoanalysis, borders on the domain of *cura*. For the moment, although we will be more specific later on, let us say that the term *desire* first became necessary as a specific semantic cover for what can logically be expressed in the *process* as a *negativity*. Defined by Lacan as "the metonymy of the want-to-be" |*manque à être*|,[40] desire organizes its logical structure on what can be called nothingness or the zero in logic. At first, "desire"'s peregrinations recall the logical labyrinth of Hegelian negativity to the extent that they posit a rationality that is similar to the synthesis of theory and practice; precisely because of this dialectical operation, mechanists accuse the notion of "desire" of arbitrariness, as seen in Lacan's statement that "what presents itself as unreasonable in desire is an effect of the passage of the rational in so far as it is real—that is to say, the passage of language—into the real, in so far as the rational has already traced its circumvallation there."[41]

On the other hand, *desire* also designates the process of the subject's advent in the signifier through and beyond needs or drives. As the crossroad between "the being of language" and "the non-being of objects,"[42] desire takes up the logic of Hegelian negativity through the notions of the first Freudian topography, but raises them out of their biological and material entrenchment into the domain of social praxis where "social" means "signifying": "Desire merely subjugates what analysis makes subjective."[43] Desire is thus the movement that leaps over the boundaries of the pleasure principle and invests an already signifying reality—"desire is the desire of the Other"—which includes the subject as divided and always in movement. Because the subject is desiring, he is the subject of a practice, which itself can be carried out only to the extent that its domain—the "real"—is impossible since it is beyond the "principle ironically called pleasure."[44] This *desire*, the principle of negativity, is essentially the *death wish* and, only as such, is it the precondition of that practice, which can be considered, in turn, an effectuation of desire. Both desire and practice exist solely on the basis of language: desire is "produced . . . by an animal at the mercy of language . . ."[45] This interdependence among *desire, death, language*, and *beyond the pleasure principle* articulates a punctual position (one that is both solid and active) for a subject, but does so to the detriment of an "objectivity," called "the real," from which this subject will forever be cut off.

Yet the negativity characteristic of the Hegelian dialectic, which emerged through the analytical theory of *desire*, ends up yielding before a Kantian agnosticism when the subject psychoanalysis has in view proves to be either the subject of Kantian understanding or that of science. More precisely and concretely, this subject's desire is founded on drives ("the psychosomatic articulation [*charnière*]") that remain unsatisfied, no matter what phantasmatic identifications desire may lead to because, unlike desire, drives "divide the subject from desire."[46] Desire's basis in drives will thus be dismissed and forgotten so that attention may be focused on *desire itself*, reactivated by the reiteration of castration. The negativity *articulating two orders* and positing the never saturated subject in process/on trial between them—the drives' status as articulation—will be replaced by a nothingness—the "lack" [*manque*] that brings about the unitary *being* of the subject. Desire will be seen as an always already accomplished subjugation of the subject to lack: it will serve to demonstrate only the development of the signifier, never the heterogeneous process that questions the psychosomatic orders. From these reflections a certain kind of *subject* emerges: the subject, precisely, of desire, who lives at the expense of his drives, ever in search of a lacking object. The sole source of his praxis is this quest of lack, death, and language, and as such it resembles the praxis of phenomenological "care."

The subject of desire, whose image par excellence is the neurotic and his fantasies, would seem to be confined within two boundaries. The first resides in the intermingling of drives in language—as opposed to the repression of drives beneath language. But in this event, in which we shall see the economy of "poetic" language, the unitary subject can no longer find his place: "When language gets into the act, the drives tend rather to proliferate, and the question (if anyone were there to ask it) would instead be how the subject will find any place whatsoever."[47] The second boundary is constituted by the stopping of desire to the extent that a subject has attempted to remain on its path. When language is not mixed with the drives and, instead, requires an extreme repression of the drives' multiplicity and/or their linearization in the development of the unitary subject, what results is a culmination of the subjugation under the Law of the Signifier in which the living person himself becomes a sign and signifying activity stops. This is the masochistic moment par excellence, auto-castration, the final mutilation joining the theological core that is one of its most perfect representations: the body becomes a "calm block here-below fallen from an obscure disaster" (Mallarmé), "the pound of flesh that life pays in order to turn it into the signifier of the signifiers" (Lacan), an ultimate signifier: "the lost phallus of the embalmed Osiris"[48]—and the catatonic body of the clinical schizophrenic.

5.

Humanitarian Desire

IN HEGEL, Desire (Begierde) is one of the moments constituting the notion of *self-consciousness*, a moment that particularizes and concretizes negativity, and represents its simultaneously most differentiated and most "superseded" movement, a *completed* dialectic. The advent of Desire takes the following path. The articulation of self-consciousness begins when it loses the object— the other—with respect to which it was posited; this object is the "simple and independent substance," the foundation of sense-certainty. Self-consciousness denies the object in order to return to itself, and loses sight of it only as a simple substance to realize its own unity with itself. (The materialist ground of this logical movement is described by Freud in the economy of *Verneinung*.) Desire is thus: the negation of the object in its alterity as "an independent life"; the introduction of this amputated object into the knowing subject; the "Assumption" of alterity and the supersession of its heterogeneity within certainty and consciousness; and the dissolution of the difference, "general dissolution," the "fluidity of the differences." This movement constitutes Life. As the movement described by "the passive separatedness of shapes" or "process," self-consciousness follows the same trajectory Life does, and self-consciousness' only meaning is found in its relation to the fluidity of Life:

The simple "I" is thus genus or the simple universal, for which *the differences are* NOT *differences* [emphasis added] only by its being the *negative essence* of the shaped independen⁻ moments; and self-consciousness is thus certain of itself only by superseding this other that presents itself to self-consciousness as an independent life; self-consciousness is Desire. *Certain of the nothingness of this other* [emphasis added], it explicitly affirms that this nothingness is *for it* the truth of the other; *it destroys the independent object* [emphasis added] and thereby gives itself the certainty of itself as a *true* certainty, a certainty which has become explicit for self-consciousness itself *in an objective manner*.[49]

We note the "paranoid" mark in the path of Desire. Self-consciousness is constituted through the supersession of the *heterogeneous* Other, and Desire is this very supersession; having always been on the path of Desire, "self-consciousness" becomes its Other, without, however, giving itself up as such. The movement of scission continues and is the very essence of self-consciousness, corresponding to Desire. But once again this dividedness is subordinated to the unity of the self in the presence of the Spirit [*Geist*]. Desire is the agent of this unity; it acts as the agent of unification by negativizing the object. Desire is the *detour of negativity toward the becoming-One*, the indispensable moment that unifies "schizoid" pulverization in one identity, albeit an infinitely divisable and fluid one.

Today it is possible to read between the lines in Hegel and find the statement of a truth about the subject: *The subject is a paranoid subject constituted by the impulse of Desire that sublimates and unifies the schizoid rupture.* Not only is paranoia therefore the precondition of every subject—one becomes a subject only by accepting, if only temporarily, the paranoid unity that supersedes the heterogeneous other—but paranoia also lies close to the fragmenting that can be called schizoid, camouflaging its secret even while drawing on its energy. Although the "fluidity of the differences" constitutes the *unity* of self-consciousness, it is also a threat to that unity, for in this fluidity alone there is no place for any *unity*, Desire, or subjection (*Unterwerfung*) to life; on the contrary, what determines this division is death, rupture, and differentiation with no unifying fluidity.

On this level, as in the whole of its trajectory, the Hegelian dialectic starts by dissolving *immediate* unity, sense-certainty. But after noting the moments of its division, doubling, and mediation with respect to the other, the dialectic comes back to the same, fills it with the other, and consolidates it. *Theology is sideswept by philosophy, only to reconstitute itself with full knowledge of the facts.* The "I" is divided and doubled only to become reunified within the unity of Self-Consciousness. This is the ambiguousness of the idealist dialectic: it posits division, movement, and process, but in the same move dismisses them in the name of a higher metaphysical and repressive truth, one that is differentiated but solely within the confines of its unity: Self-Consciousness and its juridical corollary, the State. Moreover, Hegel goes so far as to salute its statist form, that is, its unitary and unifying, centralized and controlled form, in the French Revolution and its constitution. His sun metaphor represents this development as the fulfillment of the reasoning subject, the One, in the bourgeois State:

Never since the sun had stood in the firmament and the planets revolved around him had it been perceived that man's existence centres in his head, i.e., in Thought, inspired by which he builds up the world of reality. Anaxagoras had been the first to say that νοῦς governs the World; but not until now had man advanced to the recognition of the principle that Thought ought to govern spiritual reality. This was accordingly a glorious mental dawn. All thinking beings shared in the jubilation of this epoch. Emotions of a lofty character stirred men's minds at that time; a spiritual enthusiasm thrilled through the world, as if the reconciliation between the Divine and the Secular was now first accomplished.[50]

It is as if, having glimpsed the splitting of the ego and its negative link to the elements of material and social continuity, the idealist dialectic had appropriated one of the most lucid visions of the loss of subjective and metaphysical unity and of the jouissance brought on by this loss. For, anxious to reestablish this (subjective and political) unity, riveted to it, and proceeding with that end in mind, the dialectic closes up the movement of negativity within unity. The notion of *Desire* appears, then, as the most faithful representation of this collapsing of negativity into unity. We note that the theological or metaphysical revivals of Hegel (that claim to be materialist) will take up both this notion of *Desire* and that of *man as unity* by *discarding the process of negativity dissolving unity*, which had been inherent in the notion of self-consciousness.

This is what Feuerbach's overturning of the Hegelian dialectic, which Marx would then inherit, amounts to. While criticizing the mysticism of self-consciousness and positing nature and society as productive bases of man, Feuerbach dispenses with Hegel's (furtive) dissolution of the unity of consciousness. The materialist overturning of Hegel was accomplished at the cost of a blindness to the Hegelian dialectic's potential (subjected, as we have shown, to the dominant notion of totalization) for *dissolving* the subject. In our view, this unification of the signifying process under the unitary notion of *man* reveals the "pious atheism" of Feuerbach's move. What causes the difficulty and then vanishes in this overturning is precisely Hegelian negativity: Feuerbach, attributing the unity of being and nothingness to the "oriental imagination," reduces that unity to the "*indifference* of the species or of the consciousness of the species towards the particular individual."[51] Thus the unity of being and nothingness no longer functions at the level of the individual, who is consequently deprived of contradiction and expenditure; the "subject," whose negativity has disappeared, is reduced to a desirable ego: a "human being" that only "the species" (or, at best, society) can call into question, but whose status as a speaking and signifying being can never be negatived. It is this desiring "human being" who constitutes the mainstay of religion, which presents him with various "objects" to desire, the archetype of which is God: "The basic dogmas of Christianity are the fulfilled wishes of mankind."[52] Desire unifies man and binds him to others; as such, desire serves as the foundation of anthropomorphism and the human basis of the community, society, and finally the State. Although Feuerbach is correct to reject speculative philosophy in the name of the boundary, the finite, and the real, he attenuates the driving force of the dialectic when he declares that "the essence of man is contained in community, in the unity of man with man."[53]

The mechanistic materialist overturning of the Hegelian dialectic thus makes explicit the *real basis* of its *totalizing and unifying* aspect. It reveals that certain social relations—the family, civil society, and the State—founded on this unitary subject and his desire, are the truth of Hegelian speculation in its *positivistic as-*

pect. Indeed this is what Marx retains from Feuerbach: "Family and civil society are presuppositions of the state; they are the real agents; but speculation reverses their roles. . . . The facts that are the basis of everything are not thought of as such, but as a mystical result."[54] In this reversal, the true agent of the family—civil relations and the State—will be the (lacking, suffering) subject of *desire*. With Left Hegelians, the criticism of speculative philosophy passes through a subjectification. "Hegel objectifies what is subjective, I subjectify what is objective," writes Feuerbach.[55] This subjectification, which is in fact an anthropomorphization of Hegelian negativity, transfers the cutting edge of negativity from theology to the realm of society, and would serve as the base for "communist" philosophers in the second half of the nineteenth century. The desiring subject then becomes the basis of the authoritarian State, which not only foresees but also regulates subjective anomalies. The total man is therefore best represented by "the head of state":

Man is the ground of the state. The state is the realised, complete and explicit totality of the human essence. In the state the essential goals and activities of man are realised in the different classes, but again brought to identity in the person of the head of state. The head of state has to represent all classes without distinction. Before him all are equally necessary and have equal rights. The head of state is the representative of universal man.[56]

Marx takes up the notion of "desire" in his writings of 1842 and in *The German Ideology*,[57] and even though this notion is not essential to his analysis of social relations, it emerges in the mechanistic "Marxist" (if not Marxian) conception of a society made up of individuals serving as the mainstay of relations of production and of the exchange values which alone are capable of placing these human "supports" in a contradiction that would negative their singularity. But Marx measures the limitations of this shift in emphasis by observing that when negativity is locked within the *desiring subject* (man), its impact is limited and is restricted to the conformist confines of Hegelian notions of society.

Marx's dialectical materialism will move decisively away from

Feuerbach's naturalist metaphysics by reinstating the ferment of the dialectic—the notions of *struggle, contradiction,* and *practice*—with a view toward the process that would transform not only society but man as well. Referring to a book by Eugen Dühring in an 1869 letter to Engels, Marx writes that "the gentlemen in Germany believe that Hegel's dialectic is a 'dead duck.' Feuerbach has much on his conscience in this respect."[58] Despite its development of the dialectic, Marxist doctrine inherits two fundamental moments from Feuerbach's enterprise:

(1) The anthropomorphization, better still, the subjectification of Hegelian negativity in the form of a human unity—the man of desire and of lack—is represented in Marx by the proletariat, which is viewed as the means for realizing the total man— mastered and unconflicted; man is above all a *"mastery,"* a *"solution to the conflict"*:

On the one hand, it is only when objective reality everywhere becomes for men in society the reality of human faculties, human reality, and thus the reality of his own faculties, that all objects become for him the objectification of himself. The objects then confirm and realise his individuality, they are his own objects, that is, man himself becomes the object.[59]

In Marxism, the complicity between the philosopher and the proletariat is the figure given this conception of the subject as unitary, a Janus composed of metalanguage and desire: "Philosophy is the head of this emancipation [i.e., of man] and the proletariat is its heart. Philosophy can only be realised by the abolition of the proletariat and the proletariat can only be abolished *by the realisation of philosophy.*"[60]

(2) Man is considered to be *directly and exclusively* anchored in the State or, more generally, in the social machine and social relations, that is, relations between men governed by need and suffering. Within the machine of contradictions in production and class conflicts, man remains an untouchable unity, in conflict with others but never in conflict "himself"; he remains, in a sense, neutral. He is either an oppressing or oppressed subject, a boss or an exploited worker or the boss of exploited workers, but never

a *subject in process/on trial* who is related to the *process*—itself brought to light by dialectical materialism—in nature and society.[61]

If this is the status of the individual in the bourgeois system according to Marx, and if we were to read this observation in the light of psychoanalysis, we would say that, in the State and in religion, capitalism requires and consolidates the paranoid moment of the subject: a unity foreclosing the other and taking its place. But if, after having carried it to its extreme, the proletariat resolves the contradiction between subject-thing and inalienable subject and thereby realizes philosophy, the proletariat's status as subject presupposes one of the following possibilities. Either the subject remains a unitary man, thus reinstating the paranoid subject of speculative thought, the State, and religion. Or else one takes "the realization of philosophy" to mean the realization of its moments of rupture and scission, the putting in process/on trial of unity: in this case, the proletariat would represent the factor disseminating the unity of the subject and the State, exploding it in a heterogeneity that is irreducible to the agency of consciousness. These two possibilities are not simply hypotheses; they are in fact two antagonistic notions of society and a fortiori of socialist society.

From the end of the nineteenth century, sociopolitical movements would aim to change the structure of the State or the relations between "men" and continue to regard man as a social being. But they would make no mention of speculative philosophy's other insights: the negative process of unity and the conflict threatening it, the dividedness of the unitary subject in the process of his constitution/deconstitution, and the moment that dissolves society and calls into question the unity of the subject. These insights were to remain the private domain of aesthetics, which theology would secretly or openly appropriate. In experiencing it, Lautréamont would run the risk of psychosis and death. In putting it into practice, Mallarmé was to seek its philosophical and social justification.

6.

Non-Contradiction: Neutral Peace

GRAMMATOLOGY RETAINS the essential features of a nonsubstantial, nonsemantic, and nonphenomenal device that might enable us to sort out the logocentric entanglement of substance, meaning, and phenomena, and indicate its exorbitant mobility. It is, in our view, the most radical of all the various procedures that have tried, after Hegel, to push dialectical negativity further and elsewhere. Difference, the trace, the grammè, writing [*écriture*], contain, retain, and harbor this dialectic in a way that, while avoiding totality, is nevertheless definite and very precise; "a certain dialectic," writes Derrida, echoing Artaud:

The present offers itself as such, appears, presents itself, opens the stage of time or the time of the stage only by harboring its own intestine difference, and only in the interior fold of its original repetition, in representation. In dialectics.
        . . . For if one appropriately conceives the *horizon* of dialectics—outside a conventional Hegelianism—one understands, perhaps, that dialectics is the indefinite movement of finitude, of the unity of life and death, of difference, of original repetition, that is, of the origin of tragedy as the absence of a simple origin. In this sense, dialectics is tragedy, the only possible affirmation to be made against the philosophical or Christian idea of pure origin, against "the spirit of beginnings."[62]

It is obvious that grammatology clears its way [*se fraye la route*] by attacking teleology and Hegelian semiology, and does so explicitly. What interests us here is the debt to Hegel that makes of "arche-writing" "the *movement* [emphasis added] of the *sign-*

function linking a content to an expression, whether it be graphic or not," and not just a schema.[63]

Negativity is inscribed in arche-writing as a constitutive absence: the "absence of the other," "irreducible absence within the presence of the trace"; "*différance* is therefore the formation of form."[64] As a result, we recognize in negativity the economy Derrida speaks of in "Violence and Metaphysics," that of a "strange dialogue between the Jew and the Greek, peace itself," which he finds in "the form of the absolute, speculative logic of Hegel, the living logic which *reconciles* formal tautology and empirical heterology after having *thought* prophetic discourse in the preface to the *Phenomenology of Spirit.*"[65]

Clearly, the grammatological fabric's complex elaboration and its chronologically distended and topographically uneven strategy cannot be reduced to a homogeneous system. But from the texts on Husserl or Jabès onward, Derrida takes in [*recueille*] and reinvests Hegelian negativity in the phenomenological corpus in order to expose and question it. In the course of this operation, negativity has become positivized and drained of its potential for producing breaks. It holds itself back and appears as a delaying [*retardement*], it defers and thus becomes merely positive and affirmative, it inscribes and institutes through retention: "The instituted trace cannot be thought without thinking the retention of difference within a structure of reference where difference appears *as such* and thus permits a certain liberty of variations among the full terms." "Without a retention in the minimal unit of temporal experience, without a trace retaining the other as other in the same, no difference would do its work and no meaning would appear."[66]

Through this *ingathering* [*recueillement*], the trace absorbs and, in this sense, reduces—but not phenomenologically (thus we speak of *ingathering* and not of *reduction*)—the "terms," "dichotomies," and "oppositions" that Hegelian negativity concatenates, reactivates, and generates. The trace that includes its effacement, and writing that inscribes only while under protection and by delaying[67]—both can be thought of as metaphors for a movement that retreats before the thetic but, sheltered by it, unfolds only within the stases of the semiotic *chora*. The trace thus expresses the preconditions and/or the (fetishistic, maternal) repressed element of logocentric reason and, in this sense, grammatology disturbs logic and its subject. In other words, grammatology denounces the economy of the symbolic function and opens up a space that the latter cannot subsume. But in its desire to bar the thetic and put (logically or chronologically) previous energy transfers in its place, the grammatological deluge of meaning gives up on the subject and must remain ignorant not only of his functioning as social practice, but also of his chances for experiencing jouissance or being put to death. Neutral in the face of all positions, theses, and structures, grammatology is, as a consequence, equally restrained when they break, burst, or rupture: demonstrating disinterestedness toward (symbolic and/or social) structure, grammatology remains silent when faced with its destruction or renewal.

Indeed, since *différance*[68] neutralizes productive negativity, it is conceived of as a *delay* |*retard*| that comes *before*, a (pre)condition, a possibility, becoming and become, a movement preceding the sign, *logos*, the subject, *Being*, and located within every differentiated entity. It is the path of their becoming and, as such, is itself a *becoming*; its *Being* will be under erasure: "It is thus the delay |*le retard*| which is in the beginning |*originaire*|." "*Différance*, the *pre-opening* |emphasis added| of the ontic-ontological difference . . . and of all the differences which furrow Freudian conceptuality, such that they may be organized, and this is only an example, around the difference between 'pleasure' and 'reality,' or may be derived from this difference." "Life must be thought of as trace *before* Being may be determined as presence."[69] "Without referring back to a 'nature,' the immotivation of the trace has always *become*. In fact, there is no unmotivated trace . . ." "It is that starting from which a becoming-unmotivated of the sign, and with it all the ulterior positions between *physis* and its other, is possible."[70] Or again, referring to the trace "where the relationship with the other is marked," as a possibility always already oriented toward the sign, toward beings:[71] "This formula, beside the fact that it is the questioning of metaphysics itself, describes the structure implied by the 'arbitrariness of the sign,' from the moment that

one thinks of its possibility *short of* the derived opposition between nature and convention, symbol and sign, etc. These oppositions have meaning only *after the possibility of the trace.*[72] Concealed in *Being* and all its variations, concealing the other within
itself, and concealed from itself, the trace marks *anteriority* to every
entity and thus to every position; it is the movement whose veil-
ing produces metaphysics or, more accurately, metaphysics is a
trace unknown to itself *[qui s'ignore]*. The grammatologist speaks
to transcendence and unsettles it because he states its economy:
"The primordial difference of the absolute origin. . . . That is perhaps what has always been said under the concept of 'transcendental' . . . Transcendence would be difference."[73]

   If in this way the trace dissolves every thesis—material,
natural, social, substantial, and logical—in order to free itself from
any dependence on the *Logos*, it can do so because it grasps the
formation of the symbolic function preceding the mirror stage and
believes it can remain there, even while aiming toward that stage.
Grammatology would undoubtedly not acknowledge the pertinence of this psychoanalytic staging *[stadialité]*, which depends on
the categories and entities of beings. Yet to the extent (1) that
the psychoanalytic discovery paves the way, in a certain sense, for
grammatology itself, and (2) that grammatology designates an
enclosure that is recognized as insurmountable, we may posit that
the force of *writing [écriture]* lies precisely in its return to the space-
time previous to the phallic stage—indeed previous even to the
identifying or mirror stage—in order to grasp the becoming of the
symbolic function as the drive's deferment *[différance]* faced with
the absence of the object.

   Although it begins by positing the heterogeneity in which
différance operates, doesn't grammatology forget this heterogeneous element the moment it neglects the thetic? Doesn't it indefinitely delay this heterogeneous element, thus following its own
systematic and philosophical movement of metalanguage or theory. Indeed grammatology seems to brush aside the drive "residues" that are not included in the *différance* toward the sign, and
which return, heterogeneous, to interrupt its contemplative retention and make language a practice of the subject in process/on

trial. This instinctual heterogeneity—neither deferred nor delayed, not yet understood as a becoming-sign—is precisely that which *enters into contradiction with différance* and brings about leaps, intervals, abrupt changes, and breaks in its spacing [*espacement*]. Contradiction can only be the irruption of the heterogeneous which cuts short any *différance*. Indeed, without this heterogeneous element, ideational Hegelian contradiction, which is aimed toward the presence of Being and the subject, dissolves into differences.

But materialism and Freudian practice—to the extent that the latter is a materialist practice—show that it is impossible to gather up the heterogeneous element into *différance* without leaving any remainders. The return of the heterogeneous element in the movement of *différance* (symbolic retention, delayed becoming-sign-subject-Being), through perception and the unconscious (to use Freudian categories), brings about the revolution of *différance*: expenditure, semantico-syntactic anomaly, erotic excess, social protest, jouissance. This heterogeneity breaks through the barrier of repression and censorship that writing entails since, as the trace and its effacement, it is "the original synthesis of primal *repression* and secondary repression, repression 'itself.'"[74] The heterogeneous element is a threat to repression and tosses it aside. Does this mean that it breaks through "primal" repression or repression "itself"? Or does it mean that *différance* is instituted only out of the repression which the *heterogeneous element*, precisely, may pass through in the form of the "residues of primary perceptions" or the "exceptions" of nondeferred energy charges that can no longer be held in abeyance and are expended?[75]

The disturbance of *différance* calls into question the distinction between the "pleasure principle" and the "reality principle" and, with them, the very economy by which the symbolic is established. If this distinction is "the original possibility, within life, of the detour, of deferral (*Aufschub*) and the original possibility of the economy of death,"[76] then what thwarts it, and what takes the exact opposite course, far from setting up an economy of death, abruptly introduces death: this is none other than the "principle" of jouissance as destruction, self-destruction, the return from "reality" (always symbolico-logocentric) to "matter." Through the irruption of the nondeferred and impatient drive charge in *différance*, all the "natural," "cultural," "physical," "chemical," "biological," and "spiritual" heterogeneities are introduced in logic—heterogeneities that *différance* effaces but that Derrida recognizes as "absolutely decisive," marked off by phenomenological reduction, and "indispensable to all analyses of being-heard."[77] Yet rejection no longer introduces them as phenomenological but instead as economic: as nonsymbolized material inside-outside, as mortal jouissance renewing the real, shutting down reality itself before including it in a new becoming of *différance*.

In this way sustained energetic force, substances, the world, and history, which the storing up of the negative in a deferred consumption had held back, are introduced into the semiotic device in the guise of phenomenal stases. This unleashing of the heterogeneous element as nonsymbolized and nonsymbolizable operates neither on the path of becoming-sign-subject-beings, nor in their neutralization, but in precipitating—as in a chemical reaction—the deferring stage [la scène différante] in the expenditure of the process of the subject and signifiance. A heterogeneous energy discharge, whose very principle is that of scission and division, enters into contradiction with what has been traced [le tracé], but produces only flashes, ruptures, and sudden displacements, which constitute preconditions for *new* symbolic productions in which the economy of *différance* will be able to find its place as well. But there is no guarantee that rejection will be able to maintain the scene of *différance*. Its expenditure could pierce and abolish it, and then all symbolic becoming would cease, thus opening the way to "madness." Similarly, without rejection, *différance* would be confined within a nonrenewable, nonproductive redundancy, a mere precious variant within the symbolic enclosure: contemplation adrift.

Both as a result of investigations such as these, and in rereading the theory of drives, one begins to suspect—even in psychoanalysis, where the notion has become so central that it seems incontrovertible since it revolves around the social, Stoic, and Cartesian subject—that *desire* cannot completely account for the mechanisms of the signifying process.[78] In technology and politics but also in art, areas have been found in which desire is exceeded by a "movement" that surpasses the stases of desiring structuration and displaces the frameworks of intersubjective devices where phantasmatic identifications congeal. These discoveries move us closer to a notion that will prove to be essential in borderline functionings, which produce social and cultural innovations, but more importantly, this notion appears at the very foundation of the functioning of signifiance. To understand it, we must designate an event that occurs before and within the trajectory of Hegelian negativity, an event that lies between and beneath the psychoanalytic distinction between "desire" and "need," one that moves through and is inherent in biological and signifying development but links them together. We could call it *scission, separation,* or *rejection*: "I am not dead, but I am separated."[79]

7.

Freud's Notion
of Expulsion: Rejection

REJECTION, OR expenditure, constitutes the key moment shattering unity, yet it is unthinkable outside unity, for rejection presupposes thetic unity as its precondition and horizon, one to be always superseded and exceeded. Rejection serves to bind only to
the extent that it is the *precondition* of the binding that takes place
on another scene. To posit rejection as fundamental and inherent
in every thesis does not mean that we posit it as origin. Rejection
rejects origin since it is always already the repetition of an impulse that is itself a rejection. Its law is one of returning, as opposed to one of becoming; it returns only to separate again immediately and thus appear as an impossible forward movement.
      Of the terms "rejection," "scission," and "separation," *re-
jection* is the one that best designates, archaeologically, the instinctual, repetitive, and trans-signifying aspect of the dynamics
of signifiance. It implies a pre-verbal "function," one that is pre-
logical and a-logical in the sense that the *logos* signifies a "relation," a "connection." *Scission* and *separation* are more appropriate
terms for that rupture when it is considered from the point of view
of the subject and already constituted meaning, which is to say,
within a perspective that takes into account language and the unity
of the subject—a signifying sociality dependent on norms. We shall
stress the first term (*rejection*) because it suggests the heterogeneity of signifiance we are attempting to demonstrate, and because, within the text, it opens up an a-signifying, indeed pre-
linguistic, crucible. But we shall use the other terms (*scission* and
separation) as well because they emphasize the underlying unity

which withdraws and is reconstituted in the return of rejection. They also signal the permanent logical constraint of an insurmountable *consciousness*, which ensures the reactivation of rejection in a process, thus saving it from foundering in inarticulable instinctuality, where signifying production would be impossible. Our conception of rejection will oscillate between the two poles of drives and consciousness, and this ambiguity will reveal the ambiguity of process itself, which is both divided and unitary. But to the extent that these two threads (drives and consciousness) intersect and interweave, the *unity of reason* which consciousness sketches out will always be shattered by the *rhythm* suggested by drives: repetitive rejection seeps in through "prosody," and so forth, preventing the stasis of One meaning, One myth, One logic.

In Freud's article on *Verneinung* [negation], expulsion (*Ausstossung*) is what constitutes the real object as such; it also constitutes it as lost, thus setting up the symbolic function. For the pleasure-ego, the oral ego of incorporation and unification (*Einbeziehung*), the outside does not matter. Expulsion (*Ausstossung*) establishes an outside that is never definitively separate—one that is always in the process of being posited. But in doing so, it already runs counter to the unifying pleasure principle and sets up the most radical exteriority: the struggle with the latter will represent the recipient *topos*, the mobile *chora* of the subject in process/on trial. The pleasure principle, which unifies and identifies, seems to have been conceived by Freud as an aid to repression. Expulsion (and its symbolic representation in the sign of negation), acting against the pleasure principle, acts against the consequences of repression. "The performance of the function of judgement is not made possible," writes Freud, "until the creation of the symbol of negation has endowed thinking with a first measure of freedom from the consequences of repression and, with it, from the compulsion of the pleasure principle."[80]

Significantly, in thinking the establishment of the symbolic function through the symbol of negation, Freud remarks that the symbolic function is instituted on the basis of *expulsion* (*Ausstossung*, referred to as *Verwerfung* [foreclosure] in "Wolf Man"),[81] but says nothing about the "drive bases" of this "act," or about the drive that activates this "kineme": in other words, he says nothing about rejection. As a result of this omission, Freud sets up an opposition, via expulsion, between the symbolic function and Einbeziehung—unification, incorporation—which refers to orality and pleasure. The symbolic function is thereby dissociated from all pleasure, made to oppose it, and is set up as the paternal place, the place of the superego. According to this view, the only way to react against the consequences of repression imposed by the compulsion of the pleasure principle is to renounce pleasure through symbolization by setting up the sign through the absence of the object, which is expelled and forever lost.

What this interpretation seems to rule out is the pleasure underlying the symbolic function of expulsion, a pleasure which this function represses but that can return to it and, when combined with oral pleasure, disturb, indeed dismantle, the symbolic function. In any case, it can transform ideation into an "artistic game," corrupt the symbolic through the return of drives, and make it a semiotic device, a mobile *chora*. This pleasure derives from the anal drive—anal rejection, anality—in which Freud sees the sadistic component of the sexual instinct and which he identifies with the death drive. We would like to stress the importance of anal rejection or anality, which precedes the establishment of the symbolic and is both its precondition and its repressed element. Because the process of the subject involves the process of his language and/or of the symbolic function itself, this implies—within the economy of the body bearing it—a reactivation of anality. The texts of Lautréamont, Jarry, and Artaud—among others—explicitly point to the anal drive that agitates the subject's body in his subversion of the symbolic function.

Freud's silence, both on the subject of anality and in front of Signorelli's frescos, is not just the symptom of a certain blindness toward homosexuality, which, to his credit, he nevertheless sees at the basis of social institutions. His silence is also bound up with psychoanalysis' silence about the way the literary function subverts the symbolic function and puts the subject in process/on trial. Although psychoanalysis may speak of fantasies in literature, it never mentions the economy of the subject bound up with those fantasies that dissolves the symbolic and language. If the return of rejection, by corrupting both the symbolic and sublimation in modern texts, attests to the presence of the death drive—a destruction of both the living being and the subject—how can we neglect the jouissance harbored by this "aggressivity," this "sadistic component"? The jouissance of destruction (or, if you will, of the "death drive"), which the text manifests through language, passes through an unburying of repressed, sublimated anality. In other words, before arranging itself in a new semiotic network, before forming the new structure which will be the "literary work," the not yet symbolized drive and the "residues of first symbolizations" attack, through unburied anality and fully cognizant of homosexuality, all the stases of the signifying process: sign, language, identifying family structure.

It will now be helpful to recall in more detail the role that rejection and jouissance play in the symbolic function and in putting that function in process/on trial. Although the sadistic component of the sexual instinct makes a veiled appearance in both the oral and genital phase, it dominates the anal phase and is so essential to libidinal economy that Freud recognizes that there might be such a thing as a primary sadism, one "that has been turned round upon the subject's own ego" before any object has been isolated, and would hence constitute primary masochism.[82] What we mean by *rejection* is precisely the semiotic mode of this permanent aggressivity and the possibility of its being *posited*, and thus *renewed*. Although it is destructive—a "death drive"—rejection is the very mechanism of reactivation, tension, life; aiming toward the equalization of tension, toward a state of inertia and death, it *perpetuates* tension and life.

The anal phase designated by psychoanalysis comes before the Oedipus conflict and the separation of the ego from the id in Freudian topography. This phase concludes a more extensive and more fundamental period for the infantile libido: the period called *sadistic*, which predominates before the Oedipus complex begins and constitutes an oral, muscular, urethral, and anal sadism. In all these forms, of which the anal is the last to be repressed and hence the most important, energy surges and discharges erotize the glottic, urethral, and anal sphincters as well as the kinetic system. These drives move through the sphincters and arouse pleasure at the very moment substances belonging to the body are separated and rejected from the body. This acute pleasure therefore coincides with a loss, a separation from the body, and the isolating of objects outside it. Before the body itself is posited as a detached alterity, and hence the real object, this expulsion of objects is the subject's fundamental experience of separation—a separation which is not a lack, but a discharge, and which, although privative, arouses pleasure. The psychoanalyst assumes that this jubilant loss is simultaneously felt as an attack against the expelled object, all exterior objects (including father and mother), and the body itself.

The problem then becomes how to hold this "aggressivity" in check. In other words, how does one curb the pleasure of separation caused by rejection, the ambivalence of which (the body's jouissance plus the loss of body parts) constitutes a nexus of the pleasure and threat that characterizes drives. The "normal," Oedipal way of curbing this pleasure consists in identifying the body proper with one of the parents during the Oedipal stage. At the same time, the rejected object definitively separates and is not simply rejected but suppressed as a material object; it is the "opposite other" ["l'autre en face"] with whom only one relation is possible—that of the sign, symbolic relation in absentia. Rejection is thus a step on the way to the object's becoming-sign, at which the object will be detached from the body and isolated as a real object. In other words, rejection is a step on the way to the imposition of the superego.

However, as cases of child schizophrenia prove, the violence of rejection and of the anal pleasure it produces is sometimes so powerful that Oedipal identification cannot absorb and symbolize them by setting up a signifiable, real object. In such instances, the body is unable to "defend" itself against rejection through suppression or repression and the pleasure aroused by the return of rejection immobilizes the body there. Rejection and sadism, which is its psychological side, return and disturb the symbolic chains put in place by the Oedipal complex. Melanie Klein interprets the behavior "disturbances" that result as the organism's "defenses" against the danger of aggressivity. But she recognizes that "this defense . . . is of a *violent* character and differs fundamentally from the later mechanism of repression," which symbolism establishes.[83] These "defenses" are resistances, *thetic substitutes* for the "violent" drive process, which, far from having a psychological value of prevention, *arrange* the "sadistic" drive charge, *articulate* rejection in such a way that it is not subsumed by the construction of a *superego* (as is the case in the Oedipus complex). The distortion of words, the repetition of words and syntagms, and hyperkinesia or stereotypy reveal that a *semiotic network*—the *chora*—has been established, one that simultaneously defies both verbal symbolization and the formation of a superego patterned after paternal law and sealed by language acquisition.

Indeed, the acquisition of language and notably syntactic structure, which constitutes its normativeness, is parallel to the mirror stage.[84] Language acquisition implies the suppression of anality; in other words, it represents the acquisition of a capacity for symbolization through the definitive detachment of the rejected object, through its repression under the sign. Every return of rejection and of the erotic pleasure it produces in the sphincters disturbs this symbolic capacity and the acquisition of language that fulfills it. By inserting itself into the signifying system of language, rejection either delays its acquisition or, in the case of the schizoid child, prevents it altogether. In the adult, this return to nonsublimated, nonsymbolized anality breaks up the linearity of the signifying chain, and suffuses it with paragrams and glossolalia.[85] In this sense, interjections—those semiotic devices which run through modern phenotexts,[86] and which become rhythmic expectorations in Artaud—convey the struggle of a nonsublimated anality against the superego. Ideologically, this transformation of the signifying chain attacks, provokes, and unveils repressed sadism—the anality underlying social apparatuses.

There exist two signifying modalities that seem to permit the survival of rejection to the extent that they harmonize the shattering brought about by rejection, affirm it, and make it positive without suppressing it under paranoid paternal unity. The first of these modalities is *oralization*: a reunion with the mother's body, which is no longer viewed as an engendering, hollow, and vaginated, expelling and rejecting body, but rather as a vocalic one— throat, voice, and breasts: music, rhythm, prosody, paragrams, and the matrix of the prophetic parabola; the Oedipus complex of a far-off incest, "signifying," the real if not reality. The second modality, always inseparable from the first, appears in the reunion with brothers' bodies, in the reconstitution of a *homosexual phratry* that will forever pursue, tirelessly and interminably, the murder of the One, the Father, in order to impose *one* logic, *one* ethics, *one* signified: *one*, but *other*, critical, combatant, revolutionary—the brothers in Freud's primal horde, for example, or Michelangelo's "Battle of the Centaurs" in Florence.

These two modalities—oralization and the homosexual phratry—point to the two sides—"poetic" and "mastering"—of texts, situated on the path of rejection, which carry out the signifying process by making it a production for community use. The "poetic" side of the text can be seen in the supposedly pianistic scansion of sentences in *Maldoror*, Mallarméan rhythmics, the iciness of "Hérodiade," or in the opulent chic of Méry Laurent, coveted by the Parisian poetic inner circle. Examples vary: from preciosity and snobbery (a token of the forbidden, idealized, and oralized mother) to the glottal spasm in Mallarmé; or, in Lautréamont, a mother who is oceanic and submissive though she is also the over-possessive lover of the hanged man. The Hegelian philosophy in Mallarmé's A *Throw of the Dice* and *Igitur*,[87] the monastic, sacramental, and ritual call of his *Le "Livre,"* and the broken and then restored logic of Lautréamont's *Poems* show that the second, "mastering" modality is a lining of the first, "poetic" modality.

Oralization can be a mediator between the fundamental sadism of rejection and its signifying sublimation. Melody, harmony, rhythm, the "sweet," "pleasant" sounds and poetic musicality found in "symbolist" poetry and in Mallarmé, for example, may be interpreted as oralization. This oralization restrains the aggressivity of rejection through an attempted fusion with the mother's body, a devouring fusion: Mallarmé's biography documents this attempt. A return to oral and glottal pleasure combats the superego and its linear language, which is characterized by the subject/predicate sequences of its syntagms. Suction or expulsion, fusion with or rejection of the mother's breast seem to be at the root of this erotization of the vocal apparatus and, through it, the introduction into the linguistic order of an excess of pleasure marked by a redistribution of the phonematic order, morphological structure, and even syntax: portmanteau words in Joyce and syntax in Mallarmé, for example.

The oral cavity is the first organ of perception to develop and maintains the nursing infant's first contact with the outside but also with the *other*. His initial "burrowing" movement, which is meant to establish contact—indeed biologically indispensable fusion—with the mother's body, takes on a *negative* value by the age of six months. The rotating movement of the head at that age indicates refusal even before the "semantic," abstract word "no" appears at fifteen months.[88] Fusing orality and devouring, refusing, negative orality are thus closely intermingled, as they are in the anal stage that follows. During this stage aggressivity is accentuated, ensuring the body's separation from and always already negative relation to the outside and the other. In addition, even if it is recognized as more archaic than rejection, fusing orality and the libidinal drive it supports are *borne* by rejection and, in the genesis of the subject's symbolic functioning, *determined* by it.[89]

If, through a defusion of the drives or for some other reason, *rejection* as the bearer of drives or, more precisely, their negative discharge, is accentuated, this discharge uses the muscular apparatus as a passageway for discharging energy in brief spurts:[90] pictorial or dancing gesturality may be ascribed to this mechanism. But rejection may pass through the vocal apparatus as well. The oral cavity and the glottis are the only internal organs that do not have the characteristic capacity of muscular apparatuses to restrain bound energy. Instead they free discharges through a finite system of phonemes specific to each language, by increasing their frequency, by accumulating or repeating them, and thus determining the choice of morphemes.[91] They may even condense several "borrowed" morphemes into a single lexeme.[92] In so doing, the rejection that invests the oral cavity awakens in and through it the "libidinal," "unifying," "positive" drive which characterizes, at the earliest stages, this same cavity in its initial "burrowing" movement. Through the new phonematic and rhythmic network it produces, rejection becomes a source of "aesthetic" pleasure. Thus, without leaving the line of meaning, it cuts up and reorganizes that line by imprinting on it the path of drives through the body: from the anus to the mouth.

Rejection therefore constitutes the return of expulsion— Ausstossung or Verwerfung[93]—within the domain of the constituted subject: rejection reconstitutes real objects, "creates" new ones, reinvents the real, and re-symbolizes it. Although in so doing rejection recalls a schizoid regressive process, it is more important to note that rejection positivizes that process, affirming it by introducing the process into the signifying sphere: the latter thus finds itself separate, divided, put in process/on trial. This symbolization of rejection is the place of an untenable contradiction which only a limited number of subjects can reach. Although rejection includes the moment of "excorporation,"[94] ("expectoration" in Artaud's terms, or "excretion" in Bataille's), this motorial discharge and corporeal spasm are invested in the sign—in language—which is itself already divided, reintroducing and unfolding within it the very mechanics by which the separation between words and things is produced. Rejection thus unfolds, dismantles, and readjusts both the vocal register (as in Mallarmé's texts or Lautréamont's Maldoror) and the logical register (as in Ducasse's Poems).[95] Rejection is reintroduced and reiterated in a divided language.

Characteristically, the formalist theory of symbolism simplifies the signifying process by seeing it only as a text (in the sense of a coded or deviant distribution of marks), without perceiving the drive rejection which produces it, straddling the corporeal and natural on the one hand, the symbolic and social on the other, and found in each of them specifically. By contrast, recognizing the dialectical heterogeneity of these "orders" means indicating, above all, that rejection—anal, sadistic, aggressive— posits the "object" and the "sign," and that it constitutes the real where phantasmatic or objective reality is found. From this standpoint, the subject seems to have two possibilities.

Either he goes elsewhere, which is to say, beyond rejection into reality, forever surpassing the trajectory of separation and scission, living it only as the spin-off or side aspect of a "commitment" to the real where all the logic of *meta-* is reified: meta-subject, meta-language, meta-physics. In this case, he places himself under the law of the father and takes on both this paranoia and the homosexuality connoting paranoia, the sublimation of which is all too fragile: here we see Orestes who murders his mother in the name of the laws of the city-state.

Or else the subject constantly returns to rejection and thus reaches what lies beneath the paranoid homosexuality laid bare by signifying production: the schizoid moment of scission. Mallarmé's suffering body and, later, the shattered and mummified body of Artaud attest to this loss of unity.

The representation of the "character" who becomes the place of this process is one that normative consciousness finds intolerable. For this "character"'s polymorphism is one that knows every perversion and adheres to none, one that moves through every vice without taking up any of them. Un-identical and in-authentic, his is the wisdom of artifice which has no interiority and is constant rejection. He is familiar with the social organism and its paranoid reality but makes light of it and, for them, he is an unbearable monstrosity. This has always been his traditional representation, from Heraclitus' "misanthropy" to the maliciousness of [Diderot's] Le Neveu de Rameau and his Paradoxe du comédien.

Within the Greek tradition, the extant fragments of Heraclitus seem to have come closest to grasping the process of a simultaneous "hypertrophy of a self"[96] and its separation within maintained reason. Thus, without leaving the domain of reason, Heraclitus makes of reason not a logical unity, as Plato and the Stoics have accustomed us to understanding it, but rather a divided speech, a counter-speech, sanctioning [homologuant] what stands separate: words and things, but also things among things and words among words—the word as rejection of both the thing that it utters and another word, said or unsaid. Only the "clever" one who has mastered the technique of saying can achieve this "poetic" wisdom, τὸ σοφόν, "art." This does not mean that "art" which maintains words within rejection, is a discourse on discourse: the discursive is only one of the phenomenal and linguistic manifestations of the process. Although metalanguage can apprehend this process only through language, by pursuing stylistic, logical, and etymological figures, the separation that discourse replays refers to pre-symbolic and intra-symbolic rejection, where logos and its sanction disappear. It refers to the a-symbolized and a-symbolizable scission, to the nothing that is neither one nor multiple, but rather the "infinite nothingness" spoken of by speculative philosophy, which we shall posit as matter that is always already split; from it, repeated rejections will generate not only the thetic logos but its shattering.

Heraclitean art is the practice that takes up, through the *logos*, this *separation* without beginning or end, which certain Freudian formulations assign to the unconscious.[97] "Of all the discourses I have heard," states one of the Heraclitean fragments, "not one manages to distinguish the distinct element that makes art what it is."[98] No discourse can identify the distinct element—instinctual matter—that characterizes art. Although it contradicts the One and discourse, instinctual matter is inscribed in them in order to reject them and reject itself from them. Iamblichus echoes Heraclitus, suggesting that the singular and rare man who is able to achieve rejection in reason does so on the basis of matter. Though this man is more than matter, matter is his precondition; it produces him by rejecting itself and rejecting him: "Hence I posit two kinds of sacrifice. On the one hand, those of completely purified men, which, as Heraclitus says, even a singular man can only rarely carry out, or only a numbered few; and on the other hand, those that remain material [restent dans la matière] . . ."[99]

Now that we have followed the notion of expulsion [repoussement] in Freud, let us pick it up again in Hegel who opened the way for the notion of *negativity* outlined at the beginning of this chapter.[100] In Hegel, the term *Repulsion* designates a movement within negativity that comes close to what we have called

rejection yet does not coincide with it. *Repulsion* is the negative relation of the One with itself, as opposed to *Becoming*, which is "a
transition of Being into Nothing."[101] Since it is the fundamental
determination of the One and its fragmentation, Repulsion both
ensures the preservation of the One and produces the plurality of
Ones by the Attraction it presupposes. Thus we see that Hegelian
Repulsion is always subordinate to Unicity and that, in beginning
to act within it, Repulsion calls Unicity into question only *from the*
outside, by adding multiple external meanings. There is no doubt,
and Hegel himself stresses, that Repulsion fundamentally inte-
riorizes negativity, in opposition to Kantian analytics where the
"two basic forces remain, within matter, opposed to one another,
external and independent," and where "Kant determines . . . re-
pulsive force . . . as a *superficial force*, by means of which parts of
matter can act upon one another only at the common surface of
contact."[102] But in internalizing Repulsion within the One itself,
and in making Repulsion what specifies, determines, and, in sum,
identifies the One, Hegel subordinates Repulsion to what we have
called the "symbolic function"; whereas Freud, on the other hand,
joins dialectical logic by making *expulsion* the essential moment in
the constitution of the symbolic function. The difference is that,
in Freud, what activates expulsion is "another scene" based on
the drives. Since he does not have this heteronomy in view, Hegel
can only supercede the exteriority of Repulsion that Freud has
sketched out.[103] This comes about because separation in Hegel
becomes the explanation of what the One is in itself; it gets ex-
ported outside this One, which is always already constructed, becomes exteriorized, and, as a result of the dialectic, ends up in an
exteriority:

The self-repulsion of the One is the explication of that which the
One is in itself; but infinity, as split-up, is here infinity which has
passed beyond itself: and this it has done through the immediacy of
the infinite entity, the One. It is a simple relation of One to One,
and equally, or rather, the absolute unrelatedness of the One; it
is the former according to the simple affirmative self-relation of
One, and the latter according to the same as negative. In other

words, the plurality of the One is its self-positing; the One is its own negative self-relation and nothing else, and this relation (the One itself) is many Ones. But equally, plurality is merely external to the One; for the One *also is the transcending of Otherness, Repulsion is its self-relation and simple self-identity. The plurality of Ones is infinity, as contradiction which unconcernedly produces itself.*[104]

What Hegel does not envisage is the moment the One is *shattered* in a return of Repulsion onto itself, which is to say, a turning against its own potential power for positing and multiplying the One. Nor does Hegelian logic see the heterogeneous parcelling of the symbolic, which underlies the symbolic's very constitution and constantly undermines it even while maintaining it in process; the simultaneous existence of the *boundary* (which is the One) and the a-reasonable, a-relative, a-mediating *crossing* of that boundary; or the possibility of the constitution-unconstitution of One meaning-non-meaning, passing through categorial boundaries ("inside," "one," "multiple," etc.), which is precisely what *rejection* brings about in the "schizoid" process of the text.

The ideational closure of the Hegelian dialectic seems to consist in its inability to posit negativity as anything but a repetition of ideational unity in itself. The exteriority to which it is condemned *in fact* is thus bound up with the ideational enclosure, in which, despite many detours, its trajectory ends. Repeated rejection, far from purely and simply restoring the series of many Ones, instead opens up in and through Unity—we are tempted to say beyond "signifying unity" and "subjective unity"—*the material process of repeated* (a-signifying and instinctual) *scissions*; these repeated scissions act with the regularity of objective laws and recall, through the rifts or new arrangements they produce, the pulsation of that process through symbolic unification. These are the conclusions we may draw from a materialist interpretation, opened up by the Freudian position on repetition compulsion.

Indeed, although for Freud *Ausstossung* or *Verwerfung* posits the sign, it already functions beforehand, "objectively" so to speak, in the movement of living matter subject to natural and social constraints. "In order to understand this step forward [the con-

stitution of the real as separate], we must recollect that all pre-
sentations originate from perceptions and are repetitions of
them."[105]

While establishing the sign, subject, and judgment, *Verwe-
fung* points *at the same time* toward the repeated scissions of a-
symbolized living matter and toward the inorganic. The drive that
thus takes shape operates in a trans-symbolic realm that sends
the signifying body back to biological a-signifiance and finally to
death. Moreover what is *represented* as a "death" is probably—as a
great many "literary" texts show—nothing but the verbalization
of this rejection, this multiplied rupture of all unity, including that
of the body: "Now we shall have to call it the de-corporealization
of reality, the kind of rupture intent, it would seem, on multiplying; a rupture between things and the feeling they produce in our
mind, the place they must take."[106]

Freud reveals the obstinate and constraining return of
rejection, its "repetition compulsion," as one of the "ultimate"
mechanisms of psychic functioning—more essential than the
"pleasure principle"—and characterizes it as "demonic," as "an
urge inherent in organic life" to stop the galloping evolution of
organic forms and their symbolizing capacity in order to return to
a state of inertia and constancy. Through these formulations and
beyond Freud's speculations on death (avowed as such by Freud
himself),[107] from observations about "schizophrenia," but, for our
purposes, even more so from modern texts, there emerges the
confirmation of an objective law. *Rejection*, the specific movement
of matter, produces its various forms, including their symbolic
manifestations, at the same time that it ensures, by its repetition,
a *threshold of constancy*: a *boundary*, a restraint around which difference will be set up—the path toward symbolization. But even as
it posits the symbolic and its differentiation, this expenditure of
drives returns—notably in the text—to shatter difference and introduce, through its play, what silently acts on it: the scissions of
matter. Because these scissions—which Freud situates in the *id*
or in the *unconscious*—irrupt within the differentiation of symbolic
play, we maintain that the signifying process practiced in its infinite totality has no unconscious; in other words, the text has no

unconscious. Repeated and returned rejection opposes repression and, in Freudian terms, reintroduces "free energy" into "bound energy."

We have now reached a crucial point in the notion of *signifying process*. Rejection, which is the signifying process' powerful mechanism, is heterogeneous, since it is, from a Freudian standpoint, *instinctual*, which means that it constitutes an articulation [*charnière*] between the "psychical" and the "somatic." So much so that although the dichotomy between these two "orders" is upheld, it is also dialecticized, and the "signifier" appears only as a *thesis*—a positing—of infinite repetitions of material rejections when "free energy," always already splitting, doubling, and rejecting, collides against the walls of natural and social *structures*, which Freud terms "external disturbing forces," crystallizing "unities." Freud notes that "the manifestations of a compulsion to repeat . . . exhibit to a high degree an instinctual character and, when they act in opposition to the pleasure principle, give the appearance of some 'daemonic' force at work." Further on, he continues:

But how is the predicate of being 'instinctual' related to the compulsion to repeat? At this point we cannot escape a suspicion that we may have come upon the track of a universal attribute of drives and perhaps of organic life in general which has not hitherto been clearly recognized or at least not explicitly stressed. It *seems, then, that a drive is an urge inherent in organic life to restore an earlier state of things* which the living entity has been obliged to abandon under the pressure of external disturbing forces; that is, it is a kind of organic elasticity, or, to put it another way, the expression of the inertia inherent in organic life.[108]

Conformist psychoanalysis after Freud has embarked on an attempt to "break down the id's resistances" by interpreting them and thereby suppressing drive rejection within the domain of so-called "action" in order to "signify" or "nuance" it. When established as a principle, this normalization of rejection contributes to the destruction of the "spearhead" of the signifying process. On the other hand, when rejection is brought back to its essential motor functions, when it necessarily becomes, whether unconsciously or voluntarily, the maintained and reinforced agent of the signifying process, it produces new cultural and social formations which are innovative and—under specific conditions which we shall discuss further on—subversive.

How is this return of rejection—this *surplus of rejection* that puts in process/on trial the symbolic already instituted by *Verwerfung*—represented in discourse? What is the negativity of the text, which is different from symbolic negation in judgment, and is sustained by the threatened subject? What is its libidinal organization and discursive economy?

According to Freud in his article on "Negation,"[109] symbolization implies a repression of pleasure and erotic drives. But this repression is not absolute. Freud implies that complete repression (if it were possible) would stop the symbolic function. Repression, Lacan explains, is a "*kind of discordance* between the signified and the signifier that is determined by any censorship originating in society."[110] Setting up the symbolic function requires this repression and prevents the removed truth of the real from slipping in anywhere except "between the lines," i.e., in the linguistic structure, as "negation" for instance.

"The performance of the function of judgment," Freud continues, "is not made possible until the creation of the symbol of negation has endowed thinking with a first measure of freedom from the consequences of repression . . ." Let us now return to an earlier point in the text on negation. For Freud, "negation is a lifting of the repression [*Aufhebung der Verdrängung*]," which means an "intellectual acceptance of the repressed," but not its discharge or its "consumption." As a consequence, the "intellectual function" is separated from the "affective process," which results in "a kind of intellectual acceptance of the repressed, while at the same time what is essential to the repression persists."

The appearance of the symbol of negation in the signifier thus partially liberates repression and introduces into the signifier a part of what remains outside the symbolic order: what was repressed and what Freud calls "affective." These are instinctual, corporeal foundations stemming from the concrete history of the concrete (biological, familial, social) subject. Although it is true that the "affective" can be grasped only through discursive structuration, it would be semantic empiricism to believe that it does not in some fashion exist outside it. Clearly, negation as a *symbolic function* inherent in judgment (inherent in symbolization) constitutes an intellectual sublimation (*Aufhebung*) of only one part of foreclosure (*Verwerfung*).

Negation-as-denial [*dénégation*] in cases of "obsessive ideas," writes Freud, allows "the ideational content of what is repressed . . . [to] reach consciousness." In analysis, through transference, "we succeed in conquering the negation as well, and in bringing about a full intellectual acceptance of the repressed; but the repressive process itself is not yet removed by this."

By contrast, in aesthetic productions, which do not involve transference, negation is not "conquered." Rejection operates in them and does not produce an "intellectual acceptance of the repressed" (in other words, it does not effect the passage of the repressed element into the signified, into the symbolic function). Instead it *marks signifying material* with the repressed. This observation implies, on the one hand, that setting up the symbolic function (founded on judgment) requires a transference situation. It implies, on the other hand, that the symbolic function already carries out the distinction not only between "objective" and "subjective," but also between "signifier" and "signified." The reintroduction of the symbol of negation into poetic language (as opposed to the reintroduction of negation as "denial" [*dénégation*] into analysis), *arranges the repressed element in a different way*, one that does not represent an "intellectual acceptance of the repressed," an *Aufhebung*, but instead constitutes a post-symbolic (and in this sense anti-symbolic) hallmarking of the material that remained intact during first symbolization. This "material," expelled by the sign and judgment from first symbolizations, is then withdrawn from the unconscious into language, but is not accepted there in the form of "metalanguage" or any kind of intellection. The repeated death drive (negativity, destruction) withdraws from the unconscious and *takes up a position as already positivized and erotized in a language* that, through drive investment, is organized into prosody or rhythmic timbres.[111] If, as Freud writes in the same article, "in analysis we never discover a 'no' in the unconscious and [if] that recognition of the unconscious on the part of the ego is expressed in a negative formula," then the semiotic device constructed by poetic language through the positing of language as a symbolic system constitutes third-degree negativity. It is neither the lack of a "no" (as in the unconscious), nor a negative formula (a sign of the instituted symbolic function), nor negation-as-denial (symptoms of the neurotic ego idealizing the repressed), but instead a *modification of linguistic and logical linearity and ideality*, which cannot be located in any ego. Poetic rhythm does not constitute the acknowledgement of the unconscious but is instead its expenditure and implementation.

For psychoanalysis, "the true subject is the subject of the unconscious" who appears only in the phenomenon of transference. Clearly, this is not the poetic subject. Although psychoanalysis and, hence, transference have allowed the (plural) topographies of the subject to emerge for science, the topography of poetic language appears as one that draws out, within a signifying device (which has been called "prosody," "art," and so forth), not the "ideational content" of what remains outside first symbolization, but rather its *economy*: the *movement* of rejection. This rejection may be implied in affirmative judgment (*Bejahung*) (as in Lautréamont), or in linguistic morphology and syntax (as in Mallarmé); in other words, it may appear in the symbol of negation or in morpho-syntactic destruction. Poetic negativity is third-degree rejection. As the rejection of symbolic and neurotic negation, it recalls, spatially and musically, the dialectical moment of the generating of signifiance.

In so doing, the text *momentarily* sets right the conflict between signifier and signified established by the symbol of negation and which determines all censorship originating in society—re-positing it, of course, but redistributing it as well. The text makes rejection work on and in the very place of symbolic and social censorship, which establishes language as a symbolic system with a double articulation: signifier and signified.

III.

Heterogeneity

Merely point out that heterogeneity is lacking in Freud, but put the relations between heterology and psychoanalysis (1) in the paragraph dealing with expenditure, and (2) in the paragraph where the fundamental genetic elements of heterology are to be contrasted with the Oedipus theme. . . .

Point out that historical heterology is a return to the history of wars, and that historical materialism, in its non-dialectical aspect, constitutes an explicitly bourgeois tendency.

Georges Bataille, "Zusatz," *Œuvres complètes*
(Paris: Gallimard, 1972), 2:171

1.

The Dichotomy
and Heteronomy of Drives

THE FREUDIAN theory of drives may be viewed as a transition from the psychical to the somatic, as a bridge between the biological foundation of signifying functioning and its determination by the family and society. Alongside this *heteronomy*, Freud maintains the fundamental *dichotomy* of drives as contradictory forces (life drives/death drives, ego drives/sexual drives), which are opposed and in conflict. He thus makes drives the shattered and doubly differentiated site of conflict and rejection. What interests us is the materialist dialectic he thereby establishes, hence, the heteronomy of drives—not their dichotomy. Drives are material, but they are not solely biological since they both connect and differentiate the biological and symbolic within the dialectic of the signifying body invested in a practice. Neither inside nor outside, drives are neither the ideational interior of a subject of understanding, nor the exteriority of the Hegelian Force. Drives are, instead, the repeated scission of matter that generates signifiance, the place where an always absent subject is produced.

Freud's fundamental insight into the heterogeneity of drives reveals drive activity's signifying and signifiable conflictual materiality. In a moment that constitutes a *leap* and a *rupture—separation* and *absence*—the successive shocks of drive activity produce the signifying function. Post-Freudian theories, however, generally seem to place much more emphasis on the neurobiological aspect of drives, particularly the division inherent in drive movement.

Constantin von Monakow and Raoul Mourgue propose the

term *diaschisis* (from διασχίζω, meaning "I split, tear") to denote "a special kind of trauma, which usually but not necessarily arises suddenly and originates in a local lesion." [The extent of the "separation" corresponds to the severity of the trauma and literally] "extends along the fibers that originate in and around the focal point of the lesion." They call the splitting tendency of nerve tissue *horme* (from ὁρμή, meaning "impulse" or "impetus"): the *horme* is the "matrix of instincts, . . . indeed, it was originally a property of living protoplasm." "For organisms that have a nervous system, we can define instinct as a latent propelling force stemming from the *horme*. The instinct synthesizes excitations within the protoplasm (introceptivity) with those acting from the outside (extroceptivity) to realize a process that will ensure, with adapted behavior, the vital interests of both the individual and the species."[1] In cases of schizophrenia, they write, the instincts are polarized: a unifying tendency (*klisis*) is overshadowed by a defense tendency (*ekklisis*) which is directed outside. This brings about a fragmentation of nervous energy (*diaspasis*), a "piecemeal" deconstruction of the nervous system that is reflected in changes in the verbal element itself, which is disturbed as if to deaden diaspasis and protect the organism from it. This biologism is provided with a teleology that is not radically different from Hans Driesch's vitalism.[2] It hastily erases the boundaries between the realms of biology and social practice, and encompasses them both within a notion of biological energy. The transcendental nature of this notion can be seen in this theory's presentation of religion as the supreme form of "syneidesis," i.e., "the mediating force of nature," a "regulating and compensatory principle."

Lipot Szondi also stresses the conflictual aspect of drives whose matrix proves to have four components (the result of the doubling of the two genes making up the heterozygote): "the source of all drives lies in the genes." "In Freud's words, 'a drive is the inherent impulsion of a living organism towards restoration of an earlier state.' Freud has, however, neglected to explain why the drives behave in this manner. Only the theory of genes can supply an adequate answer."[3] The amount of drive pressure (*Triebdrang*) depends on the extent of the contrast between the genes that condition the whole. Modern genetic theory has confirmed this doubling and its repetition and has made it more precise by positing the reversed selection of doubles in the constitution of new structures.[4] Yet this substantialism, removed from the field of social practice (such as it is taken into account by Freudian theory), confines the theory of drives to a mechanistic and transcendental arena, as seen in Szondi's crude and naive definitions of psychopathological types, and in the inability of contemporary authors to specify what they mean by their vague but constant reference to the impact of the "social factor" on psychosis.

It is nevertheless likely, as André Green reminds us, that "the genetic code functions as a copula between sexuality and the phenomenon of memory."[5] Similarly, processes germane to these genetic codes—notably the reproduction of nucleic acids patterned on the model of the double helix[6]—indicate the operation, which is always already doubled, shattered, and reversed (as in a film negative), of what will become a subjective and signifying "unity." The division, indeed the multiplication, of matter is thus shown as *one of the foundations* of the signifying function. This foundation will be repressed or reorganized by the constraints imposed by signifying social reality, but will nevertheless return, *projecting itself* onto the structured surface—disturbing and reorganizing it (as "poetry"), or piercing and annihilating it (in "madness").

This duality (both heterogeneity and the doubling of the drives) allows us to account for a heteronomous conflictual process; without it, we would be unable to situate psychotic experience or any kind of renewable practice. To preserve this duality is to obey a materialist methodological requirement that Freud always stressed:

Our views have from the very first been dualistic, and to-day they are even more definitely dualistic than before—now that we describe the opposition as being, not between ego drives and sexual drives but between life drives and death drives. Jung's libido theory is on the contrary monistic; the fact that he has called his one instinctual force 'libido' is bound to cause confusion, but need not affect us otherwise.[7]

But Freudian theory is more than a theory of dualism, it is a theory of *contradiction* and of *struggle*: "These speculations seek to solve the riddle of life by supposing that these two drives [the life drive and death drive] were struggling with each other from the very first."[8]

Genetic biological rejection suffuses the organic body with motility and imprints on it a "gesturality" that social needs and constraints will then structure. The Freudian *fort-da* reveals that the return of instinctual rejection is already kinetic and gestural and that it projects biological material rejection onto a rejection that constitutes a signifying space and/or a space of practice. It separates the object and constitutes the real and *absence* and, through absence, by means of repeated rejection, the unstable engram of the primary vocalic, gestural, and signifying stases. The instability and mobility of engrams can be seen during language acquisition, in the engendering of the holophrastic, fluctuating lexical system that grammar has yet to grasp or master. In the already constituted subject, the constant return of this mobility will make the linguistic texture [*tissu*] paragrammatic (see n. 85, part II, supra), indicating its "piecemeal dispersal" where the renewal of rejection looms up through the engram:

Feelings are nothing,
nor are ideas,
everything lies in motility
from which, like the rest, humanity has taken
   nothing but a ghost.[9]

2.

Facilitation, Stasis, and the Thetic Moment

REPEATED DRIVES or the shocks from energy discharges create a state of excitation. Because it remains unsatisfied, this excitation produces, through a qualitative leap, a repercussion that delays, momentarily absorbs, and posits that excitation. Repeated *rejection* thus *posits* rejection. Although repeated rejection is separation, doubling, scission, and shattering, it is at the same time and afterward accumulation, stoppage, mark, and stasis. In its trajectory, rejection must become positive: rejection engrammatizes, it marks One in order to reject it again and divide it in two again. As a step toward the development of the signifier, the engram is rejection's self-defense, its relative immobilization, which, in turn, allows the reactivation of drives: re-jection. Without this stasis (on which the symbolizing thesis will be established)—presented by Freud both in *Beyond the Pleasure Principle* and in his article on *Verneinung*—rejection could not produce something *new* and displace boundaries; it would be a merely mechanical repetition of an undifferentiated "identity." Instead, rejection generates thetic *heterogeneity* under very precise biological and social conditions: "humanity." By dint of accumulating ruptures, and through this heterogeneity, which uses the presignifying engram produced in the absence of any object isolated in itself, rejection becomes stabilized. Its tendency toward death is deferred by this symbolic heterogeneity: the body, as if to prevent its own destruction, *reinscribes* [*re-marque*] rejection and, through a leap, *represents* it *in absentia* as a sign.

This reinscription or mark is constitutive of rejection. The mark thwarts rejection in order to reactivate it and defers rejection so that it will return to divide and double the mark in turn. This mark is the "re" in re-jection and is the precondition of rejection's renewal. The quantitative accumulation of rejections nevertheless upsets the mark's stability: the mark becomes an unstable engram which ends up being rejected into a *qualitatively new space*, that of the *representamen* or the sign. Rejection destroys the stasis of the mark, breaks up its own positivity and restraint, and, in the face of this "murder," sets up a qualitatively different thetic phase: the sign. The mark is thus a step in the development of the sign since it prefigures the sign's constancy and unity. Rejection, which integrates the mark, is its destructive moment, and, in this sense, is part of the production and destruction of the sign. Although it is at the root of the symbolic function, as Freud claims in *Verneinung*, rejection is also at the root of its destruction: rejection is the mechanism both of the symbolic function's re-newal and of its demise.

Within the signifying process, rejection is thus articulated as heterogeneous: it is both material scission and the delaying of scission through the mark where the *representamen* will affix itself. Stasis (which material scission produces but also divides, jostles, and disrupts) tends to unify scission, mark One, and absorb it in the path of becoming of the desiring subject. Rejection generates the signifier and the desire adjoining it as a defense against the death that rejection brings about by carrying its logic of scission "to the end." But rejection is not simple destruction: it is re-jection. The prefix "re-" indicates not the repetition of a constant identity, but rather a renewal of division through a new unifying stoppage where something more than a mere mark—a *representamen* and an ego—will finally crystallize, and then be re-jected once again. This crystallization of an essential but temporary unity—shattered anew since it is inherent in rejection, which itself is constant—founds the *logic of renewal*—as opposed to the logic of repetition—within the signifying process: $rejection_1$—$stasis_1$—$rejection_2$—$stasis_2$—(etc.)—*Thesis*—$rejection_n$—$stasis_n$.

Free, which is to say unbound, primal energy is precisely a function of rejection, material (genetic, biological) separation. We have known since *Beyond the Pleasure Principle* that within this same movement of rejection and reversal, and under conditions specific to the human animal, free energy brings about its defensive counter-charge. This counter-charge, which makes rejection symmetrical by thwarting it, so to speak, without stopping it, and by thus perpetuating its return and nonextinction, obeys a certain regulating process, which we have called *semiotic*.

We now arrive at the heart of a contradiction, which is far from formal, between two qualitatively different heterogeneous orders: the second of which (the sign) is produced by the repeated accumulation of the successive rejections (facilitations—stases—facilitations) of the first. What is more, although this double counter-charge (engrammatic and symbolic) depends on material scission, it is by necessity *ultimately* generated by the social apparatus and the social practice in which the subject is led to function. Thus, through the transference-relation and its demonstration of the *lack* [*manque*] that constitutes desire and the symbolic, the psychoanalytic device ends up binding material, heterogeneous rejection through so-called primary processes (metonymies, metaphors) within secondary processes. This device transposes the conflict between them by linking it up within the system of the *representamen*—the system of the signifier, the sign, and, finally, the understanding.

Because it is normative, the psychoanalytic cure uniformizes and resolves heterogeneous contradiction by making it an intra-signifying, intra- and inter-subjective differentiation. The cure turns contradiction into a language and a desire. In other circumstances, for example when social and family constraints block the heterogeneous process, rejection is definitely thwarted and stopped, and cannot be repeated. Debilitated, rejection is incapable of reproducing its heterogeneous contradiction ad is thus condemned to arrested movement [*arrêt*], a well-known characteristic of schizophrenic asemia.

We stress once again that these two opposing tendencies are found in biology, in the way living matter functions: in its division and stoppage and in the principles of multiplication and constancy, the latter ensuring the preservation of the organic cell.

Not only does drive rejection follow these objective laws of living matter, they are its indispensable precondition.

But when it operates as the signifying function, the mechanism of rejection is situated at a qualitatively different level. It produces separations and renewed stases, but also brings about heterogeneous relations between *scission and material constancy*, on the one hand, and its *binding*, through a leap, in the *representamen*, on the other. Indeed, to speak of the scission and stoppage |*arrêt*| that organize the struggle characteristic of rejection, we must consider this logic in connection with the social milieu in which the *representamen* manifests itself. For identification with the other or the suppression of the other are locked within family structure; it is in the family that relations of rejection become intersubjective: they become relations of desire.

3.

The Homological Economy
of the *Representamen*

REJECTION PRINCIPALLY centers on those elements of the natural and social milieu with which the individual, under various biological and social constraints, tends to identify. In family structure, it is generally—but not always—the parent of the same sex who faces rejection.[10] That the individual seeks the complicity of the parent of the opposite sex in this struggle often leads to hasty conclusions about the fundamental role played by the transgression of the incest prohibition in free symbolic functioning (in art, for example). On a deeper level, the alliance with the parent of the opposite sex is only ephemeral, a screen set up to facilitate the rejection of the same. Indeed, if there is a fixation on the parent of the opposite sex without a rejection of the parent of the same sex, the process of rejection cannot be renewed; such a blockage not only prevents all signifying production but also brings about profound disturbances in the symbolic function itself. Within the intersubjective structure whose model is the family, rejection emerges in the fundamental narcissistic relation (in other words, the homosexual relation), and tends to break it up, or rather renew it, through a struggle against the symbolic. Although rejection corrupts the symbolic function, it does so in a struggle against the homosexual tendency, and in this sense, supposes, relies on, acknowledges, takes up, and renews that tendency. To the extent that rejection involves sexual relations between individuals—though sexuality is only one stratum of the signifying process—the subject in process/on trial recognizes the homo-sexuality which underlies these relations and is so fundamental to all intersubjective and/or transference relations. The identification and sub-jective unification carried out in opposition to the process de-pend on the relation to the parent of the *same* sex, who appears as a logically thetic identifying unity. In a society governed by pa-ternal law, this unity is the Name-of-the-Father, but, practically, it can be assumed by any power-wielding protagonist or structure (father, mother, the family, or the State). This is Lautréamont's "the Creator . . . showed a pederast in."[11] To remove rejection from the homosexual realm is to move it outside sexuality, which finally means outside the intersubjective relations that are pat-terned after family relations. It means setting the drive charge in motion—not necessarily as a sublimated force, but as one in-vested in the process of transformation of nature and society.

But the role of society's defensive structures—from the family to capitalist institutions—is to harness this rejection within identificatory, intersubjective, and sexual stases, whether they are sublimated or not. These structures locate generalized rejection in a very specific place: the homosexual relation, which is the in-tersubjective framework of the thetic phase, and hence the para-noid moment which protects the unity of the subject from being put in process/on trial. Freudianism points to this homosexual mechanism in social relations, even though Freud himself failed to do so on several occasions when his evidence remained opaque (the Signorelli frescos) or was perceived later (the case of Dora). Although psychoanalysis indicates that homosexuality is the ba-sis of social normativeness and normality, it is slow in showing that the subject in process/on trial makes his way through this fixation *knowingly* and that he conveys the charge of rejection, without sublimating it, in the very movement that makes him confront prohibitions and social institutions, which is to say, in the movement of a revolutionary (political, scientific, or artistic) *practice.*

In this sense, what is beyond the pleasure principle is be-yond sexuality if and only if it is beyond homosexuality, itself the truth behind heterosexual "relations." This statement is all the more applicable to a society in which the family, no longer the basic structure of production—is itself in the process of dissolving and is being overrun by the totality of social relations that exceed it and will even eliminate it. In such a society, rejection finds its representative stases in other articulations of social relations—in social practices (science, politics, etc.) and the social groups in which they are based—but also outside social structures in the objects and structures of the natural world. The identifications with the other or suppressions of·the other that operate in this sort of society produce jubilatory phases and pleasures for the subject who identifies and they thus become "objects" of his "desire." But they do not have the constancy and tenacity of the family structure: they cannot maintain the identificatory illusion effectively and, with it, the possibility of desirable fantasies. Within the mobility of the crossing through nature and society, which is put to the test by destructuring and renewing social practice, desire becomes a fragile element exceeded by the violence of rejection and its separating negativity.

In this social configuration, which is precisely that of capitalism, rejection emerges with all its clear-cut force, destroying all subjective, phantasmatic, and desiring unity. Rejection acts through a negativity that no longer restrains a desire. This negativity restrains only the signifying stasis and thesis within the process of practice, that is, only the positing and positive moment, which opens the way to a realization-in-practice, a production: the entire range of social practices, from aesthetics to science and politics. Hence what provides the affirmative moment of rejection and ensures its renewal is not the *object that is produced*, i.e., the metonymic object of desire; it is, instead, the *process of its production* or, let us say, its productivity. Within this process, the object is not a boundary to be reached but merely the lower threshold allowing rejection to be articulated as social practice.

4.

Through the Principle of Language

METONYMIC SLIPPAGE (of desire and of the signifier governing desire) is, then, only a logical, already secondary, movement in the subject's "becoming-One," which occurs within the specularization allowed him by the current forces of production—which is to say an intra-familial specularization. The logic of rejection not only precedes this metonymic-desiring slippage but is the basis and perhaps even the mainspring of a practice that involves jouissance and the transformation of signifying or immediately social reality. As moments binding rejection, the pleasures, desires, avoidances, and evasions the subject provides himself, belong to the process of this practice. They ensure its provisional unity; they are the compensatory representation of the destructive violence that reactivates the practice, the representative corollaries of its thetic phase. The subject of such a practice invests desire and fantasy more in its *productivity* than in its productions; but since the productions are part of the transformation of the real, the subject invests desire in the transformation itself. To identify with the *process* of signifying, subjective, social *identity* is precisely to practice process, to put the subject and his theses on trial [*en procès*] and see to it that the laws of signifiance follow objective, natural, and social laws.

The aim of philosophies used to be to explain the world. Dialectical materialism, by contrast, wants to change it, and speaks to a new subject, the only one capable of understanding it. This new subject—like the former one—explains, cogitates, and knows, but he is also elusive because he *transforms* the real. In explaining, cogitating, and knowing, he emphasizes one pole of heterogeneous contradiction over the other: he stresses *process* over identification, *rejection* over desire, *heterogeneity* over signifier, *struggle* over structure.

The practices which interest us here—those of modern texts—realize a subtle, fragile, and mobile equilibrium between these two poles of heterogeneous contradiction. Given the fragility both of the mark and of the *representamen* generated out of it, the passage of "free energy" is ensured. But the latter, under the violent attack of heterogeneous rejection, cannot be enclosed within the symbolic stereotype of a linguistic structure or an established ideology that is in accord with the dominant (family, State) or local (the analyst/analysand relation) social device. More importantly, although rejection remains close to the *representamen* and does not lose sight of its markings, it dismantles the *representamen* and, out of the heterogeneity of rejection's *practice* or *experience* (see below, in part IV, "Experience Is Not Practice"), produces new symbolizations. This is the mechanism of innovation, which displaces the frameworks of the real, and, as Marx has shown, characterizes social practice in all domains, but especially and with the most immediate violence, in politics.

When material heterogeneous rejection—free or primal energy—irrupts within the very structure of the *representamen*, when contradiction is at its most acute, when repeated drive rejection attacks what it itself has produced (signifying matter, here language) in order to check and subdue it, then practice (which is the precondition and result of this contradiction) comes close to losing the *representamen* and hence losing contradiction. But in doing so, it also verges on the most radical realization of this contradiction, which can be read either in rhythm, paragrams, and onomatopoeia, or in intellection—the logical explanation of the struggle between two heterogeneities. This practice is the site of the most radical heterogeneity (which is maintained as the struggle against the signifier), but is, at the same time, the site of the subtlest signifying differentiation. The former, which maintains rejection, takes us to the heart of jouissance and death; the latter—through subtle differences in rhythm or color, or differences made vocal or semantic in laughter and wordplay—keeps us on the surface of pleasure in a subtle and minute tension. The economy of *textual* practice would thus seem to be that most intense struggle toward death, which runs alongside and is inseparable from the differentiated binding of its charge in a symbolic texture, and which is also, as Freud emphasizes in *Beyond the Pleasure Principle*, the condition of life. The text's principal characteristic and the one that distinguishes it from other signifying practices, is precisely that it introduces, through binding and through vital and symbolic differentiation, heterogeneous rupture and rejection: jouissance and death. This would seem to be "art" 's function as a signifying practice: under the pleasing exterior of a very socially acceptable differentiation, art reintroduces into society fundamental rejection, which is matter in the process of splitting.

For the subject of metalanguage and theory, then, heterogeneity corresponds to the amount of drive left out of first symbolization. The heterogeneous element is a corporeal, physiological, and signifiable excitation which the symbolizing social structure—the family or some other structure—cannot grasp. On the other hand, heterogeneity is that part of the objective, material outer world which could not be grasped by the various symbolizing structures the subject already has at his disposal. Nonsymbolized corporeal excitation and the new object of the nonsymbolized material outer world are always already interacting: the newness of the object gives rise to drives that are not yet bound and prompts their investment, in the same way that unbound drives reject the old object in order to invest in the new one. Between these two levels, a specific exchange is carried out, regulated by the thetic phases of rejection, which will bring about the symbolization of the new object. It will thus redistribute the former signifying matrix and momentarily absorb the drive and the surrounding "objective" process in a mark and a system, which will be the representation or the "model" of the new object and at the same time the binding of a new drive charge. The subject of science will see this new model as a modification of the former symbolic system and, as a result, may describe its structure or the difference between the old and new structures.

The *heterogeneous economy* which operates in this elaboration can be deduced from only two sources: a description of the semiotic device or observations on the drive investment that occurs in the genesis and exercise of the signifying function produced by psychoanalytic practice. Having deduced this heterogeneous economy, we need no longer regard the poetic text as a modified, deformed, or incomplete variant of the linguistic structure of everyday communication between two unary subjects. Instead, through the lexical, syntactic, and prosodic specificities of this new structure, the dialectical materialist theory of signifiance will establish the specific economy of rejection that produced it. It will explore the specific ways in which symbolic and/or signifying unity is shattered, and through which a new symbolic device is constituted—a new reality [un nouveau réel] corresponding to a new heterogeneous object. This device may be situated at the level of drives or at the level of the historical and social process but most often it will be located on both these conflicting levels—each level ignoring and rejecting the other. This signifying device is precisely the one that avant-garde texts since the end of the nineteenth century have openly practiced as they go about seeking, in addition, the theory, "clear-mindedness," and laws of this practice.

5.

Skepticism and Nihilism
in Hegel and in the Text

THE MOBILE and heterogeneous but semiotizable *chora* is the place where the signifying process, rejecting stases, unfolds. In traveling the *chora*'s lines of force, the process of the subject runs the risk of becoming the very mechanism of the *chora*'s operation, its "mode" of repetition, with no signifying substance of its own, no interiority or exteriority—no subject or object, nothing but the movement of rejection. When the signifying process strives to correspond exactly to the logic of this mobile and heterogeneous *chora*, it ultimately forecloses the thetic. But in so doing, heterogeneity itself is lost; spread out in its place is the fantasy of identification with the female body (the mother's body), or even the mutism of the paralyzed schizophrenic.

The foreclosure of the subjective and representative thetic phase marks the boundary of avant-gardist experience. When this foreclosure is not merely ornamental, it leads to madness or to an exclusively experimental functioning, a mystical "inner experience." How does this occur?"

Rejection, in its excessive renewal of scission, destroys presence and annihilates the pause; as a result, there is neither ob-ject nor sub-ject, neither a "contrasting" nor a "subordinate" position, only the motility of the *chora*. Any ob-ject that may appear and be represented is nothing but the movement of rejection itself. The "referent" of such a text is merely the movement of rejection. In immediate representation it appears as pure "nothingness," although such a representation does not see that "referent" in its true economy, namely, as that from which representation itself results. Hegel denounced the immediate consciousness, fixed on its own movement, which can do no more than apprehend nothingness, and is incapable of positing the arising of a new object:

It may be remarked, in a preliminary and general way, that the exposition of the untrue consciousness in its untruth is not a merely *negative* procedure. The natural consciousness itself normally takes this one-sided view of it; and a knowledge which makes this one-sidedness its very essence is itself one of the patterns of incomplete consciousness which occurs on the road itself, and will manifest itself in due course. This is just the scepticism which only ever sees pure nothingness in its result and abstracts from the fact that this nothingness is specifically the nothingness of that *from which it results*. For it is only when it is taken as the result of that from which it emerges, that it is, in fact, the true result; in that case it is itself a *determinate* nothingness, one which has a *content*. The scepticism that ends up with the bare abstraction of nothingness or emptiness cannot get any further from there, but must wait to see whether something new comes along and what it is, in order to throw it too into the same empty abyss. But when, on the other hand, the result is conceived as it is in truth, namely, as a *determinate* negation, a new form has thereby immediately arisen, and in the negation the transition is made through which the progress through the complete series of forms comes about of itself.[12]

These remarks can be directly related to the ideological systems engaged by Mallarmé's practice and modern texts in its wake. This practice stalls the system of representation within the mechanism of heterogeneous contradiction that produces that stoppage and is unable to situate the contradiction as "determinate nothingness," one that would have a new "content" for each new thesis and each new ("natural" or "ideal") object that contradiction moves through and brings to the fore. As such, this practice can be described in Hegelian terms. Nevertheless, we should not forget that the specificity of textual practice lies in accentuating the very movement of negativity within the process, i.e., rejection. Although Hegel was the first to identify and put so much emphasis on this movement and its negativity, he subsumes it under the *presence of consciousness*, which Heidegger in turn over-emphasized, by reducing the essence of the dialectic to it. Without subscribing to this phenomenological reduction, we have on several occasions recognized in Hegel the operation that not only balances out negativity but finally closes it off within the system of dialectical consciousness. The text, by contrast, locating itself in rejection, unfolds the contradiction in rejection and represents its formation. The text does not therefore subsume rejection under the becoming of consciousness and its various scientific representations, as is the case in Hegel.

Let us now specify the difference between the Hegelian position and the practice of the text.

The limits of Hegelian *experience* become clear when its aim is the adequation of the Notion and the object. Although the search for this adequation constitutes a progression, its goal is set by the limits of the living. But in cases where what is confined within these limits is "driven beyond it|self| by something else," "this uprooting entails its death." Hegel nevertheless posits that consciousness, for its part, is capable of going beyond the limit, of transgressing its own position, and of going beyond itself. It is as if he were suggesting that, within consciousness, the transgression which is death constitutes a reactivation, a jolt, a necessary violence, consciousness' "internal cause." What we call the moment of rejection, however, is no sooner recognized than halted. For consciousness reacts to this motorial return of death with *anxiety*, which represents the arising and surpassing of death. Consciousness tends to do away with the progression of thought, aiming only for the limit that cannot be uprooted, the position that cannot be exceeded, an inertia fleeing death: consciousness "strive|s| to hold on to what it is in danger of losing." Hegel considers this fixation on the uprooting of position and this isolation of death within inertia and arrested movement futile, since thought simultaneously takes up its position again and goes beyond its limits, thereby producing its own unrest: "If |consciousness| wishes to remain in a state of unthinking inertia, then thought troubles its thoughtlessness, and its own unrest disturbs its inertia." The entire passage reads as follows:

But the *goal* is as necessarily fixed for knowledge as the serial progression; it is the point where knowledge no longer needs to go beyond itself, where knowledge finds itself, where Notion corresponds to object and object to Notion. Hence the progress towards this goal is also unhalting, and short of it no satisfaction is to be found at any of the stations on the way. Whatever is confined within the limits of a natural life cannot by its own efforts go beyond its immediate existence; but it is driven beyond |*hinausgetrieben*| it by something else, and this uprooting *Hinausgerissenwerden*| entails its death. |Was auf ein natürliches Leben beschränkt ist, vermag durch sich selbst nicht über sein unmittelbares Dasein hinauszugehen; aber es wird durch ein Anderes darüber hinausgetrieben (driven beyond), und dies Hinausgerissenwerden (uprooting) ist sein Tod.| Consciousness, however, is explicitly the *Notion* of itself. Hence it is something that goes beyond limits, and since these limits are its own, it is something that goes beyond itself. With the positing of a single particular the beyond is also established for consciousness, even if it is only *alongside* the limited object as in the case of spatial intuition. Thus consciousness suffers this violence at its own hands: it spoils its own limited satisfaction. When consciousness feels this violence, its anxiety may well make it retreat from the truth, and strive to hold on to what it is in danger of losing. But it can find no peace. If it wishes to remain in a state of unthinking inertia, then thought troubles its thoughtlessness, and its own unrest disturbs its inertia. Or, if it entrenches itself in sentimentality, which assures us that it finds everything to be *good in its kind*, then this assurance likewise suffers violence at the hands of Reason, for, precisely in so far as something is merely a kind, Reason finds it *not* to be good.[13]

By contrast, all avant-garde experience since the late nineteenth century, from the *poète maudit* to schizophrenia, demonstrates that it is possible for a signifying process to be different from the process of unifying conceptual thought. By arranging the symbolic around the jolts of rejection (or in Hegelian terms, around the "uprooting" of position, or around death), textual experience introduces death into the signifying device. Textual experience is not, however, immobilized in an unthinking inertia; instead, it shatters conceptual unity into rhythms, logical distortions (Lautréamont), paragrams, and syntactic inventions (Mallarmé), all of which register, within the signifier, the passage beyond its boundary. In these texts, it is no longer a question of mere anxiety, but of a separation, which is so dangerous for the subject's unity that, as Artaud's text testifies, signifying unity itself vanishes in glossolalia. One might say, then, that since the late nineteenth century, the avant-garde text's essential purpose has been to insert, within a non-thought and through the process of language, the violence of rejection, which is viewed as death by the unary subject and as castration by the analyst — the analyser. Expending thought through the signifying process, the text inscribes the negativity that (capitalist) society and its official ideology repress. Although it thus dissents from the dominant economic and ideological system, the text also plays into its hands: through the text, the system provides itself with what it lacks—rejection—but keeps it in a domain apart, confining it to the ego, to the "inner experience" of an elite, and to esoterism. The text becomes the agent of a new religion that is no longer universal but elitist and esoteric.

The thetic phase—that very specific mechanism of the logic of rejection—works in the service of this assimilation to the extent that it is maintained by subjective narcissism, which is the refuge of the subject's unity and the necessary compensation for the violence of the death drive. The narcissistic moment tends to attach the process of rejection to the unity of the ego, thus preventing rejection's destructive and innovative vigor from going beyond the enclosure of subjectivity and opening up toward a revolutionary ideology capable of transforming the social machine. Hegel's criticism is justified on this point:

Or, again, its fear of the truth may lead consciousness to hide, from itself and others, behind the pretension that its burning zeal for truth makes it difficult or even impossible to find any other truth but the unique truth of vanity—that of being at any rate cleverer than any thoughts that one gets by oneself or from others. This conceit which understands how to belittle every truth, in order to turn back into itself and gloat over its own understanding, which knows how to dissolve every thought and *always find the same barren Ego* instead of any content—this is a satisfaction which we must leave to itself, for it flees from the universal, and seeks only to be for itself.[14]

The modern text seeks a "universal" only in the activation and development of the social process. But it would not be able to go beyond the nineteenth-century avant-garde's ideological limitations (which are ultimately its lack of socio-historical "content") unless it took up again what the avant-garde had snatched from the unary sublimation of idealism (including dialectical idealism). In other words, the modern text had to shatter the signifying process by expending language through rejection and, as a result, take up the entire economy of the subject in this experience (fetishism, phallicization of the mother, etc.) and *reverse* it.

The text introduces into rejection a *reversal* of rejection, which constitutes signifying binding. Hence, *into rejection*, the text introduces *discourse*, thereby producing "sensuous certainty" of rejection. For this very reason, the text is a trans-subjective and transphenomenal experience. In other words, the text shatters and rebinds experience in the process—the term *experience* implying *the subject* and *presence* as its key moments. For now (we shall develop this notion later), we shall say that the text is a *practice* of rejection, since practice's key moment is *heterogeneous contradiction* and *signifying thesis* is its necessary precondition. The text moves toward scientific knowledge of the process that perturbs and exceeds it only to the extent that this latter precondition (signifying thesis) is met. We shall therefore differentiate between the *practice* of rejection and *knowledge about this practice*. The *practice* of rejection is always already signifiable, invested in the practice of the text, and is assumed by the *subject of the text*: the splitting subject in conflict who risks being shattered and is on the brink of a heterogeneous contradiction. By contrast, *knowledge about this practice* can only be organized on the basis of the text whose signifiance is already on the path toward knowledge to the extent that this path moves toward meaning. But meaning is not the same as knowledge. For knowledge, to establish itself, will proceed through a supplementary reversal of meaning, by repressing meaning's heterogeneity and by ordering it into concepts or structures based on the divided unity of its subject: *the subject of science* or *theory*.

The predicate of knowledge is the subject, "we," the addressee who salvages the "uprooting": "Yet in this inquiry [into the truth of knowledge] knowledge is *our* object, something that exists *for us*; and the *in-itself* that would supposedly result from it would rather be the being of knowledge *for us*." [15] Later, the philosophical-dialectical subject's anonymous but punctual "we" reappears as the possessor of "consciousness" in its reversal or in its conversion into "knowledge" acceptable to consciousness: "From the present viewpoint, however, the new object shows itself to have come about through a *reversal of consciousness itself*. This way of looking at the matter is something contributed by *us*, by means of which the succession of experiences through which consciousness passes is raised into a scientific progression—but it is not known to the consciousness that we are observing." [16]

The modern text combines rejection, its signifying reversal, *and* its "knowledge": it constitutes a process, but one that analyzes itself endlessly. By contrast, the nineteenth-century text, inscribing and representing the signifying process, does not summon the unary subject as a place to affix itself; what passes through the subject's shattering in the process is not a known truth but instead its expenditure.

The texts of Lautréamont and Mallarmé do *not* proceed toward the knowledge of practice, a knowledge made possible through a recasting of the Freudian discovery; instead, they set aside their representative "content" (their *Bedeutung*) for representing the mechanism of rejection itself. Thus, although they expose the repressed material of philosophical knowledge and metaphysics— the secret of what they hold sacred—these texts are condemned to be nothing but the complementary counterpart of philosophical speculation to the degree that they confine their field of practice to the experience of heterogeneous contradiction. The function of the latter, as we have seen, is to conclude and open the signifying process. But in the texts of a Lautréamont or a Mallarmé, heterogeneity does not propel the text down a long path through nature and society, thus producing vast novelistic or epic crossings. Instead, heterogeneity is gathered up within the most condensed discursive structure of contradiction—the lyric. Or it appears in the experimental evocation of its own emergence as that of the subject within the immobility of death. A tendency toward "unthinking inertia"[17] arises, which merely reflects the ego's preoccupations and diminishes the opportunities that working with language had provided rejection to give free rein to the violence of its struggles—not to founder under those blows, but instead to carry them into the clash of socio-historical contradictions. And so the path to psychosis—the foreclosure of the thetic—remains open. This situation indicates the ideological limits of the avant-garde (which we shall later discuss in more detail) and shows that the signifying process cannot be objectified by society and history. Furthermore, this situation calls attention to the crucial point textual practice reaches when it passes into the trans-linguistic, instinctual, rejecting process, and the risk it runs being immobilized there.

Constantly keeping the signifying closure open to material rejection; preventing the total sublimation of rejection and its repression by reintroducing it even in the signifying texture [tissu] and its chromatic, musical, and paragrammatic differences; and thus unfolding the gamut of pleasure in order to make heterogeneity speak: this constitutes a productive contradiction.

If this is the social-anti-social function of art, can this function confine itself to opening up contradiction through a signifying texture that represents only personal experience? Can the subtle equilibrium between heterogenous contradiction and the play of denotations (Bedeutungen) representing and signifying a story, a narrative, and a logic, confine itself to an individual, subjective representation? When social history itself breaks down and is reformulated, can heterogeneous contradiction, whose privileged terrain is the text, be absent? This is not a secondary problem: maintaining heterogeneous contradiction is essential, no matter what binding texture or ideological signified it may appear in. Indeed, this is the formalist position and also that of an esoterism to which late nineteenth-century texts succumbed, as do, if not more so, their current epigones who do not even have the advantage of precedence.

On this point, the unitary, relational, and social notion of the subject, which Marxism inherited from Feuerbach, is again relevant. In Marxism, one must take up the subject who says "I," and struggles in a social community, on the basis of his class position, and one must interpret this struggle. One must hear his *discourse* as well as the *heterogeneous contradiction* he has deferred and which "poets" have made it their task to explore. This should not be understood as a "joining" of the two sides, designed to constitute some ideal totality: instead the two sides shed light on one another; they restore the subject's internal/external motility and thus his jouissance, but in this case through the risk involved in his social conflict. They restore his freedom, but only within the implacable logical constraints of his political struggle. This means that the question of the second stage of heterogeneous contradiction, namely, that of the *interpretant* or *meaning* in which this contradiction will irrupt, is of crucial importance. What is at stake is not just the survival of the social function of "art," but also, beyond this cultural preoccupation, modern society's preservation of signifying practices that have a sizeable audience, ones that open up the closure of the *representamen* and the unary subject.

In capitalist society, where class struggle unsettles all institutions and where every subject and discourse are ultimately determined by their position in production and politics, to keep heterogeneous contradiction within a simply subjective representation is to make it inaudible or complicitous with dominant bourgeois ideology. Although the latter can accept experimental subjectivism, it can only barely tolerate—or will reject altogether—the critique of its own foundations. Combining heterogeneous contradiction, whose mechanism the text possesses, with revolutionary critique of the established social order (relations of production—relations of reproduction): this is precisely what the dominant ideology and its various mechanisms of liberalism, oppression, and defense find intolerable. It is also what is most difficult. In other words, the moment of the semantic and ideological binding of drive rejection should be a binding in and through an analytical—and—revolutionary discourse, removing the subject from signifying experience in order to situate him within the revolutionary changes in social relations and close to their various protagonists. Although, to do this, heterogeneous contradiction must accept symbolic theses, they should be rooted in practice and in the analytical—and revolutionary—discourses that shake contemporary society to its foundations. The signifying process, whose heterogeneous contradiction is the moment of a fierce struggle, should be inscribed according to a historical logic in this representational narrative, which itself attests to the historical process underway in revolutionary class struggles. Narrative is one of the forms of binding, sublimation, and repression of the drive charge against the curbs imposed by community structures. As such, and to the extent that the text plays with it, it should be able to take on the narrative of a revolutionary project. For such a project can be the defensive counter-charge that thwarts heterogeneous rejection without stopping it but it can also ensure that the struggle will last on both the instinctual and signifying levels because it ensures that their inseparability will have a historical impact.

Articulated in this way, heterogeneous contradiction suffuses or accompanies critical discourse (representative of a revolutionary social practice) and restores its mainsprings: rejection, heterogeneous contradiction, jouissance in death. Otherwise, social practice itself has a tendency to repress these mainsprings under unitary and technocratic visions of the subject. The always renewed return (which is not in the least a merely mechanical repetition) of "materiality" in "logic" ensures negativity a permanence that can never be erased by the theses of a subjective and blocking desire. Thus heterogeneity is not sublimated but is instead opened up within the symbolic that it puts in process/on trial. There it meets the historical process underway in society, brought to light by historical materialism.

IV.

Practice

It is true that today everyone's curiosity is focused on the performance, but talking about it is impossible without referring to the concept.

Mallarmé, "Hamlet," *Œuvres complètes*, p. 300

1.

Experience Is Not Practice

AVANT-GARDE TEXTS evolve within a system of representation that is exclusively corporeal, natural, or borrowed from idealist philosophy. The thetic moment of rejection invests that system in an a-social present and keeps it locked there. The text therefore signifies an experience of heterogeneous contradiction rather than a practice, which, by contrast, is always social. The proof may be seen in Mallarmé's refusal to consider the possibility of a political activity that would be simultaneous to textual activity, whatever his well-founded reasons for criticizing anarchist or social commitment.[1] Although no textual practice can exist outside the constraints imposed by the logic of the subject-in-process, when that practice claims to be only and very narrowly subjective, it condemns itself to the confines of the mirror held out to it by a coagulative, restrictive, paranoid ideology. This ideology ends up "getting the better of" the subject, making him, precisely, an "alienated subject" at the very moment the process to which this subject is submitted reaches the height of its contradiction.

"Signifying experience" must therefore be distinguished from "signifying practice." The notion of *experience* shall be reserved for practices in which heterogeneous contradiction is maintained, sought after, and put into discourse, thereby forming the essential economy of the text, but one in which heterogeneous contradiction invests, during the thetic phase, in a strictly individual, naturalist, or esoteric representation, reducing rejection to the presence of the ego, the kind of representation Bataille calls "the onanism of a funereal poem."[2] The notion of *practice*, on the other hand, would be better applied to texts in which heterogeneous contradiction is maintained *as an indispensable precondition for the di-*

mension of practice through a signifying formation, and in which, therefore, the system of representation that binds the text is also rooted in social practice, or even its revolutionary phase. Our distinction between "experience" and "practice" is drawn from a particular reading of the relation between Hegel and Marx which we would now like to elucidate.

"*Inasmuch as the new true object issues from it,*" writes Hegel, identifying experience with the dialectic, "this *dialectical* movement which consciousness exercises on itself and which affects both its knowledge and its object, is precisely what is called *experience* [*Erfahrung*]."[3] Hegel distinguishes the moment of the object's first and immediate appearance for consciousness—a moment of pure apprehension—from the moment of true experience where a new object is constituted from that first object through the turning back of consciousness upon itself, through "our own intervention." "It shows up here like this: since what first appeared as the object sinks for consciousness to the level of its way of knowing it, and since the in-itself becomes a *being-for-consciousness* of the in-itself, the latter is now the new object. Herewith a new pattern of consciousness comes on the scene as well, for which the essence is something different from what it was at the preceding stage."[4]

The first mysterious movement of "*immediate certainty*" is thus distinguished from the true realization of consciousness in *experience,* which constitutes the second moment in which immediate certainty will be introduced into the presence of consciousness through the latter's unwitting turning back upon itself ("as it were, behind its back"): "But it is just this necessity itself, or the *origination* of the new object, that presents itself to consciousness without its understanding how this happens, which proceeds for us, as it were, behind the back of consciousness [*hinter seinem Rücken vorgeht*]."[5] We know nothing about this first movement except that it is essentially negative; yet to isolate it in its negativity, without linking it to what follows, is to reduce experience to nothingness.

As we have noted, however, there emerges an instant of "uprooting" (*Hinausgerissenwerden*) or of "death" in the Hegelian conception of experience, an instant apprehended by consciousness as the cause producing the immediate *shape* and translating it into a *Notion*. In our view, this negativity—the sudden interruption of conscious presence and its finitude—is what makes Hegel's idea of experience radically different from Husserlian phenomenological experience. It comes as no surprise, then, that Hegelian *experience* leads to a *practice*; the latter is not only a subordinate moment of theoretical synthesis, it must also be a test— a confrontation with heterogeneity. In other words, a notion of experience that includes the "uprooting" entails a notion of *practice* that dialectical materialism could adapt as a way of considering not only scientific, theoretical, or "aesthetic" activities, but also all socio-historical transformation.[6]

It would thus seem that the dialectic recognizes that one moment of dialectical experience implies the annihilation of consciousness, of its presence and metaphysical unity. But since it does not recognize an objective material agency, one that is structured independently of consciousness, the idealist dialectic cannot specify objective, material relations. In a logical sense, the contradictions in those relations are what *generate* "sense-certainty" *before* the latter becomes an object of knowledge. Hegel's notion of experience thus remains an experience of knowledge. Although it is not the knowledge of science in the technical sense but rather the theological science of an absolute knowledge, Hegelian experience depends nevertheless on the same kind of *thinking subject*: the subject of a consciousness-present-to-itself. The only thing this consciousness retains from the heterogeneity working upon it is the impression of void, nothingness, lack, "as it were, behind its back."

2.

The Atomistic Subject
of Practice in Marxism

AT THE other end of the Notion's trajectory, which is to say at the end of *Science of Logic*, Hegel outlines the same movement: the *Theoretical Idea*, which is the "Idea of appearance," "cognition as such," becomes more precise, which is to say it "receives from without Individuality or determinate determinateness, or, its content,"[7] thanks to the impulse of *"the Good,"* and becomes the *Practical Idea* (*Praktische Idee*). The latter recalls and integrates the notion of "experience" (*Erfahrung*), which we came across in the Introduction to the *Phenomenology of Spirit*, at the always already reversed "beginning" of the dialectical spiral. What the Practical Idea and experience have in common is that they both involve "the determination of external being": experience separates from it; the Practical Idea reaches it. In both moments, the relation to externality is immediate; but whereas *experience* pulls away from externality in order to produce logical unity within consciousness, the *Practical Idea* returns to externality by distancing itself from self-knowledge, *without* having reached consciousness per se. Only the reintroduction of the *activity of the objective Notion* removes from actuality (apprehended thus far only as external) its "merely apparent reality, external determinability, and nullity," and posits it "as being in and for itself." Through the reintroduction of the Notion, the Idea comes about not only within the "active subject" of practice, but as "immediate actuality" and at the same time as "objectivity which is veritable": it comes about as Absolute Idea.[8]

The materialist dialectic takes up, unfolds, and overturns this point in Hegel's remarks in order to outline its theory of the primacy of practice in knowledge. Marx posits "human sensuous activity" as the foundation of knowledge; adding "practice" to "sensuous activity" is already a first step in removing the notion of practice from its subordination to a consciousness present to itself. *Human relations,* and essentially *relations of production* are, then, what take on the heterogeneity determining this practice. In his "Conspectus of Hegel's Book on *The Science of Logic,*" Lenin notes the superiority of the Practical Idea over knowledge, since the Practical Idea, bringing into existence the impulse of "the Good," has, in Hegel's view, "not only the dignity of the universal but also of the *simply actual.* . . ." In the margin Lenin writes: "*Practice is higher than (theoretical) knowledge,* for it has not only the dignity of universality, but also of immediate actuality."[9] Marxist theory, however, comments neither on the teleology of practical action, implied by "the Good," nor on the economy of "the highest contradiction," which takes hold in the Absolute Idea when the *Notion* returns within the Practical Idea. This produces "*the practical Notion*" which, according to Hegel, culminates in an "impenetrable and atomistic subjectivity"—not "exclusive individuality" but "universality and cognition" of its own alterity as objectivity: "The practical and objective Notion, *determined in and for itself, which, as person, is impenetrable and atomistic subjectivity* [emphasis added]: while at the same time it is not exclusive individuality, but is, for itself, universality and cognition, and in its Other, has its own objectivity for object."[10]

Marxism-Leninism stresses above all the orientation of *practice* toward *externality, objectivity,* and the *real.* Marx writes: "The chief defect of all hitherto existing materialism—that of Feuerbach included—is that the thing, reality, sensuousness is conceived only in the form of the *object* or of *contemplation* but not as *human sensuous activity, practice* . . . Feuerbach wants sensuous objects, really distinct from the thought objects, but he does not conceive human activity itself as *objective* activity."[11] Similarly, to Hegel's "syllogism of action," Lenin opposes the preponderance of logical *externality,* of the real: "Not, of course, in the sense that the figure of logic has its other being in the practice of man (= absolute idealism), but vice versa: man's practice, repeating itself a thousand million times, becomes consolidated in man's consciousness by figures of logic. Precisely (and only) on account of this thousand-million-fold repetition, these figures have the stability of a prejudice, an axiomatic character." [12]

Mao Tse-tung takes up Lenin's comments on Hegel in his essay "On Practice" and stresses the fact that *personal and direct experience* is the essential materialist feature of practice. While affirming that the *activity of production* determines all practical action, he adds class struggle, political life, and scientific and aesthetic activity to the range of possible practices. The moment of practice is represented according to "reverse" Hegelian logic: the "apprehension" of an "externality" in its "external" and "approximate connections." Only the repetition of phenomena within the objective continuity of social practice produces a *qualitative leap—* the *emergence of the Notion establishing internal connections.* Mao stresses two aspects of practice: it is *personal* and requires "*direct experience.*"

If you want to know a certain thing or a certain class of thing directly, you must personally participate in the practical struggle to change reality, to change that thing or class of things, for only thus can you come into contact with them as phenomena; only through personal participation in the practical struggle to change reality can you uncover the essence of that thing or class of things and comprehend them. . . . All genuine knowledge originates in direct experience.[13]

"Anyone who denies such perception [of the objective external world]," he continues, "denies direct experience, or denies personal participation in the practice that changes reality, is not a materialist." [14]

"Direct" and "personal" experience is perhaps stressed here more than anywhere else in Marxist theory and Mao's emphasis on it tends to bring to the fore a subjectivity that has become the place of the "highest contradiction"—the subjectivity Hegel calls for in the Absolute Idea. In general and at best, the notion of "practice" in Marxism implies a subjectivity which does not go beyond that of the Practical Idea (particularization, finitude, no self-reflection: in other words, it lacks the "theoretical element").

Maoism goes one step further: its "practice" is supported by a subjectivity that knows itself but only as a "practical Notion" since, although it incarnates the highest contradiction, this subjectivity remains impregnable, impersonal, atomistic, and brings about a general knowledge. Maoism, it would seem, summons and produces, above all, this kind of subjectivity, one that it views as the driving force behind the practice of social change and revolution—of course, "signifying practices" in China suggest that there might exist other kinds of subjects expending the dialectic totality . . .

3.

Calling Back Rupture
Within Practice:
Experience-in-Practice

IT SHOULD not be forgotten that the "practical Notion," which completes the Hegelian edifice and is overturned in dialectical materialism, contains, within the spiral of its elaboration, *moments that precede it*. Practice encloses and brings to knowledge the *direct experience* of reality—an immediacy Lenin notes only in passing—which incorporates the stage of *Erfahrung* (experience), that of the signifying apprehension of the new heterogeneous object. By implication, direct experience includes the border on which the subject may shatter. This shattering is not the same as the impenetrable and atomistic subject of the "practical Notion"; it constitutes instead the *precondition of his renewal*.

Mao clearly differentiates the two moments that the idealist dialectic or mechanistic materialism and the dogmatizations of Marxist thought tended to fuse. He posits a triple process (practice—truth—practice) that implies a different status for the "apprehended objects" and the "consciousness" apprehending them in each of these three phases. The emergence of the true object in *practice* should therefore be distinguished from *scientific knowledge* about it, which will render its scientific truth only to lead, in turn, to another test-in-practice. The moment of practice is thus indissolubly linked to that of true scientific knowledge, but remains distinct from it.

Since it is not a theory of the subject, Marxist theory does not deal with this moment of practice. It merely identifies the objective and logical determinations of practice, and thus evokes its conditions and structure rather than its inter- and intra-subjective dynamics. Dialectical materialism leaves behind the negativity that pervades the subject: we have already emphasized this fact and the historical justifications for this abandonment.

Nevertheless, the moment of practice dissolves the subject's compactness and self-presence. First, it puts the subject in contact with, and thus in a position to negate, various objects and other subjects in his social milieu, with which the subject enters into contradiction, whether antagonistically or not. Although an externality, the contradiction within social relations de-centers and suspends the subject, and articulates him as a passageway, a non-place, where there is a struggle between conflicting tendencies, *drives* whose stases and thetic moments (the *representamen*) are as much rooted in affective relations (parental and love relations) as they are in class conflict. Rejection, de-centering the subject, sets his pulverization against natural structures and social relations, collides with them, rejects them, and is de-posited by them. At the moment of rejection (which presupposes the phase annihilating a former objectivity), a binding, symbolic, ideological, and thus positivizing component intervenes ("we intervene," writes Hegel) in order to constitute, within language, the new object produced by the "subject" in process/on trial through the process of rejection. The fundamental moment of practice is thus the heterogeneous contradiction that posits a subject put in process/on trial by a natural or social outside that is not yet symbolized, a subject in conflict with previous theses (in other words, with those systems of representation that defer and delay the violence of rejection).

It is this very practice that includes heterogeneous contradiction as the mainspring of an infinite dialectical—material and signifying—movement. Practice is determined by the pulverization of the unity of consciousness by a nonsymbolized outside, on the basis of objective contradictions and, as such, it is the place where the signifying *process* is carried out. Out of these objective contradictions, drive rejection will bring forth the new object whose determinations exist objectively in material externality, which means that this moment of practice is not simply an "apparition," within the presence of consciousness, of the laws of "*being.*"

We would like to emphasize a logical moment previous to this return of the knowing consciousness, which is precisely the second stage of the movement of practice. We would therefore like to bring to the fore the repressed element of practice: in it, in the passage of an always already signifiable rejection—one that is nevertheless perpetually undermined by that which remains outside symbolization—what takes place is the struggle with the strictly subjective thesis, with the One, as well as with all preexisting natural, social, scientific, and political systematicities. The appearance of the new object, the new thesis, is the result of this conflict. The new object is a moment of the process whose conflict constitutes the most intense moment of rupture and renewal. Consciousness tends to repress this struggle within heterogeneity, which takes the subject into an "externality" he rejects only to posit it again, renewed. But it is this struggle that produces what consciousness will view as a *moment* of the "appearance" of this "new" object. At *the place of this struggle*, the "appearance" *does not exist*; its "moment" is "*fiction*," or even "*laughter*" because all meaning is ephemeral there, due to the pressure of rejection, which, for the subject, to repeat Freud again, is nothing other than the death drive or jouissance.

The subject of this experience-in-practice is an excess: never one, always already divided by what Sollers calls a "double causality," simultaneously "outside" and "inside" the subject, divided in such a way that the subjective "unity" in question is expended, expending, irreducible to knowledge, "bordered" by laughter, eroticism, or what has been called the "sacred."

The subject we don't want to know anything about: the effect and intersection of matter in movement? . . . The cause external to the subject leads him to undergo, without being able to master it, the effect of his internal determining cause, in other words, to be consumed by it in consuming it. The subject becomes a game that hides *through* and *in* his cause *from* his cause, the (external) *precondition* laying bare the (internal) *foundation*. Bataille gives this compressed operation a name: laughter.[15]

In this moment of heterogeneous contradiction, the subject breaks through his unifying enclosure and, through a leap (laughter? fiction?), passes into the process of social change that moves through him. In other words, the moment of practice *objectifies* the signifying process since it sets drive rejection against material contradictions (class struggle, for example) but *at the same time it introduces these material contradictions into the process of the subject.* Heterogeneous contradictions here lies between the signifying process and the objective social process: it is the excess of one by and through the other.

In this confrontation of drive rejection with the historical process, what then occurs is the entire recasting of subjective and social structuration, the reconstituting of the knowing unity [the subject] with the new object it discovered within social process. The force of drive rejection favors the reconstituted subject's rediscovery of this new object, which, we should not forget, is located in the social structure and asserts itself at the thetic moment of the signifying process. The moment of practice implies testing to what degree the process of rejection corresponds to and deviates from the objective (natural, social) process it confronts. Faced with the laws of the existing historical process (the structures of capitalist society, for example), drive rejection may invest and recognize itself in them, turning those structures into symbolic theses and becoming locked within them. Or else, by its violence, which no thesis can stop, drive rejection may reject all stasis and symbolize the objective process of transformation, according to the constraints imposed on the movement of drives, in which case it produces a revolutionary "discourse." Only a testing of that discourse (through the process of practice—truth—practice) can make it correspond to objective mobility and necessity.

The psychoanalytic device of *transference* aims to reintroduce the process of rejection into the molds of intersubjective (interfamilial) relations. It tends to ossify the subject on the basis of this reconstituted unity, even when this unity knows itself to be broken and forever inadequate to the mechanisms of rejection, which outlines the framework of the real. In contrast, *practice* calls on rejection itself and, as a replacement for the thetic phase, offers it not an identifying addressee (not even the silent, hidden analyst) to converse with, but rather processes and objective laws to discover. When these laws are those of the revolutionary transformation of society, the process of rejection finds its place in them all the more logically since its own logic is none other than that of renewed contradiction.

Practice of whatever kind—but revolutionary practice in its explicit content—knows this moment in which the race toward death—implicit jouissance—is never far behind the contradictions confronted by the subject, since he supersedes himself there, first as a unity and finally as a living being, if the objective law of struggle demands it. In order to do this, however, the subject of social practice hypostasizes the *thetic moment of rejection*, the "paranoid" moment: he offers himself, in representation, as a dilated, inflated, tenacious ego, armed with ideological and theoretical assurance, combatting, within representation, the old theses that resist rejection, whose agent this inflated ego has become. Having joined the course of historical processes—though uniquely within representation—the signifying process gives itself an agent, an ego, that of the revolutionary who has no need of knowing and even less of closely examining the mechanism of rejection that pulverizes or brings him together again, since objectively this misjudging—imaginary or ideological—ego is the module by which the mechanism of rejection in question invades the social realm.

Because they repress the moment of "sensuous" and "immediate activity," Hegel's "practical Notion" and dialectical materialism's so-called *practice* are condemned to be a mere mechanical repetition of actions without any modification of real, material and signifying, objective and subjective devices. By locking an opaque reality into a null and void atomistic subjectivity, such a "practice" blocks the very process of a practice that aims to "change [both] the objective world . . . and the subjective world."[16] On the other hand, when it rehabilitates this moment of "sensuous human experience," dialectical materialism moves toward what one might call the *analysis-in-practice* of the "impenetrable" and "atomistic" subject, the bearer of the "practical Notion." Dialectical materialism knows that this impenetrable subject is the logical and historical precondition for *action*, and that his thetic phase is complicitous with ethical teleology. It makes use of this knowledge but, fully engaged in the movement of social revolution, does not analyze it discursively. It is therefore incumbent upon particular signifying operations, both verbal and nonverbal, to introduce *into discourse* the analysis-in-practice that dissolves the impenetrable and atomistic subject. Otherwise, this analysis-in-practice may or may not come about as a real though always unstated component in the social practice governed by the contradiction in relations among atomistic subjects.

4.

The Text as Practice, Distinct from Transference Discourse

THE TEXT is able to explore the mechanism of rejection in its heterogeneity because it is a practice that pulverizes unity, making it a process that posits and displaces theses. In other words, the text exposes, for representation, the extreme moment characteristic of all process-as-practice. In so doing, it "speaks" to every subject moving through this moment of practice in various domains, even though that subject may turn away and leave it "behind his back." In every kind of society and situation, the text's function is therefore to lift the repression that weighs heavily on this moment of struggle, one that particularly threatens or dissolves the bond between subject and society, but simultaneously creates the conditions for its renewal.

In the process of transference in analysis, *discourse* establishes the subject within language precisely because transference permits the analysand to take over the (power of) discourse the analyst is presumed to hold. Although it thereby reconstructs the signifying process, this renewal of power locks it up within a discourse that tests intrafamilial relations (see above, pp. 90–93, on narrative). The text, by contrast, is not based on personified transference: its always absent "addressee" is the *site of language itself* or, more precisely, its thetic moment, which the text appropriates by introducing within it, as we have said, semiotic motility. In so doing, the text takes up strictly individual experience and invests it directly in a signification (*Bedeutung*), in other words, in an enunciation and a denotation that stem from the socio-symbolic whole. In this way, the significations (ideologies) that preoccupy the social group—the ones implied in its acts or controlling them—are put into play by the process of the subject they wanted to ignore. Indeed this is the contradiction that characterizes what we have called *experience-in-practice.*

The text's signifying practice thus retains the analytic situation's requirement that the process of the subject be realized in language. The absence of a *represented* focal point of transference prevents this process from becoming locked into an identification that can do no more than adapt the subject to social and family structures. To hamper transference, the text's analysis must produce the certainty that the analyst's place is empty, that "he" is dead, and that rejection can only attack signifying structures. This is textual practice's presupposition and its starting point. Admittedly, the designated addressees of the text are often its focus of transference, its objects of attempted seduction and aggression. But this transference relation, supposing that it exists, is controlled more by the *structure* of the text than by the *other,* the addressee, and, in any case, concerns only the writing subject and his partner; it could never exhaust the impact of the text as social practice for all its possible readers. The disadvantage of this independence from the transference relation is that it deprives the text of immediate truth criteria. On the other hand, it allows the text to operate in a much wider signifying field than it otherwise would, and to carry out much more radical subversions, which, far from stopping at desire, involve the subject's very jouissance.

There is no limit to what can be said in the text. As we know, Lautréamont and Mallarmé denied the "unspeakable that lies" and pushed back ever further the boundaries of grammar and "decency." The text's so-called *composition,* however, assigns a "boundary to the infinite," and thereby fulfills the text's first criterion: to avoid becoming a free-flow "escape" [*fuite*] of the signifier, this discourse must provide itself with guardrails [*des garde-fous*]. *Composition,* in this sense, is the index of the text as practice and the *premise* of its *truth,* the *proof* of which will be provided by the recognition of an era or of one of its structures. "An era automatically recognizes the Poet's existence," Mallarmé announces.

Now the situation becomes clearer. As the text constructed itself with respect to an empty place ("Nothing shall have taken place except the place," writes Mallarmé in A *Throw of the Dice*), it in turn comes to be the empty site of a process in which its readers become involved. The text turns out to be the analyst and every reader the analysand. But since the *structure and function of language take the place of the focus of transference* in the text, this opens the way for all linguistic, symbolic, and social structures to be put in process/on trial. The text thereby attains its essential dimension: it is a *practice* calling into question (symbolic and social) *finitudes* by proposing *new signifying devices*. In calling the text a practice we must not forget that it is a new practice, radically different from the mechanistic practice of a null and void, atomistic subject who refuses to acknowledge that he is a subject of language. Against such a "practice," the text as signifying practice points toward the possibility—which is a jouissance—of a *subject who speaks his being put in process/on trial through action*. In other words and conversely, the text restores to "mute" practice the jouissance that constitutes it but which can only become jouissance through language.

The text thus responds to an expectation buried within the communital representation of practice, an expectation that is felt most strongly at those historical moments when the gap between social practice and its representation by the dominant ideology has significantly widened and deepened. At the end of the nineteenth century, the deep dissatisfactions of the working classes—from the peasantry to the petty bourgeoisie—impoverished by the bourgeois State's accumulation of capital, erupted in a series of revolutions from 1848 to the 1871 Commune. The only representations of these dissatisfactions were to be found in the mystic positivism of an Auguste Comte and a Renan or, marginally, in the sociological theories of revolution, from Marx to the utopians or the French anarchists. Capitalism leaves the subject the right to revolt, preserving for itself the right to suppress that revolt. The ideological systems capitalism proposes, however, subdue, unify, and consolidate that revolt, bringing it back within the field of unity (that of the subject and the State). When objective conditions were not such that this state of tension could be resolved through revolution, rejection became symbolized in the avant-garde texts of the nineteenth century where the repressed truth of a shattered subject was then confined.

In the forefront of both its linguistic functioning and the representation that invests it, the modern *text* exhibits that which has always been the disguised mainspring of "art," hidden behind the appearances of phantasmatic formations or of exquisite differentiations in the signifying material. The text intensifies these formations and differentiations by unfolding them, transformed, exclusively around the principal heterogeneous construction (position/process of the subject). In so doing, the modern *text* already situates itself outside "art," through "art." The text shapes this space, which formerly belonged to religion and its dependencies, through the singular practice of a subject in process/on trial and, as a result, introduces the kind of knowledge concerning the body, language, and society that sciences today might have provided.

Having objectively rejected Christianity (whose rites, for centuries, had absorbed the Western—unitary—subject's nostalgia for contradiction), the Western petty bourgeoisie, in barely secret societies, gave itself over to a reborn occultism that was to shelter poetic "experiences" as well. The Symbolists, Wagnerians, Parnassians, and Mallarméans, up through the Surrealists and their current survivors, were to become the hesitant and stray defenders of a certain "truth" about the subject that the dominant ideologies could no longer master and that religions—in which "the race's secret" (Mallarmé) had taken refuge—had sealed up. These avant-garde texts thus offered themselves as a supplement to bourgeois society and its technocratic ideology, but within this supplement an objective truth remains hidden: the moment of struggle exploding the subject toward heterogeneous materiality. Yet the representative system of these very texts brought this moment back within subjective *experience*. The avant-garde text of the nineteenth century thus renounced any part in the contemporary social process, even while it exhibited that process' repressed yet inaugural moment—constitutive to the extent that it reveals the moment that dissolves all constituted unity. In so doing, the avant-garde text served the dominant ideology by providing it with something to replace what it lacked, without directly calling into question its system of reproduction within representation (within signification).

Could it be that social revolution, by taking charge of rejection and ensuring its social objectification, makes these texts useless? In any case, it indicates their limited aspect and confines them to being an "experience": a discovery of the heterogeneous base, the constant struggle, within the subject's "consciousness." As Bataille showed in his polemic with Sartre on Baudelaire, what justifies this experience is that it shows the subject, blinded in his social representations, the death drive that provides his jouissance and makes him reject existing shackles. Bataille recognizes the poet's "minor attitude," his infantile misery:

Though poetry may trample verbally on the established order, it is no substitute for it. When disgust with a powerless liberty thoroughly commits the poet to political action, he abandons poetry. But he immediately assumes responsibility for the order to come: he asserts the *direction* of activity, the *major attitude*. When we see him we cannot help being aware that poetic existence, in which we once saw the possibility of a *sovereign attitude*, is really a *minor attitude*. It becomes no more than a child's attitude, a gratuitous game.[17]

As a result, however, Bataille foresees that it is possible to go beyond a poetry that is incapable of assuming positivity (the "Good"); although he stresses that "even if we do so we cannot be complacent," Bataille seems to predict that the poetic practice stemming from Baudelaire will break down, dissolving in "a perfect silence of the will."[18]

Although to our mind Bataille is in the right against the Sartrean dialectic with its full subject, whose economy is never open and never negativized, the polemic between them reflects its protagonists' mutual determinations and a dichotomy (experience/practice) whose terms are mutually exclusive. Despite Lautréamont's moralist tendency, which seemed to be seeking to go beyond this dichotomy through his *Poems*, and despite Mallarmé's philosophical and journalistic leanings, the question we must ask today is one that the texts of the nineteenth century did not resolve: Is it possible to keep open the heterogeneous and contradictory moment, which is unbearable for the subject, within a text that represents, through this moment, the diversity and multiplicity of social practices which disregard that moment in their own realization? The problem is thus one of introducing the struggle of signifiance—its process—no longer just into "individual experience"—where, in any case, it already is, since it is always destroying that experience—but also into the objective process of contemporary science, technology, and social relations. This is the stake that was first proposed by the texts of the late nineteenth century.

5.

The Second Overturning of the Dialectic: After Political Economy, Aesthetics

TO VIEW texts as signifying practices is to view their signifying operation in the light of their subject in process/on trial—in light of that subject's always unsuccessful positing [*position manquée*]. To say that the text is a signifying practice implies that it has a subject, a meaning, and a logic, but the logic is one from which the subject is absent and it is through this very absence that the subject reveals himself. One could say that, as a signifying practice, the text is the active form of madness, or rather, an active, which is to say socialized, madness. For the text denounces not only the opaque, uninformed, and empty activity, which the capitalist system demands of the subject, but also the natural delirium that system allows—a delirium that abdicates any active social function. The four types of signifying devices we spoke of earlier (narrative, metalanguage, contemplation, and the text) are all signifying practices (see above, part I, section 13). Only as such can they break the signifying process out of its "natural" imprisonment (in madness) or its narcissistic imprisonment (in psychoanalysis). Signifying practices thus elude the machinations and blind alleys of that imprisonment; they do so slowly and cautiously, no doubt, but always within the public arena, always taking socio-historical activity into account.

Since the end of the nineteenth century, "poetry" has deliberately maintained the balance between sociality and madness, and we view this as the sign of a new era. After the upheavals of the French Revolution, the nineteenth century discovered history: the Hegelian dialectic showed that history constitutes a history of reason or, more profoundly, a history of the subject, and Marxism proved that history is a succession of struggles and ruptures within relations of production. This "discovery" opened up the modern episteme—a historical one—which philosophers today are still exploring. Establishing the bourgeois Republic in the second half of the last century showed not that history was closed but rather that its logic was henceforth *thinkable*—which is not to say controllable. For a certain "residue" continues to elude the control of the historical *ratio*: the subject. History is not the history of a subject always present to himself; it is a history of modes of production. This is the Marxist correction of the dialectic. But what then becomes of the subject? This is the question that remains unanswered.

The subject never *is*. The *subject* is only the *signifying process* and he appears only as a *signifying practice*, that is, only when he is absent *within the position* out of which social, historical, and signifying activity unfolds. There is no science of the subject. Any thought mastering the subject is mystical: all that exists is the field of a practice where, through his expenditure, the subject can be anticipated in an always anterior future: "Nothing will have taken place but the place."[19] This is the "*second overturning*" of the Hegelian dialectic, which came about toward the end of the last century and was as fundamentally radical as the Marxist overturning of the dialectic—if not more so. If history is made up of modes of production, the subject is a *contradiction* that brings about practice because practice is always both signifying and semiotic, a crest where meaning emerges only to disappear. It is incumbent upon "art" to demonstrate that the subject is the absent element of and in his practice, just as it was incumbent upon political economy to prove that history is a matter of class struggle: ". . . in order to close the gap created by our lack of interest in what lies outside the realm of aesthetics.—Everything can be summed up in Aesthetics and Political Economy."[20]

The subject's absence in practice is demonstrated first and

foremost through the practice of language, which was what *objectively* prepared the way for Freud's discovery. This discovery sought the truth of the subject in the transference relation, which can be viewed as a subset of practice relations. Only today can we see that this truth must be applied to all social practice, including political practice, but also, and increasingly, everyday, scientific, and technical practice. It is as if, after the emphasis Freud placed on the subject's impossible coincidence with himself in sexuality, a return toward the practice of the text were necessary to recall not only that "poets" had already discovered this impossibility but also that, as the precondition of their practice, the contradiction inherent in the signifying process is the precondition of all practice. Consequently, poetry ceased to be "art" and claimed other functions: showing the heterogeneity that works on all practice and furnishing every disappearance of meaning with a signifying device and practical scope.

6.

Maldoror and Poems: Laughter as Practice

LAUTRÉAMONT WAS undoubtedly the first to state explicitly that poetry must be oriented toward a "truth-in-practice" [*vérité pratique*].[21] He made poetry the link between what he calls "first principles" and the "secondary truths of life"—terms that we believe can be understood as "semiotic processes" and "symbolic processes" (ones that are thetic, capable of truth). In requiring that poetry give the thetic its due, Lautréamont would have it disclose the laws inherent in sociopolitical activity and theory:

Poetry must have for its object practical truth [*vérité pratique*]. It expresses the relation between the first principles and the secondary truths of life. Everything remains in its place. The mission of poetry is difficult. It is not concerned with political events, with the way a people is governed, makes no allusion to historical periods, *coups d'état*, regicides, court intrigues. It does not speak of those struggles which, exceptionally, man has with himself and his passions. It discovers the laws by which political theory exists, universal peace, the refutations of Machiavelli, the cornets of which the work of Proudhon consists, the psychology of mankind. A poet must be more useful than any other citizen of his tribe. His work is the code of diplomats, legislators and teachers of youth. We are far from the Homers, the Virgils, the Klopstocks, the Camoëns, the liberated imaginations, the ode-producers, the merchants of epigrams against the deity. Let us return to Confucius, Buddha, Jesus Christ, those moralists who went hungry through the villages. From now on we have to reckon with reason which operates only on those faculties which watch over the category of the phenomena of pure goodness.[22]

To understand this maxim we must add the definition of "good-ness" given in *Maldoror*: "goodness is nothing but a couple of so-norous syllables"; as well as some of the numerous references to *reason* as a "prohibition" and a "discourse": "We are not free to do evil," and "the soul being one, sensibility, intelligence, will, reason, imagination and memory can be introduced into our dis-course."[23]

The poetry Lautréamont strove for can thus be understood as the heterogeneous practice we spoke of earlier: the positing of the unary subject, and, through this unity, an exploration of the semiotic operation that moves through it. In Lautréamont's text, the musical scanning of sentences and complex logical operations[24] inscribe this relation between "goodness" and "law." *Poems* stresses the need for an attitude rooted in practice—which is affirmative above and beyond negation—and rejects the strictly verbal analy-sis adopted by a Mallarmé or a Joyce. Yet such an attitude im-poses a limit on romantic flow, just as—beyond its law-giving and apparently unpolished formulation—it reminds Mallarméan sym-bolism of its affected limitations and fetishistic pitfalls. In declar-ing that "reason," "consciousness," the "unity of the soul," and the "judgment of poetry" are superior to poetry, Lautréamont af-firms the positing and insistence of the subject in poetry and, by this means alone, makes it a *practice*. Thus, "it will not always be a negation;"[25] but this does not mean that Lautréamont's *Poems* advocate worship of morality, the Good, or even affirmation. His play with the logical reversals of the moralists tends to mitigate such a suspicion since it points out the *irony* of the gesture and the process of negativity, which works on the text even in its most aphoristic or totalizing formulation.

Several explicit statements by Lautréamont have the same effect: "A student could acquire a considerable amount of literary knowledge by saying the opposite of what the poets of this cen-tury have said. He would replace their affirmations with nega-tions. If it is ridiculous to attack first principles, it is even more ridiculous to defend them against the same attacks. I will not de-fend them." The true is not a set affirmation, it is merely the path of correction and transformation, one and the other (in our terms:

the true is both the symbolic and the semiotic, both *Bedeutung* and what breaks through it): "If these sophisms were corrected by their corresponding truths, only the corrections would be true; while the work which had been thus revised would no longer have the right to be called false. The rest would be outside the realm of the true, tainted with falsehood, and would thus necessarily be considered null and void."[26]

The true is not the absolute positing of a transcendental ego; it is instead that part of it registered in a relation with the other. Truth is thus an alteration, a positing but an altered, imaginary one. Lautréamont values this imaginary truth, in opposition to Pascal's moralism which belittles this alteration. "We are not content with the life within us," Lautréamont writes. "We wish to lead an imaginary life in other people's minds. We strive to appear to be what we are. We make every effort to preserve this imaginary being, which is simply the real one."[27]

Although it constitutes a totality, this practice is always a heterogeneous totality and, for this reason, it is unbearable at the precise moment it lifts inhibitions and offers us aid: "Reason and feeling counsel and supplement each other. Whoever knows only one of these, renouncing the other, is depriving himself of *all* of the aid which has been granted us to guide our actions."[28]

In the split but indivisible unity they form, *Maldoror* and *Poems* both complement and contest each other (see note 95, part II, supra). *Maldoror* puts the subject in process/on trial into a hallucinatory narrative that has the linguistic resources of poetry. *Poems*, on the other hand, affirms the thetic place from which every textual organization sets forth but which, when consciously accepted and elaborated upon, guarantees "poetry"'s dimension in practice. Finally and above all, the unity of *Maldoror* and *Poems* articulates a new experience-in-practice for "poetry"—one that flees psychosis and aims to invest, within social discourse, the truth of the subject thus put to test. Many factors limited the impact of Lautréamont's text: Napoleon III's Empire was ending; Lautréamont's life was cut short, and various personal limitations prevented the signifying process from joining together the two sketched-out sections of his text; furthermore, Lautréamont tends to privilege mastery and to glorify metalanguage over laughter in the loss of meaning during process. Despite these inhibiting factors, Lautréamont's gesture inaugurated a new phase in the status of "literature." Only today, now that we are beyond surreal-. ism's fascination with Lautréamont, can we question, carry out, and go beyond this text.

To question Lautréamont's text as a practice one must address its heterogeneity—unique in the history of literature. For the heterogeneity of this particular text is designated by the complementary opposition (in our terms, the "non-synthetic joining") of the two sections of the text (*Maldoror/Poems*), which are signed by two different names: the pseudonym and the father's name. It is in deciphering the *unity* within this contradiction of texts and names that we can see that they are *moments* in the subject's experience-in-practice. Indeed the transition from Lautréamont to Ducasse, from narrative to law, from the domination by the semiotic to that of the symbolic, designates the scission in the process of the subject, which is the precondition of signifying practice. One may interpret this doubling the way Marcelin Pleynet does: ". . . the pseudonym (Lautréamont) allowed the proper name to refer to something other than its paternal heritage (which is its obvious referent). From then on Ducasse was the son of his own works."[29] This doubling thus represents a second birth, a self-engendering, eliminating the family and usurping all its roles. (Artaud was to do the same: "I am my son, my father, my mother/and myself"; and so would Mallarmé in the *Notes pour un Tombeau d'Anatole*).[30]

Although this doubling may be read as the process of psychotic totalization, it also represents something else. First of all, the pseudonym does not foreclose the name of the father since the name of the father only appears after the pseudonym has allowed the breach of the symbolic in *Maldoror*. Hence, *Maldoror* may be read as transgressions that have never abolished the law they pass through. Second, there is no biography—not a single personal reference—to hypostasize or create paranoia in the signifying process that has been brought out. In this way, the pseudonym assigned to *Maldoror* introduces the negativity or the putting-to-death of the subject; whereas the name of the father in *Poems* posits the rupture or boundary within which the subject exists but only in that he is absent. This double articulation is what Philippe Sollers calls a "thanatography": although he writes through the boundary of the name of the father and thus through the symbolic boundary, the subject of writing retains this boundary as a means of access to enunciation and denotation (*Bedeutung*) but transgresses it in order to position himself through it, nowhere, within the "imaginary" process where he is a subject-to-death [*un sujet à la mort*]. One can therefore understand why the subject of such a writing practice is not solely a subject of the utterance [*énoncé*] or a subject of enunciation [*énonciation*], and is, perhaps, neither of these:

In fact, what the literal practice of writing reveals is not an enounced/enunciation [*énoncé/énonciation*] duality, but—by means of a disjunction, a specific decentering and dissymmetry—*the enounced of the enunciation of the enounced*, or an infinite perpetuation of the enounced; or again, since the verb 'to enounce' remains too closely linked to the speaking stage, a generalized *disenunciation* continually demonstrating the absence of any subject whatsoever . . .[31]

Sollers's book, *Lois*, elaborates upon and displaces this articulation of literary practice.[32] Sollers transforms the two divided spaces of Lautréamont into a *shattered book* whose musicality and mimesis are a veritable thanatography, putting to death the positing of the subject through the orchestrated violence of a process which no aspect of the subject's experience can escape. The *social*[33] enunciation and denotation of this process involves the most acute social contradictions of the seventies, not just in France but throughout the world. Today *Maldoror* and *Poems*, subjectivity and objectivity, the universe of the ego and that of society, negativity and positivity are no longer separate. Instead they interpenetrate, call each other into question, and prevent the narcissistic-literary fall of the first set of terms, and the repressive-metalinguistic assumption of the second set. Lautréamont is no stranger to today's "thanatography-truth-in-practice" for his own statements are reversed (in the same way those of Pascal and Vauvenargues are reversed in *Poems*): neither true nor false, their truth consists in the ability to participate in the process of contradiction which, logically and historically, both includes and goes beyond them.

There is one inevitable moment in the movement that recognizes the symbolic prohibition and makes it dialectical: *laughter*. Practice, as we have defined it, posits prohibitions, the ego, "meaning," etc., and makes them dialectical, and *laughter* is the operation that attests to this mechanism. Freud views witticisms as the simultaneous preservation of the ego and the socialization of psychic activity (which makes it different from dreaming).[34] But here, in the heterogeneous articulation of the pseudonym and the name—fiction and law—where semiotic motility becomes a formula and where that formula dissolves within the negativity that produces it, what is involved is much more than a witticism.

A witticism is merely an epiphenomenon of the more general trajectory located at the junction of the two sides of the signifying process. This trajectory is common to all practice to the extent that a subject is posited there only to make himself absent. Hegel defines this trajectory as the endpoint of the dialectic of the Idea, which is turned back upon itself in self-interrogation, but only after having asserted its authority. According to Hegel, this is the reason comedy can only be undertaken by a sovereign people, such as the Greek δῆμος.[35] But outside this democratic objectification and following it, the "artist" is the one called upon to pursue the doubling process in which he (as subject) posits himself as sovereign at the very moment he shatters within the process encompassing this position.

Baudelaire[36] emphasizes the contradictory structure of laughter which embraces an infinite "pride" and "misery" and rebels against theological authority: "The Word Incarnate never laughed;" laughter is "one of the numerous pips contained in the symbolic apple," and as a result, it is "generally the prerogative of madmen" precisely because it designates an irruption of the drives against symbolic prohibition: "Melmoth is a living contradiction. He has parted company with the fundamental conditions of life; his bodily organs can no longer sustain his thought." Although laughter thus indicates one of the internal laws governing meaning only a few rare philosophers can become the *subject* of laughter (whereas anyone can be its *object*). It is above all the "artist" who must accomplish, in each of his actions, what the instant of laughter reveals to the philosopher only in rare privileged moments. Consequently Baudelaire writes that laughter "comes into the class of all artistic phenomena which indicate the existence of a permanent dualism in the human being—that is, the power of being oneself and someone else at one and the same time." Laughter is thus merely the *witness of a process* which remains the privileged experience of the "artist": a sovereignty (of the subject and of meaning, but also of history) that is simultaneously assumed and undermined. Thus, since "the nations of the world will see a multiplication of comic themes in proportion as their superiority increases," it is clearly up to the "artist" to guide them on this path.[37]

At this point one could speak at length about Lautréamont's debt to "satanic" romantic laughter, to Melmoth, or to the Gothic novel in general. But what is interesting here is that Lautréamont goes far beyond his precursors by displacing the "phenomenon of laughter" onto a *more general logic*—a logic which Baudelaire had already considered characteristic of the "class of all artistic phenomena." Lautréamont makes laughter the *symptom of rupture* and of the heterogeneous contradiction within signifying practice when he requires that poetry *bring about an explosion of laughter within metalanguage* at the same time he *refuses the laughter* that is a phenomenon of psychological decompression (or compensation) or narcissistic compromise. Thus he writes: "The theorem is in its nature a form of mockery. It is not indecent"; yet he also says, "I despise and execrate pride and the indecent delights of that extinguishing irony which disjoints the precision of our thought."[38]

We now understand why laughter is given only negative connotations in *Maldoror*: "laugh like a rooster"; "[Maldoror] eventually burst out laughing. It was too much for him! . . . he laughed as sheep do"; and, in the following opposition between laughter and poetry: "But know this: poetry happens to be wherever the stupidly mocking smile of duck-faced man is not." Laughter always indicates an act of aggression against the Creator, or rather, a rejection of the Creator: "anathemata—specialists in provoking laughter";[39] "Wielding my terrible ironies in my firm untrembling hand, I warn you [O Creator] that my heart will contain enough to keep on attacking you until my existence ends. I shall strike your hollow carcass . . . cunning bandit . . . This I have done and now they no longer fear you."[40]

Laughter is what lifts inhibitions by breaking through prohibition (symbolized by the Creator) to introduce the aggressive, violent, liberating drive.[41] Yet when this contradiction takes place within a subject, it can hardly be said to make him laugh: "My reasoning will sometimes jingle the bells of madness and the serious appearance of what is, after all, merely grotesque (although according to some philosophers, it is quite difficult to tell the difference between the clown and the melancholic man, life itself being but a comic tragedy or a tragic comedy)."[42]

Contradiction provokes laughter only when at least one of its terms is removed from the one who laughs; whereas nothing is funny (except the *effect*, which in such a case is one of supreme comedy) when the subject himself is the theater of contradiction: "Seeing these exhibitions I've longed to laugh, with the rest, but that strange imitation was impossible." "I do not know what laughter is, true, never having experienced it myself." "I have just proved that nothing on this planet is laughable. Droll but lofty planet."[43] There is a strange problem in the way laughter works: the ego that laughs through the irruption of the drive charge tearing open the symbolic, is not the one that observes and knows. In order to make the irruptive charge pass into discourse so that the addressee may laugh, the instigator of laughter, just like the artist, must bind or rebind the charge. This new binding is already a dis-position, a new prohibition which prevents a drifting-into-non-sense [*dérive*] as well as pleasure. Freud remarked that "the expenditure on the joke-work is in every case deducted from the yield resulting from the lifting of the inhibition . . . We are not, it seems, in a position to see further on this point."[44] The laughter of the one who produces that laughter is thus always painful, forced, black: both the prohibition to be lifted and the prohibition necessary to the articulation of the utterance weigh heavily on him. In other words, he replaces the effect of laughter with the production of new devices (new texts, a new art): "But know this: poetry happens to be wherever the stupidly mocking smile . . . is not"; and, conversely, the new devices contain the rupture from which laughter bursts forth.

The practice of the text is a kind of laughter whose only explosions are those of language. The pleasure obtained from the lifting of inhibitions is immediately invested in the production of the new. Every practice which produces something new (a new device) is a practice of laughter: it obeys laughter's logic and provides the subject with laughter's advantages. When practice is not laughter, there is nothing new; where there is nothing new, practice cannot be provoking: it is at best a repeated, empty act. The novelty of a practice (that of the text or any practice) indicates the jouissance invested therein and this quality of newness is the equivalent of the laughter it conceals. Beyond merely laughable phenomena and through prohibition, Lautréamont's text bears this message for social practice.

7.

The Expenditure
of a Logical Conclusion:
Igitur

MALLARMÉ'S IGITUR points toward the specific arena of this social practice: a hazardous act putting into play the disappear-
ances of the symbolic; Mallarmé calls it "chance" [*le hasard*]. In
order to come about, this practice incorporates the symbolic, but
expends itself while bringing it about. Such a practice is neither
science nor madness, neither the familial, national, or racial historical lineage, nor the anachronistic ego—neither time nor its loss.
Indeed the character in this scene is logic itself—*Igitur* [in Latin:
therefore]—which has become its interdependent opposite—
madness—in order to call attention to what is lacking in both:
active chance, which cannot be discursively, linearly stated—A
Throw of the Dice will be its realization in language. In this movement from logic to madness to active chance, madness is necessary.

Mallarmé calls madness useful because it foils the piracy
of a certain logic whose order is dependent upon the social order,
which is to say the familial, ancestral, and reproductive order
handed down through the ages. Madness places the infinity of
signifiance within a subject who then imagines he possesses it;
as a result, he splits off from his family and its history, which had
relegated infinity to the Absolute of religion. In making himself
the living representative of infinity, the subject (Igitur) immobilizes it, immobilizes himself, and dies the victim of the logic he
had contested. Even so, to "personify" signifying infinity is an act

which, as such, not only includes but also binds *chance*: that "drop of nothingness lacking in the sea," the impossibility of completing, circumscribing, harnessing, and assimilating signifying infinity. This is why only the act (by which we mean the poetic act) can bring about the expenditure of infinity through chance and prevent infinity from turning in on itself, knowing itself, making itself logical as an insane Igitur. Igitur is, then, the truth behind the Hegelian subject of absolute knowledge: madness is what the syllogism stumbles against on its way toward mastering the infinite. Thus, for Mallarmé, the madman who had transgressed prohibitions (notably, ones his mother had imposed) is the accomplice or the underside of the learned family, to the extent that both the madman and the learned family deny—though differently—the hazardous expenditure inherent in the signifying process: the madman in identifying with that expenditure (on the edges of obsessional neurosis and paranoia), the learned family by excluding it.

The alternative is to attempt to perform the signifying and thetic act (a "throw of the dice") anyway, but by shattering the essential unity of the throw into a multiplicity of chancy and chance-determined fragmentations [*brisures hasardées*] that are nevertheless arranged in "numbers" and in a "constellation" as if they designated through and beyond their fixed position what we have called the dangerous motility of the semiotic *chora*: "(The empty vial, madness, all that remains of the castle?) Nothingness having departed, only the castle of purity remains."—"*or the dice—absorbed chance.*"[45]

A CONSTELLATION

cold with forgetfulness and disuse
not so much
that it does not enumerate
on some vacant and superior surface
the successive shock
siderally
of a count total in formation

    watching
        doubting
            rolling
                shining and meditating

                            before stopping
            at some last point which sanctifies it

            Every Thought Gives Forth a Throw of the Dice.[46]

    This "last point which sanctifies" the throw of the dice is
what we have called a thetic moment of the signifying process
and is precisely what makes this game a practice. But this practice (this "Act") is acted upon by "chance"—the nonsymbolic expenditure, the very semiotic game of dice: this is what poetic
practice means to Igitur, the logical madman:

*In short, in an act where chance is in play, it is always chance which accom-
plishes its own Idea by affirming or denying itself. Faced with the existence of
chance, negation and affirmation come to naught.*[47] *Chance contains the
Absurd—implies it, though in a latent state,—and prevents it from existing,
which allows the Infinite to be.*

    The Dicehorn is the Horn of the unicorn—of the unihorn. [Le Cornet
est la Corne de la licorne—de l'unicorne.][48]

    The unity, the phallic unicity of the horn [*corne*] is a dice-
horn [*cornet*]: a body born [*corps né*], a dice game. If this unity is
accomplished in the act, then the latter, to its credit, improves
society and history, but for the subject, the act's sole function is
to make him coincide with the infinite (as does Hegel's "absolute
knowledge"):

Whereupon his self becomes manifest in that he takes up Madness once again: accepts the act and, willingly, takes up the Idea
as Idea: and since the Act (guided by whatever power) denied
chance, he concludes that the Idea was necessary.
. . . .

    All that this means is that his race has been pure, that it
took purity away from the Absolute in order to be it and leave

nothing but its Idea, itself culminating in Necessity; and that, as for the Act, it is prefectly absurd except as a (personal) movement rendered to the Infinite, but that the Infinite is finally *fixed in place*.[49]

To personify infinity is to deny chance, abolish ruptures, immobilize the infinite, make it exist, and represent it: the infinite, Igitur, is "an anachronism, a character, the supreme incarnation of this race." Such is the "madman" who possesses the future: the prophet, "a throw of the dice that fulfills a prediction," "no chance in any sense."[50] Although he constitutes the logical conclusion of his race, Igitur is nevertheless engaged in an internal struggle with its piracy:

The infinite emerges out of chance, which you have denied. You, mathematicians, have died—I am projected as the absolute. I was to finish as the Infinite. Simply speech |*parole*| and gesture. As for what I tell you, to explain my life. Nothing of you shall remain— The infinite finally escapes the family, which has suffered from it—old space—no chance. The family was right to disavow him— his life—so that he might be the absolute.[51]

Unable to see himself in the mirror, disappearing there, Igitur is "made unstable by the mania for idealism: this ennui." The heir to symbolic mastery has only one choice: ennui and the impotence of the obsessive or the simultaneous disappearance of the mirror and time ("He separates himself from indefinite time and he is!") Logic would have him be everything at once: the victim, the madman, the dead man in the family. The subject of logic is merely death, the arrested process.—"On the ashes of the stars, those undivided ashes of the family, / the poor character was lying down, having / drunk the drop of nothingness lacking in the sea."[52]

Yet there are "several sketches of the exit from the bedroom"[53] and the most radical consists in transgressing the mother's order not to play in the tombs. The mother is the keeper of the last, the most radical, the most insidious prohibition, the one that safeguards the race's continuity by maintaining the mystery around the process of the subject (which Freud was to unveil by analyzing sexuality and which Mallarmé explores through the language of madness denied).

Disregarding this prohibition—though we shall see that his transgression of it remains ambiguous—Igitur descends the "other side" of the "notion" where there is no longer any symbolic, but where there reigns instead a "perverse and unconscious confusion" as well as the "Nothingness-as-substance" leading to death. With an accuracy that no psychoanalysis has yet been able to match, Mallarmé evokes what Freud would later clarify and describe: the transgression of this prohibition, laid down by the mother, causes the rupture of symbolic binding and, through perversion and substantialism, leads to madness and death—a trajectory whose nucleus can be found in infantile traumatism.

(His *mother's prohibition against descending that way—his mother who told him what he was supposed to accomplish. For him he is also moving in a childhood memory, if he killed himself, on that favored night, he could not, grown up, carry out the act.*)[54]

He proceeds despite his mother's prohibition:

He can go forward because he is surrounded in mystery. . . . This is the reverse course of the *notion* whose ascent he did not know, having arrived, adolescent, at the Absolute: spiral, at the top of which he remained as Absolute, incapable of moving . . . Finally he arrives at the place where he must arrive and sees the act that separates him from death.
　　Another childish antic.
　　He says: I cannot do this seriously: but the pain I am suffering is horrible, from living: at the core of this perverse and unconscious confusion of things that isolates his absoluteness—he feels the absence of the self, represented by the existence of Nothingness-as-substance, I must die, and since this vial contains the nothingness which my race deferred until me . . .[55]

Sexual and generalized impotence or death in madness: this is the alternative bequeathed to Igitur by "the race" which thought of itself as the subject *present* in the infinity of his history.

　　Yet there is one act that can serve to denounce the inanity of "their madness": it attests to the existence of this madness and, in so doing, streaks speech, opens up its unity and its "process-of-becoming-mad" toward a "matter" that exceeds it. This Mallarméan act sums up the import of the signifying practice as the place of a contradiction whose sole witness is the subject. This Mallarméan act is, in a sense, *Igitur*: the logical conclusion of an expenditure, the expenditure of a logical conclusion, the throw and the dice—

the absurd act which attests to the inanity of their madness. . . .
Do not hiss because I spoke of the inanity of your madness! silence, none of this lunacy that you purposely want to show. So! it's so easy for you to go back up there to seek out time—and to become—are the doors closed?
I alone—I alone—I shall know nothingness. You, you come back to your amalgam.[56]

What is this "knowledge" of negativity that has no learned, familial, or insane amalgams?—"I say the word [*Je profère la parole*] in order to plunge it back into inanity." It will be a timely, just, unified word and even, as the ancestors wanted it, a prediction. Yet in its positing, the act (which is always in some sense mad because it is transgressive), will inscribe the hazardous discontinuities that are played straight out of matter: "He throws the dice, the move is made, twelve, the time (Midnight)—the one who created once again becomes matter, blocks, dice—. . . certainly this is an act—it is my duty to proclaim it: this madness exists. You were right (noise of madness) to show it: do not think that I will plunge you back into nothingness."[57] In this sense, *Igitur*—the wild panic of reason, the logical conclusion of madness—will not take place: what takes its place so as to bring about the expenditure of logic is the syntax of A *Throw of the Dice*. But what is it that checks a definitive submersion into the semiotic *chora*? What prevents the foreclosure of the symbolic?
The means by which the subject is able to face up to the death drive turns out to be filial affection: "I do not want to know Nothingness until I have given back to my forebears that for which they engendered me."[58] Genealogy reclaims its rights, and there the subject takes shelter in order to posit himself, if only temporarily, so that he may throw the dice of expenditure-in-practice. This means that the forbidden mother does not in fact lose her

rights. She reappears as the race, ancestral lineage, and species whose survival must be ensured and whose knowledge must be carried on. Although the law of this gynaeceum sustains Igitur's play in the tombs and thus saves him from death, it makes him, necessarily, fetishistic. At the same time, through this genealogical angle, Igitur, who thinks he is joining his game to history, is actually introducing into history the "absurd act," expenditure-in-practice. All of the ambiguities, limits, and advances of the modern text can be seen in this loop that perpetuates history and at the same time expends it, thus constituting the dawn of a new era: that of failed delirium, the insane excess of "those raging in the pursuit of intelligence" |*furieux d'intelligence*| who will try all possible transgressions in order to turn them into new devices so that, through this practice, history may rediscover its mainspring in "matter, blocks, dice."

As Sollers has written, this practice no longer has anything to do with the concept of literature. How, then, can we talk about it?

A COMPREHENSIVE THEORY |THEORIE D'ENSEMBLE| IS CALLED FOR, DERIVED FROM THE PRACTICE OF WRITING.
. . . .
From the practice signifies that it has become impossible, beginning with a rupture that can be precisely situated in history, to make writing an object that can be studied by any means other than writing itself (its exercise, under certain conditions). In other words, the specific problematic of writing breaks decisively with myth and representation to think itself in its literality and its space. Its practice is to be defined on the level of the "text," a word which henceforth refers to a function writing does not "express," but of which it *disposes*. A dramatic economy whose "geometrical locus" is not representable (it is performed |*il se joue*|).[59]

Faced with this expenditure-in-practice of history, theoretical discourse can only mark off its scansions. *The only way theoretical discourse itself can be a practice* is to become the historian of these practices that streak through historical reasoning.[60]

Here we arrive at the heart of the question concerning the *ethical function* of the text, or the ethical function of art in general.

Abandoned by formalism, transformed into a moralist humanism by idealist philosophy and vulgar sociologism, the question cannot be asked again except from a new perspective that takes into account the process/trial of the subject in language or, more generally, in meaning. "Ethics" should be understood here to mean the negativizing of narcissism within a *practice*; in other words, a practice is ethical when it dissolves those narcissistic fixations (ones that are narrowly confined to the subject) to which the signifying process succumbs in its socio-symbolic realization. Practice, such as we have defined it, positing and dissolving meaning and the unity of the subject, therefore encompasses the ethical. The text, in its signifying disposition and its signification, is a practice assuming all positivity in order to negativize it and thereby make visible the *process* underlying it. It can thus be considered, precisely, as that which carries out the ethical imperative. Given this insight, one cannot ask that "art"—the text—emit a message which would be considered "positive": the univocal enunciation of such a message would itself represent a suppression of the ethical function as we understand it. By stating scientific truths about the process of the subject (his discourse, his sexuality) and the tendencies of current historical processes, the text fulfills its ethical function only when it pluralizes, pulverizes, "musicates" these truths, which is to say, on the condition that it develop them to the point of laughter.

This conception of the ethical function of art separates us, in a radical way, from one that would commit art to serving as the representation of a so-called progressive ideology or an avant-garde socio-historical philosophy. The latter view denies the specificity of "art," which is its position between metalanguage or contemplation on the one hand and the irruption of drives on the other.

This notion of "art" 's ethical function also separates us from Hegel's idealist position, which sees art as a means of repressing or "purifying" the passions as it represents them: "Art by means of its representations, while remaining within the sensuous sphere, liberates man at the same time from the power of sensuousness." Hegelianism leads to an ethical subordination of art to philosophy, since only the latter is thought to be capable of absorbing both sides of the nature/law contradiction; art, by contrast, is believed to accentuate their "universal and thoroughgoing opposition."[61]

Finally, our notion of the ethical as coextensive with textual practice separates us from the "scientific morality" that would like to found a normative, albeit apparently libertarian, ethics based on knowledge. As we have perhaps already overstated, such a moralism preaches the foreclosure of the subject-as-model, provided that the uniformity of a transcendental ego is still cast there. The stated ethic betrays the leader who advocates it: the Good he professes, backed up with scientific proofs, denotes the teleology of the necessarily oppressive System. And thus, in terms of results, mechanistic rationalism joins Hegel's normative idealism.

The ethical cannot be stated, instead it is practiced to the point of loss, and the text is one of the most accomplished examples of such a practice. Mallarmé writes: "I revere Poe's opinion, no trace of a philosophy, ethics or metaphysics will show through, but let me add that it must be included and latent."[62]

Notes

TRANSLATOR'S PREFACE

1. "Homage and parricide" is Gayatri Spivak's formulation; I have extended it here to refer not only to the translator's preface but to the act of translating itself. See also her discussion of the uncertain epistemological status of "original" and "secondary" texts in her "Translator's Preface," Jacques Derrida, *Of Grammatology* (Baltimore: Johns Hopkins University Press, 1976), p. xi. The figurative parricide is further complicated in the present case by the gender of the author and the translator.

2. Kristeva has written a "memoir" of that period, published in French on the occasion of the demise of *Tel Quel* and the first issue of *L'Infini*; see "Mémoire," *L'Infini* (Winter 1983), 1:39–54. The article was originally written for the issue of *New York Literary Forum* entitled "The Female Autograph" (1984), edited by Domna C. Stanton, where it appears in translation.

3. Kristeva, "Preface," *Desire in Language* (New York: Columbia University Press, 1980), p. ix.

4. "Interview with Perry Meisel," Margaret Waller, tr., a portion of which has been published in *Partisan Review* (Winter 1984) 51(1):128–132.

5. Philip Lewis, "Revolutionary Semiotics," *Diacritics* (Fall 1974), 4(3):28–32. For an example of the more detailed and "concretized" textual analyses in the latter portion of *La Révolution*, see Caren Greenberg's translation, "Phonetics, Phonology, and Impulsional Bases," *ibid.*, pp. 33–37.

6. See part I, section 13B.

7. See the useful explanation of Kristeva's terms and of the rationale behind their English translation in the introduction to *Desire in Language*, pp. 1–12.

8. Kristeva explained in a note to me that "the 'subject' in this book is so abstract or universal that it concerns both sexes. We can therefore keep the 'he' . . . In reality, feminine 'subjectivity' is a different question but it does not elude the general realm of *subjecthood* [*subjecticité*], or of subjectivation."

9. *The Language of Psycho-Analysis*, Daniel Lagache, introd., Donald Nicholson-Smith, tr. (London: Hogarth Press, 1973).

10. Grange Woolley, *Stéphane Mallarmé* (Madison, N.J.: Drew University, 1942; rpt. New York: AMS Press, 1981); *Mallarmé: Selected Prose Poems, Essays, and Letters*, Bradford Cook, tr. and introd. (Baltimore: Johns Hopkins University Press, 1956); and *Igitur*, Jack Hirschman, tr. (Los Angeles: Press of the Pegacycle Lady, 1974). Elizabeth Seawell's *The Structure of Poetry* (London: Routledge and Kegan-Paul, 1951) also includes translations from Mallarmé. Robert Greer Cohn offers a line-by-line reading of *Igitur* in his *Mallarmé: Igitur* (Berkeley: University of California Press, 1981).

INTRODUCTION BY LEON S. ROUDIEZ

1. For example, La Révolution du langage poétique appeared in 1974 and a German translation came out four years later, in 1978. A little over ten years separate the present English translation from the French original. Works previously translated into English include On Chinese Women (New York: Urizen Books, 1977); a selection of essays, Desire in Language (New York: Columbia University Press, 1980); and Powers of Horror (New York: Columbia University Press, 1982).

2. Louis Althusser, Lire le Capital (Paris: FM/Petite collection Maspero, 1970), 1:12.

3. Roman Jakobson, Essais de linguistique générale (Paris: Minuit, 1963), p. 218.

4. Julia Kristeva, Recherches pour une sémanalyse (Paris: Seuil, 1969), pp. 178–79.

5. Jean-Paul Sartre, "L'Engagement de Mallarmé," Obliques (1979), 18–19:169–94; the quotation is from p. 183n.

6. Jacques Lacan, Ecrits (Paris: Seuil, 1966), p. 257.

7. Julia Kristeva, Jean-Claude Milner, and Nicolas Ruwet, eds., Langue, discours, société (Paris: Seuil, 1975), p. 230.

8. Susan Sontag, Under the Sign of Saturn (New York: Vintage, 1981), p. 25.

9. Evelyn H. Zepp, "The Criticism of Julia Kristeva: A New Mode of Critical Thought," Romanic Review (January 1982), 73(1):80–97.

10. Cf. Lotfi A. Zadeh et al., editors. Fuzzy Sets and Their Applications to Cognitive and Decision Processes (New York: Academic Press, 1975).

11. Julia Kristeva, Le Texte du roman (The Hague: Mouton, 1970), p. 50.

12. Jean-Paul Sartre, Situations II (Paris: Gallimard, 1948), p. 103.

13. For a preliminary examination of some of these points, see Leon S. Roudiez, "Absalom, Absalom!: The Significance of Contradictions," The Minnesota Review (Fall 1981), NS17:58–78.

14. Roland Barthes, "To Write: An Intransitive Verb?" in Richard Mackey and Eugenio Donato, eds., The Languages of Criticism and the Sciences of Man (Baltimore: The Johns Hopkins Press, 1970), pp. 134–45.

15. Julia Kristeva, La Révolution du langage poétique (Paris: Seuil, 1974), p. 338.

16. Francois-René Buleu, "Tel Quel à l'amphi," Le Monde, July 5, 1973, p. 15.

PROLEGOMENON

1. "Device" is Kristeva's own choice for the translation of "dispositif": something devised or constructed for a particular purpose.—Trans.

2. The expression "le renversement de Hegel" refers to a complex series of visions and revisions of the materialist debt to Hegel's dialectic. Kristeva's use of the term would seem to be informed by Althusser's "symptomatic reading" of Marx. In "Contradiction and Overdetermination," Althusser questions Marx's ambiguous and metaphorical statement that the Hegelian dialectic is "standing on its head" and "must be turned right side up again," and he argues that the materialist "inversion" of Hegel is no inversion at all. For Marx, Ben Brewster, tr. (New York: Random House, 1969), pp. 89–116. I have therefore translated "renversement" as "overturning" to convey the notion of a radical transformation that may or may not consist in a "reversal" of Hegel's dialectic.—Trans.

3. Gilles Deleuze and Félix Guattari, Anti-Oedipus: Capitalism and Schizophrenia, Robert Hurley et al., tr. (New York: Viking Press, 1977).

I. THE SEMIOTIC AND THE SYMBOLIC

1. See Zellig Harris, *Mathematical Structures of Language* (New York: Interscience Publishers, 1968). See also Maurice Gross and André Lentin, *Introduction to Formal Grammars*, M. Salkoff, tr. (Berlin: Springer-Verlag, 1970); M.-C. Barbault and J.-P. Desclés, *Transformations formelles et théories linguistiques*, Documents de linguistique quantitative, no. 11 (Paris: Dunod, 1972).

2. On this "object" see *Langages* (December 1971), vol. 24, and, for a didactic, popularized account, see Julia Kristeva, *Le Langage cet inconnu* (Paris: Seuil, 1981).

3. Edmund Husserl, in *Ideas: General Introduction to Pure Phenomenology*, W. R. Boyce Gibson, tr. (London: Allen & Unwin, 1969), posits this subject as a subject of intuition, sure of this universally valid unity [of consciousness], a unity that is provided in *categories* itself, since transcendence is precisely the immanence of this "Ego," which is an expansion of the Cartesian *cogito*. "We shall consider conscious experiences," Husserl writes, "*in the concrete fullness and entirety* with which they figure in their concrete context—the *stream of experience*—and to which they are closely attached through their own proper essence. It then becomes evident that every experience in the stream which our reflexion can lay hold on has *its own essence open to intuition*, a 'content' which can be considered in its *singularity in and for itself*. We shall be concerned to grasp this individual content of the *cogitatio* in its *pure singularity*, and to describe it in its general features, excluding everything which is not to be found in the *cogitatio* as it is in itself. We must likewise describe the *unity of consciousness* which is demanded *by the intrinsic nature of the cogitationes*, and so necessarily demanded that they could not be without this unity" (p. 116). From a similar perspective, Benveniste emphasizes language's dialogical character, as well as its role in Freud's discovery. Discussing the I/you polarity, he writes: "This polarity does not mean either equality or symmetry: 'ego' always has a position of transcendence with regard to *you*." In Benveniste, "Subjectivity in Language," *Problems in General Linguistics*, Miami Linguistics Series, no. 8, Mary Elizabeth Meek, tr. (Coral Gables, Fla.: University of Miami Press, 1971), p. 225. In Chomsky, the subject-bearer of syntactic synthesis is clearly shown to stem from the Cartesian *cogito*. See his *Cartesian Linguistics: A Chapter in the History of Rationalist Thought* (New York: Harper & Row, 1966). Despite the difference between this Cartesian-Chomskyan subject and the transcendental ego outlined by Benveniste and others in a more clearly phenomenological sense, both these notions of the act of understanding (or the linguistic act) rest on a common metaphysical foundation: consciousness as a synthesizing unity and the sole guarantee of Being. Moreover, several scholars—without renouncing the Cartesian principles that governed the first syntactic descriptions—have recently pointed out that Husserlian phenomenology is a more explicit and more rigorously detailed basis for such description than the Cartesian method. See Roman Jakobson, who recalls Husserl's role in the establishment of modern linguistics, "Linguistics in Relation to Other Sciences," in *Selected Writings*, 2 vols. (The Hague: Mouton, 1971), 2:655–696; and S.-Y. Kuroda, "The Categorical and the Thetic Judgment: Evidence from Japanese Syntax," *Foundations of Language* (November 1972), 9(2):153–185.

4. See the work of Ivan Fónagy, particularly "Bases pulsionnelles de la phonation," *Revue Française de Psychanalyse* (January 1970), 34(1):101–136, and (July 1971), 35(4):543–591.

5. On the "subject of enunciation," see Tzvetan Todorov, spec. ed., *Langages* (March 1970), vol. 17. Formulated in linguistics by Benveniste ("The Correlations of Tense in the French Verb" and "Subjectivity in Language," in *Problems*, pp. 205–216 and 223–230), the notion is used by many linguists, notably Antoine Culioli, "A propos d'opérations inter-

venant dans le traitement formel des langues naturelles," *Mathématiques et Sciences Humaines* (Summer 1971), 9(34):7–15; and Oswald Ducrot, "Les Indéfinis et l'énonciation," *Langages* (March 1970), 5(17):91–111. Chomsky's "extended standard theory" makes use of categorial intuition but does not refer to the subject of enunciation, even though the latter has been implicit in his theory ever since *Cartesian Linguistics* (1966); see his *Studies on Semantics in Generative Grammar*, Janua Linguarum, series minor, no. 107 (The Hague: Mouton, 1972).

    6. See John R. Searle, *Speech Acts: An Essay on the Philosophy of Language* (London: Cambridge University Press, 1969).

    7. See Robert D. King, *Historical Linguistics and Generative Grammar* (Englewood Cliffs, N.J.: Prentice-Hall, 1969); Paul Kiparsky, "Linguistic Universals and Linguistic Change," in *Universals of Linguistic Theory*, Emmon Bach and Robert T. Harms, eds. (New York: Holt, Rinehart and Winston, 1968), pp. 170–202; and Kiparsky, "How Abstract Is Phonology?" mimeograph reproduced by Indiana University Linguistics Club, October 1968.

    8. S.-Y. Kuroda distinguishes between two styles, "reportive" and "non-reportive." "Reportive" includes first-person narratives as well as those in the second and third person in which the narrator is "effaced"; "non-reportive" involves an omniscient narrator or "multi-consciousness." This distinction explains certain anomalies in the distribution of the adjective and verb of sensation in Japanese. (Common usage requires that the adjective be used with the first person but it can also refer to the third person. When it does, this agrammaticality signals another "grammatical style": an omniscient narrator is speaking in the name of a character, or the utterance expresses a character's point of view.) No matter what its subject of enunciation, the utterance, Kuroda writes, is described as representing that subject's "*Erlebnis*" ("experience"), in the sense Husserl uses the term in *Ideas*. See Kuroda, "Where Epistemology, Style, and Grammar Meet," mimeographed, University of California, San Diego, 1971.

    9. Even the categories of dialectical materialism introduced to designate a discourse's conditions of production as essential bestowers of its signification are based on a "subject-bearer" whose logical positing is no different from that found in Husserl (see above, n. 3). For example, Cl. Haroche, P. Henry, and Michel Pêcheux stress "the importance of linguistic studies on the relation between utterance and enunciation, by which the 'speaking subject' situates himself with respect to the representations he *bears*—representations that are put together by means of the linguistically analyzable 'pre-constructed.'" They conclude that "it is undoubtedly on this point—together with that of the syntagmatization of the characteristic substitutions of a discursive formation—that the contribution of the theory of discourse to the study of ideological formation (and the theory of ideologies) can now be most fruitfully developed." "La Sémantique et la coupure saussurienne: Langue, langage, discours," *Langages* (December 1971), 24:106. This notion of the subject as always already there on the basis of a "pre-constructed" language (but how is it constructed? and what about the subject *who constructs* before *bearing* what has been constructed?) has even been preserved under a Freudian cover. As a case in point, Michel Tort questions the relation between psychoanalysis and historical materialism by placing a subject-bearer between "ideological agency" and "unconscious formations." He defines this subject-bearer as "the biological specificity of individuals (individuality as a biological concept), inasmuch as it is the material basis upon which individuals are called to function by social relations." "La Psychanalyse dans le matérialisme historique," *Nouvelle Revue de Psychanalyse* (Spring 1970), 1:154. But this theory provides only a hazy view of how this subject-bearer is produced through the unconscious and within the "ideological" signifier, and does not allow us to see this production's investment in ideological repre-

sentations themselves. From this perspective, the only thing one can say about "arts" or "religions," for example, is that they are "relics." On language and history, see also Jean-Claude Chevalier, "Langage et histoire," *Langue Française* (September 1972), 15:3–17.

10. On the phenomenological bases of modern linguistics, see Kristeva, "Les Epistémologies de la linguistique," *Langages* (December 1971), 24:11; and especially: Jacques Derrida, "The Supplement of Copula: Philosophy Before Linguistics," Josué V. Harari, tr., *Textual Strategies*, Josué V. Harari, ed. (Ithaca, N.Y.: Cornell University Press, 1979), pp. 82–120; *Of Grammatology*, Gayatri Chakravorty Spivak, tr. (Baltimore: Johns Hopkins University Press, 1976), pp. 27–73; and *Speech and Phenomena, and Other Essays on Husserl's Theory of Signs*, David B. Allison, introd. and tr. (Evanston, Ill.: Northwestern University Press, 1973).

11. The term *"chora"* has recently been criticized for its ontological essence by Jacques Derrida, *Positions*, Alan Bass, annotator and tr. (Chicago: University of Chicago Press, 1981), pp. 75 and 106, n. 39.

12. Plato emphasizes that the receptacle ($\dot{v}\pi o\delta o\chi\epsilon\hat{i}ov$), which is also called space ($\chi\dot{\omega}\rho\alpha$) vis-à-vis reason, is necessary—but not divine since it is unstable, uncertain, ever changing and becoming; it is even unnameable, improbable, bastard: "Space, which is everlasting, not admitting destruction; providing a situation for all things that come into being, but itself apprehended without the senses by a sort of bastard reasoning, and hardly an object of belief. This, indeed, is that which we look upon as in a dream and say that anything that is must needs be in some place and occupy some room . . ." (*Timaeus*, Francis M. Cornford, tr., 52a–52b). Is the receptacle a "thing" or a mode of language? Plato's hesitation between the two gives the receptacle an even more uncertain status. It is one of the elements that antedate not only the *universe* but also *names* and even *syllables*: "We speak . . . positing them as original principles, elements (as it were, letters) of the universe; whereas one who has ever so little intelligence should not rank them in this analogy even so low as syllables" (*ibid.*, 48b). "It is hard to say, with respect to any one of these, which we ought to call really water rather than fire, or indeed which we should call by any given name rather than by all the names together or by each severally, so as to use language in a sound and trustworthy way. . . . Since, then, in this way no one of these things ever makes its appearance as the *same* thing, which of them can we steadfastly affirm to be *this*—whatever it may be—and not something else, without blushing for ourselves? It cannot be done" (*ibid.*, 49b–d).

13. There is a fundamental ambiguity: on the one hand, the receptacle is mobile and even contradictory, without unity, separable and divisible: pre-syllable, pre-word. Yet, on the other hand, because this separability and divisibility antecede numbers and forms, the space or receptacle is called *amorphous*; thus its suggested rhythmicity will in a certain sense be erased, for how can one think an articulation of what is not yet singular but is nevertheless necessary? All we may say of it, then, to make it intelligible, is that it is amorphous but that it "is of such and such a quality," not even an index or something in particular ("this" or "that"). Once named, it immediately becomes a container that takes the place of infinitely repeatable separability. This amounts to saying that this repeated separability is "ontologized" the moment a *name* or a *word* replaces it, making it intelligible: "Are we talking idly whenever we say that there is such a thing as an intelligible Form of anything? Is this nothing more than a word?" (*ibid.*, 51c). Is the Platonic *chora* the "nominability" of rhythm (of repeated separation)?

Why then borrow an ontologized term in order to designate an articulation that antecedes positing? First, the Platonic term makes explicit an insurmountable problem for discourse: once it has been named, that functioning, even if it is pre-symbolic, is brought back into a symbolic position. All discourse can do is differentiate, by means of a "bastard reasoning," the receptacle from the motility, which, by contrast, is not poşited as being "a *certain* something" ["une *telle*"]. Second, this motility is the precondition for symbolicity, heterogeneous to it, yet indispensable. Therefore what needs to be done is to try and differentiate, always through a "bastard reasoning," the specific arrangements of this motility, without seeing them as recipients of accidental singularities, or a *Being* always posited in itself, or a projection of the *One*. Moreover, Plato invites us to differentiate in this fashion when he describes this motility, while gathering it into the receiving membrane: "But because it was filled with powers that were neither alike nor evenly balanced, there was no equipoise in any region of it; but it was everywhere swayed unevenly and shaken by these things, and by its motion shook them in turn. And they, being thus moved, were perpetually being separated and carried in different directions; just as when things are shaken and winnowed by means of winnowing baskets and other instruments for cleaning corn . . . it separated the most unlike kinds farthest apart from one another, and thrust the most alike closest together; whereby the different kinds came to have different regions, even before the ordered whole consisting of them came to be . . . but were altogether in such a condition as we should expect for anything when deity is absent from it" (*ibid.*, 52d–53b). Indefinite "conjunctions" and "disjunctions" (functioning, devoid of Meaning), the *chora* is governed by a necessity that is not God's law.

14. The Platonic space or receptacle is a mother and wet nurse: "Indeed we may fittingly compare the Recipient to a mother, the model to a father, and the nature that arises between them to their offspring" (*ibid.*, 50d); "Now the wet nurse of Becoming was made watery and fiery, received the characters of earth and air, and was qualified by all the other affections that go with these . . ." *Ibid.*, 52d; translation modified.

15. "Law," which derives etymologically from *lex*, necessarily implies the act of judgment whose role in safeguarding society was first developed by the Roman law courts. "Ordering," on the other hand, is closer to the series "rule," "norm" (from the Greek γνώμων, meaning "discerning" [adj.], "carpenter's square" [noun]), etc., which implies a numerical or geometrical necessity. On normativity in linguistics, see Alain Rey, "Usages, jugements et prescriptions linquistiques," *Langue Française* (December 1972), 16:5. But the temporary ordering of the *chora* is not yet even a *rule*: the arsenal of geometry is posterior to the *chora*'s motility; it fixes the *chora* in place and reduces it.

16. Operations are, rather, an act of the subject of understanding. [Hans G. Furth, in *Piaget and Knowledge: Theoretical Foundations* (Englewood Cliffs, N.J.: Prentice-Hall, 1969), offers the following definition of "concrete operations": "Characteristic of the first stage of operational intelligence. A concrete operation implies underlying general systems or 'groupings' such as classification, seriation, number. Its applicability is limited to objects considered as real (concrete)" (p. 260).—Trans.]

17. Piaget stresses that the roots of sensorimotor operations precede language and that the acquisition of thought is due to the symbolic function, which, for him, is a notion separate from that of language per se. See Jean Piaget, "Language and Symbolic Operations," in *Piaget and Knowledge*, pp. 121–130.

18. By "function" we mean a dependent variable determined each time the independent variables with which it is associated are determined. For our purposes, a function is what links stases within the process of semiotic facilitation.

19. Such a position has been formulated by Lipot Szondi, *Experimental Diagnostic of Drives*, Gertrude Aull, tr. (New York: Grune & Stratton, 1952).

20. See James D. Watson, *The Double Helix: A Personal Account of the Discovery of the Structure of DNA* (London: Weidenfeld & Nicholson, 1968).

21. Throughout her writings, Melanie Klein emphasizes the "pre-Oedipal" phase, i.e., a period of the subject's development that precedes the "discovery" of castration and the positing of the superego, which itself is subject to (paternal) Law. The processes she describes for this phase correspond, *but on a genetic level*, to what we call the semiotic, as opposed to the symbolic, which underlies and conditions the semiotic. Significantly, these pre-Oedipal processes are organized through projection onto the mother's body, for girls as well as for boys: "at this stage of development children of both sexes believe that it is the body of their mother which contains all that is desirable, especially their father's penis." *The Psycho-analysis of Children*, Alix Strachey, tr. (London: Hogarth Press, 1932), p. 269. Our own view of this stage is as follows: Without "believing" or "desiring" any "object" whatsoever, the subject is in the process of constituting himself vis-à-vis a non-object. He is in the process of separating from this non-object so as to make that non-object "one" and posit himself as "other": the mother's body is the not-yet-one that the believing and desiring subject will imagine as a "receptacle."

22. As for what situates the mother in symbolic space, we find the phallus again (see Jacques Lacan, "La Relation d'objet et les structures freudiennes," *Bulletin de Psychologie*, April 1957, pp. 426–430), represented by the mother's father, i.e., the subject's maternal grandfather (see Marie-Claire Boons, "Le Meurtre du Père chez Freud," *L'Inconscient*, January–March 1968, 5:101–129).

23. Though disputed and inconsistent, the Freudian theory of drives is of interest here because of the predominance Freud gives to the death drive in both "living matter" and the "human being." The death drive is transversal to identity and tends to disperse "narcissisms" whose constitution ensures the link between structures and, by extension, life. But at the same time and conversely, narcissism and pleasure are only temporary positions from which the death drive blazes new paths [*se fraye de nouveaux passages*]. Narcissism and pleasure are therefore inveiglings and realizations of the death drive. The semiotic *chora*, converting drive discharges into stases, can be thought of both as a delaying of the death drive and as a possible realization of this drive, which tends to return to a homeostatic state. This hypothesis is consistent with the following remark: "at the beginning of mental life," writes Freud, "the struggle for pleasure was far more intense than later but not so unrestricted: it had to submit to frequent interruptions." *Beyond the Pleasure Principle*, in *The Standard Edition of the Works of Sigmund Freud*, James Strachey, ed. (London: Hogarth Press and the Institute of Psychoanalysis, 1953), 18:63.

24. Mallarmé, *Œuvres complètes* (Paris: Gallimard, 1945), pp. 382–387.

25. *Ibid.*, p. 383.

26. *Ibid.*, pp. 383 and 385.

27. *Ibid.*, pp. 385–386.

28. See John Lyons, "Towards a 'Notional' Theory of the 'Parts of Speech,' " *Journal of Linguistics* (1966), 2(2). The metaphysical elaboration of this position can be found in P. F. Strawson, *Individuals: An Essay in Descriptive Metaphysics* (Garden City, N.Y.: Doubleday, 1959; 1963).

29. Husserl, *Ideas*, pp. 261–262.

30. J. N. Findlay, tr., 2 vols. (London: Routledge & Kegan Paul; New York: Humanities Press, 1970).

31. Following the distinction made between the two concepts in *Ideas*. [See partic-

ularly *Ideas*, p. 278. For the purposes of this translation, these terms will follow the French: "meaning" for *Sinn* and "signification" for *Bedeutung.—*Trans.|

32. *Ibid.*, pp. 246–247. [The same term, *Triebe*, is translated as "impulses" in Husserl and as "instincts" or "drives" in Freud.—Trans.|

33. *Ibid.*, pp. 363, 364–365, and 375.

34. *Ibid.*, pp. 332 and 339; translation modified.

35. The term "meaning" |*Sinn*| is thus used as a synonym for "proposition" |*Satz*|: "pure meaning |or| proposition" (*Ideas*, p. 380). Meaning is the bearer of position and positing is always rational: "*meaning* . . . *functions as the foundation of the noematic character of positionality*, or, which here means the same thing, the ontical character" (p. 380). Likewise: "The main groups of problems of the reason (problems of self-evidence) relate to the main types of theses, and the positing material (*Setzungsmaterien*) which these essentially demand. At the head, of course, come the protodoxa, the doxic modalities with the ontical modalities that correspond to them" (p. 406). And then, even more clearly, on the dependence of doxic and thetic varieties on propositional predication: "More specifically there lie in the pure forms of the *predicative* (analytic) synthesis *a priori* conditions of the possibility of *doxic rational certainty*, or in noematic terms, of *possible truth*. In thus setting it out objectively, we obtain Formal Logic in the narrowest sense of the word; *formal Apophansis* (the formal Logic of 'judgments') which thus has its basis in the formal theory of these 'judgments' " (pp. 406–407).

36. There is much that distinguishes this question from "transcendental egology." Husserl reveals within the Cartesian discovery of subjective consciousness the beginning of a new problematic: how this consciousness operates and produces. "Yet one should have realized that the terms 'external' and 'being in itself' draw their meaning exclusively from cognition, and that every affirmation, foundation, and cognition of an external existence is an operation of judgment and cognition, produced within cognition itself . . . Wasn't it true, then, that all the obscurities and difficulties which came from considering the knowing consciousness and from referring—necessarily—all objectivities and verities to a possible cognition, that all the unintelligibilities (*Unverständlichkeiten*) and enigmas in which one was more and more deeply mired, stemmed from the fact that, until then, consciousness had not been studied as an operating consciousness." *Philosophie première*, Arion L. Kelkel, tr. (Paris: Presses Universitaires de France, 1970), 1:94. What we are asking is: How did this consciousness manage to posit itself? Our concern, therefore, is not the operating and producing consciousness, but rather the producible consciousness.

37. Chomsky, *Studies on Semantics*.

38. *Ibid.*, p. 198.

39. Hjelmslev, *Prolegomena to a Theory of Language*, Francis J. Whitfield, tr. (Baltimore: Waverly Press, 1953), pp. 31–32; translation modified.

40. *Ibid.*, pp. 36, 79, and 34.

41. Although at the moment we cannot specify these relations within the constituting of different national languages, we can begin to envisage doing so on the basis of different signifying systems or practices.

42. Hjelmslev, p. 5.

43. Benveniste's reflections on the need to distinguish different signifying systems by whether their constitutive "units" are or are not *signs*, and his consequent criticism of glossematics anticipate and converge with our own analysis of this point. See Emile Benveniste, "Sémiologie de la langue (2)," *Semiotica* (1969), 1(2):127 et sq.

44. Here we shall sketch out only a few relations in this connection, those that stem from our reading of texts by Lautréamont and Mallarmé.

45. On this aspect of linguistic structuralism, see Kristeva, "Du sujet en linguistique," *Langages* (December 1971), 24:111–114; rpt. in *Polylogue* (Paris: Seuil, 1977), pp. 300–304; see also Roman Jakobson, "Two Aspects of Language and Two Types of Aphasic Disturbances," in *Selected Writings*, 2:239–259.

46. "The unconscious . . . is always empty . . . As the organ of a specific function, the unconscious merely imposes structural laws upon inarticulated elements which originate elsewhere—drives, emotions, representations, and memories. We might say, therefore, that the subconscious is the individual lexicon where each of us accumulates the vocabulary of his personal history, but that this vocabulary becomes significant, for us and for others, only to the extent that the unconscious structures it according to its laws and thus transforms it into discourse." (Claude Lévi-Strauss, "The Effectiveness of Symbols," in *Structural Anthropology*, 2 vols., Claire Jacobson and Brooke Grundfest Schoepf, trs. (New York: Basic Books, 1963), 1:203; translation modified.

47. Husserl, *Ideas*, p. 342.

48. In *Ideas*, posited meaning is "the unity of meaning and thetic character." "The concept of proposition (*Satz*)," Husserl writes, "is certainly extended thereby in an exceptional way that may alienate sympathy, yet it remains within the limits of an important unity of essence. We must constantly bear in mind that for us the concepts of meaning (*Sinn*) and posited meaning (or position) (*Satz*) contain nothing of the nature of expression and conceptual meaning, but on the other hand include all explicit propositions and all propositional meanings" (*Ideas*, p. 369). Further on, the inseparability of posited meaning, meaning, and the object is even more clearly indicated: "According to our analyses these concepts indicate an abstract stratum belonging to the *full tissue of all noemata* [emphasis added]. To grasp this stratum in its all-enveloping generality, and thus to realize that it is represented in *all act-spheres*, has a wide bearing on our way of knowledge. Even in the plain and simple *intuitions* the concepts meaning (*Sinn*) and posited meaning (*Satz*) which belong inseparably to the concept of object (*Gegenstand*) have their necessary application . . . (pp. 369–370).

49. On the matrix of the sign as the structure of a logical proof, see Emile Bréhier, *La Théorie des incorporels dans l'ancien stoicisme* (Paris: J. Vrin, 1970).

50. "The fact is that the total form of the body by which the subject anticipates in a mirage the maturation of his power is given to him only as *Gestalt*, that is to say, in an exteriority in which this form is certainly more constituent than constituted, but in which it appears to him above all in a contrasting size (*un relief de stature*) that fixes it and in a symmetry that inverts it, in contrast with the turbulent movements that the subject feels are animating him." Lacan, "The Mirror Stage as Formative of the Function of the I," in *Ecrits: A Selection*, Alan Sheridan, tr. (New York: Norton, 1977), p. 2.

51. "The Subversion of the Subject and the Dialectic of Desire in the Freudian Unconscious," *Ecrits: A Selection*, p. 319.

52. In Lacan's terminology, castration and the phallus are defined as "position," "localization," and "presence": "We know that the unconscious castration complex has the function of a knot: . . . (2) in a regulation of the development that gives its *ratio* to this first role: namely, the *installation* in the subject of an unconscious *position* without which he would be unable to identify himself with the ideal type of his sex . . ." ("The Signification of the Phallus," *Ecrits: A Selection*, p. 281; emphasis added). "We know that in this term

Freud specifies the first genital maturation: on the one hand, it would seem to be characterized by the imaginary dominance of the phallic attribute and by masturbatory *jouissance* and, on the other, it *localizes* this *jouissance* for the woman in the clitoris, which is thus raised to the function of the phallus" (p. 282; emphasis added). "[The phallus] is the signifier intended to *designate* as a whole the effects of the signified, in that the signifier conditions them by its *presence* as a signifier" (p. 285; emphasis added).

53. Lacan himself has suggested the term "want-to-be" for his neologism (*manque à être*). Other proposed translations include "want-of-being" (Leon S. Roudiez, personal communication) and "constitutive lack" (Jeffrey Mehlman, "The 'Floating Signifier': From Lévi-Strauss to Lacan," *Yale French Studies*, 1972, 48:37).—Trans.

54. *Ecrits: A Selection*, p. 299.

55. *Ibid*.

56. Our definition of language as deriving from the death drive finds confirmation in Lacan: "From the approach that we have indicated, the reader should recognize in the metaphor of the return to the inanimate (which Freud attaches to every living body) that margin beyond life that language gives to the human being by virtue of the fact that he speaks, and which is precisely that in which such a being places in the position of a signifier, not only those parts of his body that are exchangeable, but this body itself" ("The Subversion of the Subject and the Dialectic of Desire in the Freudian Unconscious," *Ecrits: A Selection*, p. 301). We would add that the symbolism of magic is based on language's capacity to store up the death drive by taking it out of the body. Lévi-Strauss suggests this when he writes that "the relationship between monster and disease is internal to [the patient's] mind, whether conscious or unconscious: It is a relationship between symbol and thing symbolized, or, to use the terminology of linguists, between signifier and signified. The shaman provides the sick woman with a *language*, by means of which unexpressed and otherwise unexpressible psychic states can be immediately expressed. And it is the transition to this verbal expression—at the same time making it possible to undergo in an ordered and intelligible form a real experience that would otherwise be chaotic and inexpressible—which induces the release of the physiological process, that is, the reorganization, in a favorable direction, of the process to which the sick woman is subjected." "The Effectiveness of Symbols," in *Structural Anthropology*, 1:197–198; translation modified.

57. See Lacan, "On a Question Preliminary to Any Possible Treatment of Psychosis," in *Ecrits: A Selection*, p. 197.

58. "The theory of textual writing's history may be termed 'monumental history' insofar as it serves as a 'ground' [*'fait fond'*] in a literal way, in relation to a 'cursive,' figural (teleological) history which has served at once to constitute and dissimulate a written/exterior space. . . . Writing 'that recognizes the rupture' is therefore irreducible to the classical (representational) concept of 'written text': what it writes is never more than one part of itself. It makes the rupture the intersection of two sets (two irreconcilable states of language)," Philippe Sollers writes, "Program," in *Writing and the Experience of Limits*, David Hayman, ed. Philip Barnard and David Hayman, trs. (New York: Columbia University Press, 1983), p. 7. Our reading of Lautréamont and Mallarmé will attempt to follow these principles, see *La Révolution du langage poétique* (Paris: Seuil, 1974), pp. 361–609. [This is the first of many references to the latter portion of *La Révolution du langage poétique*, which has not been translated.—Trans.]

59. Indeed, even Lacanian theory, although it establishes the signifier as absolute master, makes a distinction between two modalities of the signifier represented by the two levels of the "completed graph" (*Ecrits: A Selection*, p. 314). On the one hand, the *signifier*

as "signifier's treasure," as distinct from the *code*, "for it is not that the univocal correspondence of a sign with something is preserved in it, but that the signifier is constituted only from a synchronic and enumerable collection of elements in which each is sustained only by the principle of its opposition to each of the others" (p. 304). Drives function within this "treasure of the signifiers" (p. 314), which is also called a signifying "battery." But from that level on, and even beforehand, the subject submits to the signifier, which is shown as a "punctuation in which the signification is constituted as finished product" (p. 304). In this way the path from the treasure to punctuation forms a "previous site of the pure subject of the signifier," which is not yet, however, the true place |*lieu*| of the Other. On that level, the psychotic "dance" unfolds, the "pretence" |*feinte*| that "is satisfied with that previous Other," accounted for by game theory. The fact remains that this *previous site* does not exhaust the question of signification because the subject is not constituted from the code that lies in the Other, but rather from the message emitted by the Other. Only when the Other is distinguished from all other partners, unfolding as signifier and signified—and, as a result, articulating himself within an always already sentential signification and thus transmitting messages—only then are the preconditions for language ("speech") present.

At this second stage, the signifier is not just a "treasure" or a "battery" but a *place* |*lieu*|: "But it is clear that Speech begins only with the passage from 'pretence' to the order of the signifier, and that the signifier requires another locus—the locus of the Other, the Other witness, the witness Other than any of the partners—for the Speech that it supports to be capable of lying, that is to say, of presenting itself as Truth" (p. 305). Only from this point will the ego start to take on various configurations. What seems problematic about this arrangement, or in any case what we believe needs further development, is the way in which the "battery," the "treasure" of the signifier, functions. In our opinion, game theory cannot completely account for this functioning, nor can a signification be articulated until an alterity is *distinctly posited* as such. One cannot speak of the "signifier" before the positing or the thesis of the Other, the articulation of which begins only with the mirror stage. But what of the previous processes that are not yet "a site," but a *functioning*? The thetic phase will establish this functioning as a signifying *order* (though it will not stop it) and will return in this order.

60. "On Sense and Reference," Max Black, tr., in *Translations from the Philosophical Writings of Gottlob Frege*, Peter Geach and Max Black, eds. (New York: Philosophical Library, 1952), p. 65; emphasis added; translation modified. |To maintain consistency with Kristeva's terminology and with the French translations of Frege she cites, I have changed "sense" to "meaning" (*sens*) and "reference" to "denotation" (*dénotation*) throughout.—Trans.| Indeed, analogous remarks can be found in Husserl: "Every synthetically unitary consciousness, however many special theses and syntheses it may involve, possesses the *total object* which belongs to it as a synthetically *unitary* consciousness. We call it a total object in contrast with the objects which belong intentionally to the lower or higher grade members of the synthesis . . ." "|These| noetic experiences |have| a quite determinate essential content, over which, despite the endlessness, a proper oversight can still be kept, all the experiences agreeing in this that they are a consciousness of 'the same' object. This *unanimity* is evidenced in the sphere of consciousness itself . . ." (*Ideas*, pp. 335 and 375; emphasis added).

61. "By combining subject and predicate, one reaches only a thought, never passes from meaning to denotation, never from a thought to its truth value. One moves at the same level but never advances from one level to the next. A truth value cannot be a part

of a thought, any more than, say, the Sun can, for it is not a meaning but an object." Frege, "On Sense and Reference," p. 64; translation modified.

62. Brentano, Venn, Bayn, and Russell, among others, have argued the possibility of converting existential assertions into predicative assertions. Existence in this case is understood as the existence of a subject that has a predicate and not simply as an existence of the predicate within the subject. Frege clearly distinguishes the two levels: denotation as the existence of the logical subject as denoted object, meaning as the existence of a predicate for a subject (ibid., pp. 64–65).

63. "If now the truth value of a sentence is its denotation, then on the one hand all true sentences have the same denotation and so, on the other hand, do all false sentences." Ibid., p. 65; translation modified.

64. "It may perhaps be granted that every grammatically well-formed expression representing a proper name always has a meaning." Ibid., p. 58; translation modified.

65. The functioning of the verb 'to be' in several non-Indo-European languages shows the course the signifying process follows before it posits an existence. In this respect, these languages are different from Greek and Indo-European languages in general, which unhesitatingly posit existence and thereby tend to make it a metaphysical category. (Heidegger and Benveniste, to name only two, thought they had proved the complicity between the category of being and the verb 'to be.') These languages lead us to identify semiotic *stages* or *modalities* that precede or take place within the thetic, but are distinct from existence: designation, accentuation, reminders of the unicity or the accuracy of the act of enunciating, and so forth. Thus, in modern Chinese, the "illogical" functioning of *shi* ('to be') in its position as copula is resolved by supposing that, in most of these "illogical" cases, 'to be' is simply a substitute for the verbal function per se and is called a "pro-verb." See Anne Yue Hashimoto, "The Verb 'To Be' in Modern Chinese," in *The Verb 'Be' and Its Synonyms: Philosophical and Grammatical Studies*, John W. M. Verhaar, ed. (Dordrecht, Holland: D. Reidel, 1969), part 4, pp. 90ff. Since, as it could be shown, *shi* assumes the function of pro-verb in several cases other than those indicated by Hashimoto, we could say that its function is to indicate the logical moment of enunciation and denotation, to mark the *positing* of the act of enunciation-denotation, and the relational *possibilities* deriving from it (before there is any affirmation of the existence of the subject or denoted object and their modalities). In our view, the *emphatic* function of *shi*, which is common in Chinese, as well as its semantic functions, such as those indicating the *accuracy* or the truth of the utterance, confirm this interpretation. We might add that *shi* was not used as a verb in classical Chinese until the second century. Before that time it was used solely as a *demonstrative*; only its negative form had a verbal function.

On the other hand, in Arabic, there is no verb 'to be.' Its function is filled—as translations from Arabic into Indo-European languages and vice-versa show—by a series of morphemes. These include: the verb *kana* (with its two meanings, 'to exist' and 'to be such and such'), which indicates a genetic process and not something already in existence; the assertive particle, *inna*, which means 'indeed'; the incomplete verb *laysa*, which is a negative copula; the third-person pronoun, *huwa*, which refers to an extra-allocutory moment but nevertheless ensures the unity of the discursive act and is, according to standard metaphysical interpretation, God; and, finally, the verbal root *wjd*, which means 'to find,' a localization that, by extension, indicates truth. See Fadlou Shedadi, "Arabic and 'To Be,' " *ibid.*, pp. 112–125.

In summary, semantically as well as syntactically, explicitly in these languages but implicitly in others (Indo-European languages, for example), 'to be' condenses the different modalities of the predicative function. The most fundamental of these modalities seems to be *position* (the thetic) or localization, from which the others—the enunciation of an existence, a truth, a spatio-temporal differentiation effected by the subject of enunciation, and so forth—derive. See John Lyons, "A Note on Possessive, Existential and Locative Sentences," *Foundations of Language* (1967), 3:390–396; Charles H. Kahn, *The Verb 'Be' in Ancient Greek*, in *The Verb 'Be' and Its Synonyms*, suppl. series, vol. 16, John W. M. Verhaar, ed. (Dordrecht, Holland: D. Reidel, 1973).

66. On the predicative function as the foundation of a complete utterance, see Jerzy Kuryłowicz, *Esquisses linguistiques* (Wroclaw, Cracow: Zakład Narodowy Imienia Ossolińskich, Wydawnictwo Polskiej Akademii Nauk, 1960), pp. 35ff.; S. K. Shaumyan and P. A. Soboleva, *Osnovanija porozdajuščej grammatiki ruskovo jazyka* [Foundations of generative grammar in Russian] (Moscow: Nauka, 1968). On this same problem with respect to the utterance's relation to what is extra-linguistic, see Benveniste, "The Nominal Sentence," in *Problems*, pp. 131–144; Strawson, *Individuals*.

67. Comparative linguistics generally used to consider the *verb* as the predominant element of language and as the one from which the *noun* derived. Generative linguistics revalorizes the *noun* by making it an essential component of deep structure, while including the *verb* in another no less essential component, the *predicate*. Some linguists tend to give the *noun* a determining role because it particularizes the utterance by giving it a concrete referent. From this point of view, predication is determinative only for the act of enunciation and only if it is completed by the *noun*. See Lyons, "A Note on Possessive, Existential and Locative Sentences"; Strawson, *Individuals*; and so forth. For others, the noun always appears under the "nexus of the predicate," which follows the assertion of certain logicians (Russell, Quine) that every "particular" is replaced by a variable linked to existential quantification.

We thus see that predication is defined as being coextensive with every act of naming. What we call a *thetic* function is none other than the speaking subject's positing of enunciation through a syntagm or proposition: the distinctions between noun and verb, etc., are posterior to this function and concern only the surface structure of certain languages. But we would emphasize that (logically) even *before* this distinction, enunciation is thetic, no matter what the morphology of the syntagms used, and that it is "predicative" in the sense that it situates the act of the subject of enunciation with respect to the Other, in a space and time preceding any other particularization. This thetic (predicative) act is the *presupposition* of every simple nominal utterance, which, in its turn, will select a specific predicative morpheme. See C.-E. Bazell, "Syntactic Relations and Linguistic Typology," *Cahiers Ferdinand de Saussure* (1949), 8:5–20. On a genetic level, Benveniste observes a "pre-inflectional period" of Indo-European in which the noun and the verb, "set up on a common basis," are not differentiated. *Origines de la formation des noms en indo-européen* (Paris: Maisonneuve, 1935).

68. On the traumatizing object which hinders the positing of the thetic, see "La Transposition, le déplacement, la condensation," *La Révolution du langage poétique*, pp. 230–239.

69. See "Le Dispositif sémiotique du texte," *ibid.*, pp. 209–358.

70. See "Instances du discours et altération du sujet," *ibid.*, pp. 315–335, where we establish that it is a nonrecoverable deletion.

71. "*Effraction*," in French, is the juridical term for "breaking and entering"; in Kris-

teva's sense it also means a "breaking into" or "breaking through." I have translated it as "breach": the act or result of breaking and, more significantly, an infraction or violation as of a law.—Trans.

72. It has recently been emphasized that *mimesis* is not an imitation of an object but a reproduction of the trajectory of enunciation; in other words, *mimesis* departs from denotation (in Frege's sense) and confines itself to meaning. Roland Barthes makes this explicit: "The function of narrative is not to 'represent,' it is to constitute a spectacle still very enigmatic for us . . . Logic has here an emancipatory value—and with it the entire narrative. It may be that men ceaselessly re-inject into narrative what they have known, what they have experienced; but if they do, at least it is in a form which has vanquished repetition and instituted the model of a process of becoming. Narrative does not show, does not imitate; the passion which may excite us in reading a novel is not that of a 'vision' (in actual fact, we do not 'see' anything). Rather it is that of meaning . . . ; 'what happens' is language alone, the adventure of language, the unceasing celebration of its coming." Barthes, "Introduction to the Structuralist Analysis of Narratives," in *Image, Music, Text*, Stephen Heath, tr. (New York: Hill and Wang, 1977), pp. 123–124. This is also what Goethe means when he writes: "In your own mode of rhyme my feet I'll find,/ The repetitions of pleasures shall incite:/ At first the sense and then the words I'll find [Erst werd ich Sinn, sodann auch Worte finden]/ No sound a second time will I indite / Unless thereby the meaning is refined / As you, with peerless gifts, have shown aright!" But this analysis of meaning through sounds must result in a new device that is not just a new meaning but also a new "form": "Measured rhythms are indeed delightful,/ And therein a pleasing talent basks;/ But how quickly they can taste so frightful,/ There's no blood nor sense in hollow masks [Hohle Masken ohne Blut und Sinn]/ Even wit must shudder at such tasks / If it can't, with new form occupied,/ Put an end at last to form that's died." "Imitation" [*Nachbildung*], *West-Eastern Divan/West-Oestlicher Divan*, J. Whaley, tr. (London: Oswald Wolff, 1974), pp. 34–37.

73. This is why Lacan stated in his spring 1972 seminar that the expression "*Die Bedeutung des Phallus*" is a tautology.

74. See Jakobson, "L'importanza di Kruszewski per lo sviluppo della linguistica generale," *Ricerche Slavistiche* (1967), 14:1–20.

75. See Lacan, *Ecrits: A Selection*, pp. 156–157, et passim.

76. See Kristeva, *Le Texte du roman: Approche sémiologique d'une structure discursive transformationnelle* (The Hague: Mouton, 1970).

77. "We have not yet referred to any other sort of displacement [*Verschiebung*]. Analyses show us, however, that another sort exists and that it reveals itself in a change in the *verbal expression* of the thoughts concerned . . . One element is replaced by another [ein Element seine Wortfassung gegen eine andere vertauscht]. . . . Any one thought, whose form of expression may happen to be fixed for other reasons, will operate in a determinant and selective manner on the possible forms of expression allotted to the other thoughts, and it may do so, perhaps, from the very start—as is the case in writing a poem [Der eine Gedanke, dessen Ausdruck etwa aus anderen Gründen feststeht, wird dabei verteilend und auswählend auf die Ausdrucksmöglichkeiten des anderen einwirken, und dies vielleicht von vorneherein, ähnlich wie bei der Arbeit des Dichters]." *The Interpretation of Dreams, Standard Edition*, 5:339–340; *Gesammelte Werke* (London: Imago, 1942), 2–3:344–345. See "La Transposition, le déplacement, la condensation," *La Révolution du langage poétique*, pp. 230–239.

78. Goethe speaks of this when, describing the Arabic tradition, he calls to mind the poet whose role is to express "Undeniable truth indelibly:/ But there are some small

points here and there/ Which exceed the limits of the law [Ausgemachte Wahreit unaus-löschlich:/ Aber hie und da auch Kleinigkeiten/ Ausserhalb der Grenze des Gesetzes]." "Fetwa," West-Eastern Divan, pp. 30–33.

79. "Yet this 'object of perspective,' may be handled in different ways. In fetishism (and, in my view, in art works), it pushes itself into the great ambiguous realm of dis-avowal, and materializes . . . As a result, we see . . . that all scientific or esthetic obser-vation or activity has a part to play in the fate reserved for the 'perspective object,'" writes Guy Rosolato, "Le Fétishisme dont se 'dérobe' l'objet," Nouvelle Revue de Psychoanalyse (Autumn 1970), 2:39. [For a more complete account of this concept in English, see Rosolato, "Symbol Formation," International Journal of Psychoanalysis (1978), 59:303–313.—Trans.]

80. As Jean Pouillon remarks, "if words were merely fetishes, semantics would be reduced to phonology." "Fétiches sans fétichisme," Nouvelle Revue de Psychoanalyse (Autumn 1970), 2:147.

81. By contrast, discourse in Molière's "Femmes savantes" is an exemplary case of the fetishizing process since it focuses exclusively on the signifier. "It is indeed the sign that becomes an erotic object and not the 'erotic' signified of discourse, as is usual in simple cases of repression (obscene talk or graffiti). It is not obsession but perversion." Josette Rey-Debove, "L'Orgie langagière," Poétique (1972), 12:579.

82. See John von Neumann, The Computer and the Brain (New Haven: Yale University Press, 1958).

83. Anthony Wilden, "Analog and Digital Communication," Semiotica (1972), 6(1):50–51. [Kristeva gives a loose translation of these passages in French. I have restored the original English quotation. Wilden, it should be noted, uses "computer" in the broad sense, whether the device actually computes in the strict sense or not.—Trans.]

84. Ibid., p. 55.

85. Benveniste has taught us not to confuse these two operations, but rather to call something a language only when it has a double articulation; the distinction between phonemes devoid of meaning and morphemes as elements—for which no code is perti-nent—is a social, specifically human occurrence. See "Animal Communication and Human Language," Problems, pp. 49–54.

86. This is what Hegel believes. At the end of the "Larger Logic," describing neg-ativity as that which constructs absolute knowledge, he writes: "This negativity, as self-transcending contradiction, is the reconstitution of the first immediacy, of simple universality; for, immediately, the Other of the Other and the negative of the negative is the positive, identical, and universal." Hegel's Science of Logic, W. H. Johnston and L. G. Struthers, trs., 2 vols. (London: Allen & Unwin, 1929; 1966), 2:478; emphasis added.

87. Moses and Monotheism, Standard Edition, 23:7–137.

88. The two roles have often merged, as Georges Dumézil reminds us in Mitra-Va-runa (Paris: Gallimard, 1948). See "Deux conceptions de la souveraineté," La Révolution du langage poétique, pp. 545–552.

89. Lévi-Strauss, "Structural Analysis in Linguistics and Anthropology," in Structural Anthropology, 1:51; emphasis added; translation modified.

90. Lévi-Strauss, "Introduction à l'œuvre de M. Mauss," in Mauss, Sociologie et an-thropologie (Paris: Presses Universitaires de France, 1950), pp. xlv–xlvii.

91. René Girard, Violence and the Sacred, Patrick Gregory, tr. (Baltimore: Johns Hopkins University Press, 1977).

92. Henri Hubert and Marcel Mauss, in their famous Essai sur la nature et la fonction du sacrifice, first published in Année sociologique (1889), vol. 2, study the logical—as opposed

to the chronological—succession of sacrificial forms, and place sacrifice of the deity at the culmination of animal, vegetable, and human sacrifice: "Indeed, it is in the sacrifice of a divine personage that the idea of sacrifice attains its highest expression. Consequently it is under this guise that it has penetrated into the most recent religions and given rise to beliefs and practices still current. In this respect the Christian sacrifice is one of the most instructive to be met with in history." Mauss, *Sacrifice: Its Nature and Function*, W. D. Halls, tr. (Chicago: University of Chicago Press, 1964), pp. 77 and 93.

93. Mauss, *Sacrifice*, pp. 100, 101, 102, and 103.

94. Sacrifice has a "social function" because "sacrifice is concerned with social matters." Mauss, *Sacrifice*, p. 102.

95. *Encyclopedia Britannica*, s.v. "Sacrifice," and Robertson Smith, *Religion of Semites*, Gifford Lectures (n.p., 1890; 2nd ed., 1894), as cited by Mauss, *Œuvres* (Paris: Minuit, 1968), p. 194.

96. "The raw and the cooked, hunt and sacrifice converge precisely at the point where man is no longer anything but an animal. The οἰκεία βορά is, in sum, the equivalent of incest." Pierre Vidal-Naquet, "Chasse et sacrifice dans l'*Orestie* d'Eschyle," in Jean-Pierre Vernant and Pierre Vidal-Naquet, *Mythe et tragédie en Grèce ancienne* (Paris: Maspero, 1972), p. 148. The same can be said of Philoctetes, the ephebe, who "acquired as it were a kinship with the animal world." H. C. Avery, "Heracles, Philoctetes, Neoptolemus," *Hermes* (1965), 93:284. "The very evil that tortues him, *agrios*, is his own savagery. Philoctetes is thus on the borderline between the human and the savage . . ." "Le *Philoctète* de Sophocle et l'ephébie," in Vernant and Vidal-Naquet, *Mythe et tragédie*, p. 170.

97. Lévi-Strauss, *The Savage Mind* (Chicago: University of Chicago Press, 1966), pp. 222–228; L'*Homme nu* (Paris: Plon, 1971), p. 608.

98. "The resemblance is conceptual, not perceptual. The 'is' rests on qualitative analogy," quoted by Lévi-Strauss, *The Savage Mind*, p. 224.

99. *Ibid.*, p. 227.

100. We agree with René Girard, who writes that "even the crudest of religious viewpoints acknowledges a truth ignored by even the most lucid [*pessimiste*] nonreligious system," but that there exists "an incapacity in religion," which is "religion's own misapprehensions in regard to violence [and] . . . the nature of the threat this violence poses for human society" (*Violence and the Sacred*, p. 259). Surprisingly, however, Girard rejects the sexual nature of this violence, which Freud's work, to its credit, reveals beneath the ethnological heap. This revelation opened the way to rational knowledge of that violence, not through the abstraction of civilizations phantasmatically or mimetically reconstructed, but in the concrete practice of the subject—or subjects—within the realm of contemporary social forces.

101. Here the term *dépense* is a reference to Georges Bataille's essay, "La Notion de dépense," *Œuvres complètes* (Paris: Gallimard, 1970), 1:302–320; 2:147–158. *Dépense* is any *un*productive, wasteful, or destructive "expenditure." As examples, Bataille cites luxury, wars, cults, sumptuous monuments, games, the arts, and any sexual activity not intended for reproduction. Elsewhere Kristeva will also use the term as it is understood in drive theory and analytical theory. See particularly "Expenditure of a Logical Conclusion," in part IV below.—Trans.

102. See Godrey Leinhardt, *Divinity and Experience*, cited by Girard, *Violence and the Sacred*, p. 97.

103. We will understand "ideology" to mean any cognitive synthesis that stems from the order of the logical Idea. Within that order, we do not valorize "knowledge"—which

would devalorize "ideology"—instead, we believe that ideology underlies every act of enunciation and that the distinction between "good" and "bad" ideology can only depend on a specific position within socioeconomic contradictions.

104. But Hegel was already using the term "dialectic" in a sense that previous philosophers had not: "*Dialectic* is one of those ancient sciences which have been most misjudged in modern metaphysics and in the popular philosophy of ancients and moderns alike. . . . Dialectic has often been considered an *art*, as though it rested upon a subjective talent and did not belong to the objectivity of the Notion. The shape and result which it had in Kant's philosophy have been shown by the definite examples which express his view of it. It must be regarded as a step of infinite importance that dialectic has once more been recognized as necessary to reason, although the opposite conclusion must be drawn to that which was reached by Kant." *Hegel's Science of Logic*, 2:473, emphasis added.

105. Bataille, "Etre Oreste," in *Œuvres complètes*, (Paris: Gallimard, 1971), 3:220.

106. In his article, "Creative Writers and Daydreaming" (*Standard Edition*, vol. 9), Freud writes that "a piece of creative writing, like a day-dream, is a continuation of, and a substitute for, what was once the play of childhood" (p. 152). The advantage of this "play" is that it helps us enjoy our own fantasies "without self-reproach or shame." By what means? This question persists because Freud did no more than evoke aesthetic, "formal pleasure," and "technique." These he calls "fore-pleasure." (But where does this fore-pleasure come from?) "Fore-pleasure" is designed to serve as "the intermediary mak[ing] possible the release of still greater pleasure arising from deeper psychical sources" (p. 153). Yet other texts by Freud point out other possible directions in the search for the mechanism of this "(esthetic) fore-pleasure." "The Moses of Michelangelo," "Leonardo Da Vinci and a Memory of His Childhood," and *Delusions and Dreams in Jensen's "Gradiva"* direct our attention to childhood traumas, and to the subject's relation to castration or imaginary identification, as the instigators of fantasies. *Jokes and Their Relation to the Unconscious*, on the other hand, opens up, across the scene of language, the scene of non-sense which, emerging within the texture of signification, lifts the inhibition that creates signification, and thus produces pleasure. In this way, "esthetic technique" can be related to "jokes" since both lift the inhibition that establishes language, and retrieve, through language's constantly maintained order, the working of drives that precedes the positing of meaning.

107. Bataille, *Œuvres complètes*, 3:218.

108. See "Shifters. Verbal Categories, and the Russian Verb," in Jakobson, *Selected Writings*, 2:130–147.

109. See Joseph Needham, *Science and Civilisation in China*, 4 vols. (Cambridge: Cambridge University Press, 1960), vol. 1.

110. From a similar perspective, Edgar Morin writes: "We can think of magic, mythologies, and ideologies both as mixed systems, making affectivity rational and rationality affective, and as outcomes of combining: a) fundamental drives, b) the chancy play of fantasy, and c) logico-constructive systems. (To our mind, the theory of myth must be based on triunic syncretism rather than unilateral logic.)" He adds, in a note, that "myth does not have a single logic but a synthesis of three kinds of logic." "Le Paradigme perdu: La Nature humaine," paper presented at the "Invariants biologiques et universaux culturels" Colloquium, Royaumont, September 6–9, 1972.

111. Lacan presented this typology of discourse at his 1969 and 1970 seminars.

112. See Kristeva, *Le Texte du roman*.

113. Michel de M'Uzan. "Le Même et l'identique," *Revue Française de Psychanalyse* (May 1970), 34(3):444 and 447.

114. We say "barely" because so-called stylistic effects, characteristic of all narratives, are evidence of this crossing of boundaries.

115. Jolles, *Les Formes simples*, Antoine Marie Buguet, tr. (Paris: Seuil, 1972).

116. "Every historical event thus becomes a saga in which the dying out of a people is the dying out of the family; a people's victory is crystallized, by a verbal act, as the victory of the paterfamilias or of the hero of the legend; the clash between two peoples, whether an encounter between migrant groups or their clash with a settled population, can be thought of only in this way" (Jolles, p. 72).

117. Jolles, pp. 96–97.

118. See Freud's article on "Negation," in *Standard Edition*, 19:235–242.

119. For an explanation of this term, see Ben Brewster's glossary at the end of Althusser's *For Marx* (New York: Random House, 1969), p. 255.—Trans.

120. Victor Goldschmidt, *Le Système stoïcien et l'idée du temps*, 2d ed. (Paris: J. Vrin, 1969). On the formation of syntax in grammar, see Jean-Claude Chevalier, *Histoire de la syntaxe: Naissance de la notion de complément dans la grammaire française, 1530–1750* (Geneva: Droz, 1968).

121. P. Smith, "Principes de la personne et catégories sociales," Etudes sur les Diakhanke, *Colloque international sur la notion de personne en Afrique noire*, October 11–17, 1971 (Paris: Editions du CNRS, 1973).

122. The term is used by Joseph Needham and involves both social and biological organisms. *Science and Civilisation in China*, Vol. IVa, sec. 27c, et passim.

123. See Ion Banu, "La Formation sociale 'asiatique' dans la perspective de la philosophie orientale antique," in *Sur le "mode de production asiatique"* (Paris: Editions Sociales, 1969), pp. 285–307.

124. Freud and Breuer, "Studies on Hysteria," *Standard Edition*, 2:7 and 53.

125. See Gisela Pankow, *L'Homme et sa psychose* (Paris: Aubier-Montaigne, 1969).

126. Freud and Breuer, "Studies on Hysteria," *Standard Edition*, 2:8.

127. Marx, *Capital*, 3 vols. (New York: International Publishers, 1974), 3:820.

128. Marx, *Œuvres* (Paris: Gallimard, 1968), 2:289 and 311.

II. NEGATIVITY: REJECTION

1. Hegel's terminology poses a problem. Whereas the French translations Kristeva cites are generally consistent in their rendering of key terms, no such "standards" inform the various English translations of either *Phenomenology of Spirit*—even the title is a point of contention—or *Science of Logic*. Both texts, for example, refer to *Nichts*, commonly translated as "*néant*" in French but as "Nothing" in Johnson and Struthers's *Science of Logic* or as "nothingness" in A. V. Miller's *Phenomenology*. The same problem arises with "*le devenir*" ("Becoming" or "process of Becoming"), "*extériorisation*" ("exteriorization" or "expression"), and other such terms. I have not standardized these two different translations. When the discussion of Hegel does not refer to a specific work, I have generally selected French cognates.—Trans.

2. Lenin, "Conspectus of Hegel's Book on *The Science of Logic*," Clemens Dutt, tr. *Collected Works*, Stewart Smith, ed. (Moscow: Foreign Languages Publishing House, 1961), 38:230.

3. *Ibid.*, p. 97.

4. See "Religion in the Form of Art" in Hegel, *Phenomenology of Spirit*, A. V. Miller, tr. (Oxford: Oxford University Press, 1977), pp. 424–453.

5. Hegel, *Encyclopédie des sciences philosophiques*, vol. 1, *Science de la logique* (1817), B. Bourgeois, tr. (Paris: Vrin, 1970), p. 203.

6. Lenin, "Conspectus," *Collected Works* 38:229.

7. Hegel's *Science of Logic*, W. H. Johnston and L. G. Struthers, trs. (London: Allen & Unwin, 1929; 1966), 1:95: emphasis added.

8. *Ibid.*, p. 96.

9. *Ibid.*, p. 97.

10. *Ibid.*, 2:478–479.

11. *Ibid.*, 1:104.

12. *Phenomenology of Spirit*, p. 81. "Diese Bewegung ist aber dasjenige, was Kraft gennant wird: das eine Moment derselben, nämlich sie als Ausbreitung der selbstständigen Materien in ihrem Sehn, ist ihre Aeusserung; sie aber als das Verschwundensehn derselben ist die in sich aus ihrer Aeusserung zurückgedrängte, oder die eigentliche Kraft. Aber erstens die in sich zurückgedrängte Kraft muss sich äussern; und zweitens in der Aeusserung ist sie eben so in sich selbst sehende Kraft, als sie in diesem Insichselbstsehn Aeusserung ist." Hegel, *Sämtliche Werke* (Stuttgart: Fr. Frommans Verlag, 1927), pp. 110–111.

13. Hegel, *Phenomenology of Spirit*, p. 82.

14. *Ibid.*, pp. 88–89.

15. Artaud, "L'Automate personnel," in *Œuvres complètes*, 2 vols. (Paris: Gallimard, 1970), 1:179.

16. Hegel, *Phenomenology of Spirit*, p. 86.

17. See Gilles Deleuze, *Différence et répétition* (Paris: Presses Universitaires de France, 1968).

18. See Dominique Dubarle and André Doz, *Logique et dialectique* (Paris: Larousse, 1971), p. 36.

19. Frege, *Logical Investigations*, P. T. Geach, ed., P. T. Geach and R. H. Stoothoff, trs. (New Haven: Yale University Press, 1977), pp. 25, 30, 37. [The German "*Träger*" is closer to "bearer" and the French "*porteur*" than it is to "owner." I have substituted "bearer" for "owner" throughout.—Trans.]

20. *Ibid.*, p. 44.

21. *Ibid.*, p. 38.

22. See the commentaries by Jean Hyppolite, and by Lacan in *Ecrits* (Paris: Seuil, 1965), pp. 879–888 and 369–400.

23. Viviane Alleton, *Eléments de grammaire du chinois moderne* (Paris: Université de Paris VII, UER Extrême-Orient, 1969).

24. See Jean Dubois, Luce Irigaray, and Pierre Marcie, "Transformation négative et organisation des classes lexicales," *Cahiers de Lexicologie* (1965), 7:3–32.

25. René Spitz, *The First Year of Life: A Psychoanalytical Study of Normal and Deviant Development of Object Relations* (New York: International Universities Press, 1965), p. 193.

26. Hermina Sinclair-de Zwart, *Acquisition du langage et développement de la pensée: Soussystèmes linguistiques et opérations concrètes* (Paris: Dunod, 1967), p. 130.

27. Frege, *Logical Investigations*, p. 31; translation modified.

28. See Dubois, Irigaray, Marcie, "Transformation négative et organisation des classes lexicales"; Irigaray, "Négation et transformation négative chez les schizophrènes," *Langages* (1967), 5:84–98.

29. In French, "*minus*," which comes from the Latin "*minus habens*," means "dimwit" or "moron."—Trans.

30. Since "*minus*" literally means "less" in Latin, the word calls up its Latin antonym, "*magis*," meaning "more."—Trans.

31. "A 'signifying differential' . . . is, briefly put, the place and the means by which

254 / II. Negativity: Rejection

the genotext penetrates the phenotext at the level of the signifier." Leon S. Roudiez, tr., *Desire in Language* (New York: Columbia University Press, 1980), p. 208. See Kristeva, "L'Engendrement de la formule," in Σημειωτιχή: *Recherches pour une sémanalyse* (Paris: Seuil, 1969), pp. 299ff.—Trans.

32. The morphemes "*ne*" and "*pas*" negate the verb in modern, written French. "Originally *ne* was used without an accompanying particle (*pas, point,* etc.), but very early it began to be strengthened by the addition of a substantive or an adverb." Alfred Ewert, *The French Language* (London: Faber & Faber, 1961), p. 260.—Trans.

33. This is a reference to Philippe Sollers's essay, "The Novel and the Experience of Limits," in *Writing and the Experience of Limits*, David Hayman, ed., Philip Barnard with David Hayman, trs. (New York: Columbia University Press, 1983), pp. 185–207.—Trans.

34. See "Syntaxe et composition" and "Le Contexte présupposé" in *La Révolution du langage poétique* (Paris: Seuil, 1974), pp. 265–291 and 337–358.

35. See Kierkegaard, *Papirer*, IV, C. 97, 1.

36. Heidegger, *Being and Time*, John Macquarrie and Edward Robinson, trs. (New York: Harper & Row, 1962), pp. 244 and 241.

37. "Unius bonum natura perficit, dei scilicet, alterius cura, hominis." *Ibid.*, p. 243.

38. Karel Kosík, *Dialectics of the Concrete*, Karel Kovanda and James Schmidt, trs. (Boston: D. Reidel, 1976), pp. 37 sq.

39. *Ibid.*, p. 86.

40. Lacan, *Ecrits: A Selection*, Alan Sheridan, tr. (New York: Norton, 1977), p. 274.

41. Ibid., p. 272.

42. "The being of language is the non-being of objects," *ibid.*, p. 263.

43. *Ibid.*, p. 260; translation modified.

44. Lacan, *Ecrits* (Paris: Seuil, 1965), p. 851.

45. *Ecrits: A Selection*, p. 264.

46. *Ecrits* (Paris: Seuil, 1965), p. 853.

47. *Ibid.*, p. 662.

48. *Ecrits: A Selection*, p. 265.

49. Hegel, *Phenomenology of Spirit*, p. 109.

50. Hegel, *The Philosophy of History*, J. Sibree, tr. (New York: Willey, 1944), p. 447.

51. "Towards a Critique of Hegel's Philosophy," in *The Fiery Brook: Selected Writings of Ludwig Feuerbach*, Zawar Hanfi, tr. (Garden City, N.Y.: Doubleday, 1972), p. 93. "Man is self-consciousness." See Feuerbach, *Sämtliche Werke*, Wilhelm Bolin and Friedrich Jodl, eds., 2nd ed., 10 vols. (Stuttgart: Fromann, 1959), 2:242, as quoted and translated by David McLellan in *The Young Hegelians and Karl Marx* (London: Macmillan, 1969), p. 112.

52. Feuerbach, *Das Wesen des Christentums*, 2nd ed. (Leipzig: P. Reclam, 1843), pp. xix f.; *The Young Hegelians*, p. 89.

53. Feuerbach, *Sämtliche Werke*, 2:320; *The Young Hegelians*, p. 100.

54. Marx, *Die Frühschriften* (Stuttgart: A. Kröner, 1962), 1:262ff.; *The Young Hegelians*, p. 103.

55. Feuerbach, *Kleine philosophische Schriften*, Max Gustav Lange, ed. (Leipzig: F. Meiner, 1950), pp. 34ff.; *The Young Hegelians*, p. 94.

56. Feuerbach, *Sämtliche Werke*, 2:233; *The Young Hegelians*, p. 114.

57. "A miracle is the realisation of a natural or human wish in a supernatural manner" (*Die Frühschriften*, 1:107; *The Young Hegelians*, p. 97). Similarly, in his polemic with Max Stirner in *The German Ideology*, Marx uses the term "desire" in a crossed-out passage in the manuscript, where he hesitates between "fluid desires" and "fixed desires": "The communists are the only people through whose historical activity the liquefaction of the fixed

desires and ideas is in fact brought about . . . . The communists have no intention of abolishing the fixedness of their desires and needs . . . they only strive to achieve an organisation of production and intercourse which will make possible the normal satisfaction of all needs, i.e., a satisfaction which is limited only by the needs themselves." *The German Ideology* (Moscow: Progress Publishers, 1964), p. 277.

58. Marx and Engels, *Gesamtausgabe* (Berlin: Marx-Engels Verlag, 1927), 3:11; *The Young Hegelians*, p. 112.

59. Marx, *Die Frühschriften*, 1:600f.; *The Young Hegelians*, p. 108.

60. *Die Frühschriften*, 1:505; *The Young Hegelians*, p. 106; emphasis added.

61. Hyppolite quotes Hegel: "The liberty of bourgeois society is unique, but it merely buries the individual in individualism; he can only save himself through the State and Religion." *Studies on Marx and Hegel*, John O'Neill, ed. and tr. (New York: Harper & Row, 1969), p. 80

62. Derrida, *Writing and Difference*, Alan Bass, tr. (Chicago: University of Chicago Press, 1978), p. 248.

63. Derrida, *Of Grammatology*, Gayatri Chakravorty Spivak, tr. (Baltimore: Johns Hopkins University Press, 1976), p. 60.

64. Ibid., pp. 47, translation modified, and 63. [For an explanation of the term *"différance,"* see below, n. 68.—Trans.]

65. *Writing and Difference*, p. 153; translation modified.

66. *Of Grammatology*, pp. 46–47 and 62.

67. See "Freud and the Scene of Writing," in *Writing and Difference*, pp. 196–231.

68. In his introduction to *Writing and Difference*, Alan Bass explains that Derrida's term, *différance*, "combines in neither the active nor the passive voice the coincidence of meanings in the verb *différer*: to differ (in space) and to defer (to put off in time, to postpone presence). Thus, it does not function simply either as *différence* (difference) or as *différance* in the usual sense (deferral), and plays on both meanings at once," p. xvi.—Trans.

69. *Writing and Difference*, pp. 203, 198, and 203; emphasis added.

70. *Of Grammatology*, pp. 47 and 48.

71. In their translation of Heidegger's *Being and Time*, Macquarrie and Robinson render *Sein* as "Being" and *Seiendes* as "entity" or "entities." In keeping with the standard French translations of the terms ("*être*" and "*étant*") and the practice of more recent translators, I have kept "Being" but use "beings" (lower case, plural) for the French *étant* (*Seiendes*).—Trans.

72. *Of Grammatology*, p. 47; emphasis added.

73. Derrida, *Edmund Husserl's "Origin of Geometry": An Introduction*, John P. Leavey, Jr. tr. (Stony Brook, N.Y.: Nicolas Hays, 1978), p. 153; translation modified.

74. *Writing and Difference*, p. 230; emphasis added; translation modified.

75. On the notion of expenditure, see Georges Bataille, *Œuvres complètes*, (Paris: Gallimard, 1970), 1:302–320; 2:147–158.

76. *Writing and Difference*, p. 198.

77. *Of Grammatology*, p. 63.

78. "But culture is yet something else again: it implies a technological and political development which partly eludes desire," writes André Green, in "La Projection: De l'identification projective au projet," *Revue Française de Psychanalyse* (September–December 1971), 35(5–6):958.

79. Artaud, "The New Revelations of Being" in *Selected Writings*, Helen Weaver, tr. (New York: Farrar, Straus and Giroux, 1976), p. 414.

80. Freud, "Negation," *Standard Edition*, 19:239.

81. "Foreclosure," write J. Laplanche and J.-B. Pontalis, is a "term introduced by Jacques Lacan denoting a specific mechanism held to lie at the origin of the psychotic phenomenon and to consist in a primordial *expulsion* of a fundamental 'signifier' (e.g., the phallus as signifier of the castration complex) from the subject's symbolic universe." *The Language of Psychoanalysis*, Daniel Lagache, introd., Donald Nicholson-Smith, tr. (London: Hogarth Press, 1973), p. 166; emphasis added.—Trans.

82. See *Beyond the Pleasure Principle*, *Standard Edition*, 18:54–55.

83. Melanie Klein, "The Importance of Symbol-Formation in the Development of the Ego," in *Contributions to Psychoanalysis* (London: Hogarth Press, 1948), p. 237.

84. Psychoanalysis places the mirror stage between the ages of 6 and 18 months, after which the so-called phallic stage begins. Observations have shown that around the latter period (age 2), language acquisition is inhibited despite the accelerated maturation of the brain and its lateralization. After this period of inhibition until the end of the Oedipus complex, and thus the decline of the phallic stage (between the ages of 4 and 5), the major elements of linguistic competence are acquired at an accelerated rate. After this, in the latency period, the curve of language acquisition becomes less steep, rising only slightly. See Eric H. Lenneberg, *Biological Foundations of Language* (New York: Wiley 1967), pp. 168, 376.

85. A text is paragrammatic, writes Leon S. Roudiez, "in the sense that its organization of words (and their denotations), grammar, and syntax is challenged by the infinite possibilities provided by letters or phonemes combining to form networks of significations not accessible through conventional reading habits . . . ," "Twelve Points from Tel Quel," *L'Esprit Créateur* (Winter 1974), 14(2):300. See Kristeva's essay, "Pour une sémiologie des paragrammes," in Σημειωτιχὴ, pp. 174–207.—Trans.

86. See "Le Dispositif sémiotique du texte," *La Révolution du langage poétique*, pp. 209–358.

87. On Mallarmé, Hegel, and the "wife-concept," see *La Révolution du langage poétique*, pp. 534–540.

88. See Spitz, *The First Years of Life*, p. 193.

89. "In my opinion, in the normal state of fusion of the two drives, aggression plays a role which is comparable to that of a carrier wave. In this way the impetus of aggression makes it possible to direct both drives toward the surround. But if the aggressive and libidinal drives do not achieve fusion or, alternately, if a defusion has taken place, then aggression is returned against the own person; and in this case libido also can no longer be directed toward the outside" (*ibid.*, p. 288).

90. See Freud, "The Economic Problem of Masochism," *Standard Edition*, 19:159–170.

91. Alliteration, assonance, etc. See *La Révolution du langage poétique*, pp. 210–219.

92. Portmanteau words, see *ibid.*

93. Freud on the "Wolf Man" in "Inhibitions, Symptoms and Anxiety," *Standard Edition*, 20:104ff.

94. See André Green, "La Projection."

95. Isidore Ducasse' *Maldoror*, first published in its entirety in 1869, was signed: comte de Lautréamont. The following year, under his own name, Ducasse published *Poems*.—Trans.

96. Jean Bollack and Heinz Wismann, *Héraclite ou la séparation* (Paris: Minuit, 1972), p. 14.

97. The theory of drives, for example.

98. Bollack and Wismann, *Héraclite*, p. 30. [Bollack and Wismann interpret σοφόν as "ingeniousness and savoir-faire." "Art" therefore refers to "a way of fashioning discourse

and the disposition of its material," (p. 306). Compare the English translation by G. S. Kirk: "Of all whose accounts I have heard no one reaches the point of recognizing that wise is separated from all." *Heraclitus: The Cosmic Fragments* (Cambridge: Cambridge University Press, 1954), p. 398.—Trans.]]

99. Bollack and Wismann, *Héraclite*, p. 226. See also p. 69.

100. Although the French translators use the term *"repoussement"* for both Freud's *Ausstossung* and Hegel's *Repulsion*, I maintain the standard English translation of these terms, "expulsion," and "Repulsion," respectively.—Trans.

101. See *Hegel's Science of Logic* 1:180–183. Hegel uses the terms *"abstossen"* (to repulse), *"repellieren"* (to repel) and *"Repulsion"* (repulsion). [In French, both verbs are translated as *"repousser"* and the noun as *"repoussement."*—Trans.] See Hegel, *Science de la logique*, Pierre-Jean Labarrière and Gwendoline Jarczyk, trs. (Paris: Aubier-Montaigne, 1972), vol. 1, Book 1 (1812), pp. 138 sq.

102. *Hegel's Science of Logic*, 1:195; emphasis added.

103. We shall return to this point in part III.

104. *Hegel's Science of Logic*, 1:182; emphasis added.

105. "Negation," *Standard Edition*, 19:237.

106. Artaud, "Description d'un état physique," *Œuvres complètes*, 1:75. In Part C of *La Révolution du langage poétique* ("L'Etat et le mystère"), we stress the a-theological function of this shattering of the One (notably pp. 579 et seq.). We recall the statement noted by Gisela Pankow in the "dream of the 'non-existent God' ": "Schizophrenia is synonymous with atheism," in *L'Homme et sa psychose* (Paris: Aubier-Montaigne, 1969), p. 220.

107. "In the works of my later years (*Beyond the Pleasure Principle* [1920g], *Group Psychology and the Analysis of the Ego* [1921c], and *The Ego and the Id* [1923b]), I have given free reign to the inclination, which I have kept down for so long, to speculation . . ." "An Autobiographical Study," *Standard Edition*, 20:57.

108. *Beyond the Pleasure Principle, Standard Edition*, 18:35 and 36; translation modified.

109. *Standard Edition*, 19:235–239.

110. Lacan, "Introduction au commentaire de Jean Hyppolite," in *Ecrits*, p. 372.

111. See "Rhythmes phoniques et sémantiques," *La Révolution du langage poétique*, pp. 209–263.

III. HETEROGENEITY

1. Von Monakow and Mourgue, *Introduction biologique à l'étude de la neurologie et de la psychologie* (Paris: F. Alcan, 1928), pp. 87, 33, and 38.

2. Driesch, *The Science and Philosophy of the Organism*, 2 vols. (London: Adam and Charles Black, 1908).

3. Szondi, *Experimental Diagnostic of Drives*, Gertrude Aull, tr. (New York: Grune & Stratton, 1952), pp. 6 and 7.

4. Thus, certain modern psychiatric and biological theories of schizophrenia maintain that this is "basically caused by major gene differences which express themselves regularly in homozygotes (*i.e.*, in a recessive manner) and occasionally in heterozygotes (*i.e.*, in a dominant manner)." Jan A. Böök, "Genetical Aspects of Schizophrenic Psychoses," in *The Etiology of Schizophrenia*, Don D. Jackson, ed. (New York: Basic Books, 1960), p. 29.

5. André Green, "Répétition, différence, réplication," *Revue Française de Psychanalyse* (May 1970), 34:479.

258 / III. Heterogeneity

6. See James D. Watson, *The Double Helix: A Personal Account of the Discovery of the Structure of* DNA (London: Weidenfeld & Nicholson, 1968).

7. "Beyond the Pleasure Principle," in *The Standard Edition of the Works of Sigmund Freud*, James Strachey, ed., 24 vols. (London: Hogarth Press and the Institute of Psychoanalysis, 1953), 18:53; emphasis added; translation modified.

8. *Ibid.*, p. 61; translation modified.

9. Antonin Artaud, "Notes pour une 'Lettre aux Balinais,'" *Tel Quel* (Summer 1971), 46:10.

10. "The attack on the mother's body, which is timed psychologically at the zenith of the sadistic phase, implies also *the struggle with the father's penis in the mother*. A special intensity is imparted to this danger-situation by the fact that a union of the two parents is in question. According to the earlier *sadistic super-ego*, which has already been set up, these united parents are extremely cruel and much dreaded assailants," writes Melanie Klein, in "Infantile Anxiety-Situations Reflected in a Work of Art and in the Creative Impulse," in *Contributions to Psychoanalysis* (London: Hogarth Press, 1948), p. 230; emphasis added.

11. Lautreámont, *Maldoror and Poems*, Paul Knight, tr. (London: Penguin, 1978), p. 198.

12. Hegel, *Phenomenology of Spirit*, A. V. Miller, tr. (Oxford: Oxford University Press, 1977), pp. 50–51.

13. *Ibid.*, pp. 51–52.

14. *Ibid.*, p. 52; emphasis added.

15. *Ibid.*, p. 53.

16. *Ibid.*, pp. 55–56.

17. *Ibid.*, p. 51.

IV. PRACTICE

1. See *La Révolution du langage poétique* (Paris: Seuil, 1974), pp. 361–440.

2. Bataille, *Literature and Evil*, Alastair Hamilton, tr. (London: Calder & Boyars, 1973), p. 33.

3. Hegel, *Phenomenology of Spirit*, A. V. Miller, tr. (Oxford: Oxford University Press, 1977), p. 55.

4. *Ibid.*, p. 56.

5. *Ibid.*, p. 56. See Heidegger's commentary, "Hegel et son concept de l'expérience," in *Chemins qui ne mènent nulle part*, Wolfgang Brokmeier, tr. (Paris: Gallimard, 1962), pp. 101–172.

6. Indeed, this is not at all the case with the Husserlian phenomenological notion of experience, which does not concern itself with the *moment of negativity* Hegel mentions in passing. For Husserl, "experience itself is accounted as judgment in the broadest sense." Even if, genetically, experience is related to "non-predicative evidence," "this founding experience has its style of syntactical performances," the status of which nevertheless remains obscure since it is not yet due to the "conceptual and grammatical formings that characterize the categorial as exemplified in the predicative judgment and the statement." *Formal and Transcendental Logic*, Dorion Cairns, tr. (The Hague: Martinus Nijhoff, 1969), pp. 211–212. As a result, one may well wonder whether the Heideggerian critique of Hegel's notion of *experience* does not first and foremost concern Husserl rather than *Phenomenology of Spirit*.

7. Hegel's Science of Logic, W. H. Johnston and L. G. Struthers, trs., 2 vols. (London: Allen & Unwin, 1929), 2:424.

8. Ibid., p. 465.

9. Lenin, "Conspectus of Hegel's Book on The Science of Logic," (Moscow: Foreign Languages Publishing House, 1961), Clemens Dutt, tr., Collected Works, Stewart Smith, ed. 38:213.

10. Hegel's Science of Logic, p. 466; translation modified.

11. Marx "Theses on Feuerbach," I, in The German Ideology, S. Ryazanskaya, ed. (Moscow: Progress Publishers, 1964), p. 645.

12. Lenin, "Conspectus," Collected Works, 38:217.

13. "On Practice," in Selected Readings from the Works of Mao Tsetung (Peking: Foreign Languages Press, 1971), p. 71.

14. Ibid., p. 72.

15. Philippe Sollers, "L'Acte Bataille," Tel Quel (Winter 1972), 52:44.

16. Mao, Selected Readings, p. 81.

17. Bataille, Literature and Evil, pp. 23–24; emphasis added.

18. Ibid., p. 42; translation modified.

19. Stéphane Mallarmé, Grange Wooley, tr. (Madison, N.J.: Drew University, 1942; rpt. New York: AMS Press, 1981), p. 185; translation modified.

20. Mallarmé, "La Musique et les lettres," Œuvres complètes (Paris: Gallimard, 1945), p. 656.

21. For Lautréamont's "vérité pratique" in this instance, and throughout for the adjective "pratique" (practical), a hyphenated noun form is used to convey more forcefully the notion of practice, which is central to Kristeva's argument.—Trans.

22. Lautréamont, Maldoror and Poems, Paul Knight, tr. (London: Penguin Books, 1978), p. 271.

23. Ibid., pp. 104, 270, and 275–276.

24. See La Révolution du langage poétique, pp. 337–358.

25. Maldoror and Poems, p. 265.

26. Ibid., pp. 269 and 265.

27. Ibid., p. 281. Pascal, by contrast, repudiates this imaginary alteration in the name of the subject's identity: "Not content with our own proper and individual life, we want to live an imaginary life in the minds of others, and to this end we struggle to make a show. We labour ceaselessly to improve and preserve our imaginary being, and neglect the real." Pascal's Pensées, H. F. Stewart, tr. and ed. (London: Routledge and Kegan Paul, 1950), pp. 45–47.

28. Maldoror and Poems, p. 275.

29. Marcelin Pleynet, Lautréamont par lui-même (Paris: Seuil, 1967), p. 157.

30. See La Révolution du langage poétique, pp. 592–599.

31. Sollers, "Lautréamont's Science," Writing and the Experience of Limits, David Hayman, ed., Philip Barnard and David Hayman, trs. (New York: Columbia University Press, 1983), pp. 138–139.

32. Sollers, Lois (Paris: Seuil, 1972).

33. Lautréamont would say "useful."

34. Jokes and Their Relation to the Unconscious, The Standard Edition of the Works of Sigmund Freud, James Strachey, ed. (London: Hogarth Press & the Institute of Psychoanalysis, 1960), 8:179–180.

35. "The movement of this abstraction is the consciousness of the dialectic con-

tained in these maxims and laws themselves, and, consequently, the consciousness of the vanishing of the absolute validity previously attaching to them." Hegel, *Phenomenology of Spirit*, p. 451. This statement is directly applicable to Lautréamont's *Poems*.

36. Lautréamont undoubtedly read Baudelaire; see Pleynet, *Lautréamont par lui-même*, p. 92.

37. Baudelaire, "On The Essence of Laughter, and, in General on the Comic in the Plastic Arts," Jonathan Mayne, tr. in *Comedy: Meaning and Form*, Robert Willoughby Corrigan, ed. (San Francisco: Chandler, 1965), pp. 450, 453, 450 (translation modified), 454, 465, and 455.

38. *Maldoror and Poems*, pp. 281 and 258.

39. *Maldoror*, Alexis Lykiard, tr. (New York: Crowell, 1970; 1972), pp. 195, 176, and 172–173.

40. *Maldoror and Poems*, p. 70.

41. On laughter and presupposition in Lautréamont, see *La Révolution du langage poétique*, pp. 337–358.

42. *Maldoror and Poems*, p. 150.

43. *Maldoror*, Alexis Lykiard, tr., pp. 3, 149, and 176.

44. Freud, *Jokes and Their Relation to the Unconscious, Standard Edition*, 8:150.

45. Mallarmé, "Igitur," *Œuvres complètes*, p. 443.

46. Mallarmé, "A Throw of the Dice," in *Stéphane Mallarmé*, p. 187.

47. See part II, section 3, where we contrasted the logical interdependence of negation and affirmation with the negativity of the process.

48. Mallarmé, "Igitur," *Œuvres complètes*, p. 441.

49. *Ibid.*, pp. 441–442.

50. *Ibid.*, p. 442.

51. *Ibid.*, p. 434.

52. *Ibid.*, pp. 440 and 443.

53. *Ibid.*, p. 445.

54. *Ibid.*, p. 450.

55. *Ibid.*

56. *Ibid.*, p. 451.

57. *Ibid.*

58. *Ibid.*

59. Sollers, "Program," *Writing and the Experience of Limits*, p. 5; translation modified.

60. The work of Michel Foucault, from *Madness and Civilization* to "La Société punitive," best illustrates this tendency.

61. Hegel, *Aesthetics: Lectures on Fine Art*, T. M. Knox, tr. 2 vols. (Oxford: Clarendon Press, 1975), 1:49 and 54.

62. "Sur Poe," *Œuvres complètes*, p. 872.

Index